ELECTORAL DYNAMICS

ELECTORAL DYNAMICS
in Britain since 1918

William L. Miller

St. Martin's Press · New York

PREFACE

This book represents an attempt, firstly, to quantify the relationship between social and party divisions in Britain, primarily at the level of the parliamentary constituency electorate rather than the individual elector; secondly, to chart the trends in that relationship since the establishment of universal (male) suffrage in 1918. The University of Strathclyde provided the facilities for computerising all constituency election results since 1918 and for manipulating and analysing all the data files. The Social Science Research Council gave a grant towards computerising selected social data from the Registrar General's Censuses since 1921 and merging the census and voting files. Since census and parliamentary boundaries did not match, merging was not an easy task. Although my principal concern was with the behaviour of electorates I have made extensive use of sample survey data from the Butler and Stokes' study; this was made available through the Inter-university Consortium for Political Research. F. W. S. Craig was the basic source for constituency election results but I must also thank him for a wealth of additional information on minor parties, candidates, cross-voting and other details.

Keith Britto searched the Census tables for relevant information on social divisions and on the spatial match between census and parliamentary areas. Gillian Raab wrote most of the file-handling programmes. Ann Mair of Strathclyde's Social Statistics Laboratory provided a whole range of computing support services. All three participated in the computer analysis, most of which was done using SPSS (Statistical Package for the Social Sciences) routines.

I am grateful to many colleagues outside Strathclyde for comments, criticism and advice, but particularly to Hugh Berrington, Graham Kalton, Antony King and L. J. Sharpe for their comments on the working papers and articles that preceded this text. It will be obvious to any reader that I owe a large intellectual debt to David Butler and Donald Stokes. Wherever possible I have tried to make the analyses of constituency electoral behaviour directly comparable with their analyses for individuals and I have used their data for additional analyses of individual behaviour. Special thanks must go to Richard Rose for his continuous encouragement throughout the study. Despite all the assistance and advice responsibility for the project remains solely my own.

William L. Miller

CONTENTS

43595

Introduction

The outcome of a British General Election is determined by the way the constituencies, not the voters, voted. With the single exception of 1923 the party winning the most constituencies has formed the Government. In 1929, 1951 and February 1974 the party that gained the most constituencies did not win the most votes, but the political consequences of this fact were negligible.

This book discusses the ways in which different constituency electorates voted. We will look at how different categories of individuals voted but only in order to explain why certain electorates voted in the way they did.

In extreme situations it may be correct to view social groups as generating parties or conversely to see parties as only the political expression of social groups. At the other extreme social groups may be irrelevant to partisanship. Possibly the Catholic/Protestant division in Northern Ireland is an example of the one extreme and support or opposition to the Scottish Nationalist Party within Scotland comes near to the other. However most of British voting since the advent of manhood suffrage in 1918 has lain between these poles. Social groups have been very relevant to partisan choices but the extent of that relevance has been determined by party appeals to the electorate. It has not been automatic. For most voters in mainland Britain social divisions have not been so deep that there were any prescribed or proscribed choices among the three major parties.

This brings us to the second aspect of our theme: the choice was usually between three major parties. In 1918, 1922 and the early thirties it could be argued that Britain had a four party system, while in the early fifties the trend was towards a two party one. But looking at the period from 1918 to 1974 as a whole we can simply describe the system as varying around a pure three party system.

The difference between a three party and a two party system is far greater than the one between a three party and a multi party system. It is a difference of kind. In a two party system influences on voting are purely quantitative: they help one party and damage the other. However once there are more than two parties, we must specify the political orientation of social effects, as well as their size. This orientation can change even when the size does not. So, for example, measuring the increase or decrease in class polarisation is of secondary importance to establishing whether the orientation of class polarisation altered or remained constant.

The plan of the book is to move from intensive to extensive analysis: to begin with one election result and work outwards to the full range of seventeen elections between 1918 and 1974. No single election could be described as completely typical but we have chosen the election of 1966 for intensive analysis. This year, although some way from the mid-point of our overall period, was half-way between the times when the Liberals were at their weakest and at their strongest. It was the first year in which census data was available for parliamentary constituencies and only the second election for which there was a nationwide Social Science Research Council (SSRC) election study using sample survey methods. The first was only two years earlier in 1964.

Chapter One reviews the issues in politics and the explicit appeals by the parties to the electors from 1918 onwards. From this review we can identify some perennial party issues and deduce the likely trends in patterns linking social groups and parties. Chapter Two uses the 1966 Election Survey to check for empirical evidence of these patterns. It presents a model of class voting and attitudes which applies both to individuals and constituency electorates alike. It investigates the communal nature of constituency voting and quantifies the power of environmental influences. How people voted depended significantly more on where they lived than on their occupations.

Chapter Three looks at social, spatial and short term temporal variations from the patterns of 1966. In particular it examines the dynamic behaviour of the basic class model. The same processes that magnify the power of class influence in a spatial context appear to dampen rather than amplify, temporal fluctuations in class polarisation. In this chapter a total of nine measures of partisanship are related to forty three social measures at five elections both for Britain as a whole and within the nations and the regions of England. However very simple models explain much of what can be explained by social divisions.

Chapter Four sets out the units, data and methods needed for the long term analysis presented in Chapters Five and Six. Over the longer term we do not have the option of using constituencies as units of analysis. Their boundaries changed over time and did not coincide with the census boundaries prior to 1966. However constituencies can be grouped into what we call 'constant units' suitable for long term analysis. This chapter describes some empirical tests on the effects of using these units instead of constituencies. It also describes how we constructed measures of class and religion from the censuses of 1921, 1931 and 1951 and compares our measures with those used previously. Finally it presents variants of factor analysis and regression analysis which are specially suited to the analysis of three party systems. It would be difficult to follow Chapters Five and Six without reading this section.

Chapter Five traces the trends in class, sectarian, religiosity and rural polarisations from 1918 to 1974 using contemporary election results and census data. It compares these findings with the patterns found in cohort analyses of the 1966 Election Survey. The Survey is also used to examine the effect of the sectarian environments. Finally it looks at the influence of candidature patterns on voting behaviour. Partly because the social structure of candidature was so very sharply defined, social alignments in British elections began at their most extreme and moderated later. Class polarisation declined rapidly until the end of the twenties and then stabilised. Sectarian and rural polarisation declined until the early fifties but then partially recovered.

Chapter Six describes variations in and around the basic model of Chapter Five. It treats varieties of non-conformity within England, restricts the model to central England and extends it to England and Wales in a search for homogeneous responses to heterogeneous social backgrounds. The model is applied to Scotland, taking account of the different sectarian divisions and the results compared with those for England. Finally there is a search for deviations from the basic model within England using fifty five social indicators, four partisan measures and all seventeen elections. At the end of each chapter there is a point by point summary which some readers may find helpful to read before the chapter itself.

At first glance our findings on the voting behaviour of local electorates appear similar to those in sample survey studies of individual voting. There is agreement on the important influence of social divisions on British voting and on which divisions were the most significant. However the differences are perhaps more noticeable than the similarites. First, the power of social divisions can be accurately quantified and compared between the two levels; social divisions were vastly more powerful influences on constituency voting than on individual voting. Second, the critical social predictors of constituency voting referred not to large quantities of people but to small quantities of rather special people. It is difficult to state this finding in terms of individual voting. Third, the trends in social alignments at the constituency level did not follow the trends in individual polarisation either in the short or long term.Fourth, it is far easier to see the effects of candidature patterns on the social alignments of electorates than of individuals. Finally no survey data can give direct evidence about interwar voting since no interview surveys were taken then.

In general, the differences between the findings in survey and constituency studies should not be regarded as discrepancies. They can be explained and we have tried to make the required connections between individual and electoral behaviour, but the differences are real and important; they need explanation and cannot be ignored. Understanding the way categories of individuals voted is not sufficient to explain how the constituencies voted.

CHAPTER 1

The Historical and Political Context of Electoral Trends since 1918

1 The Watershed

It is tempting to look back to pre-war days for the origins of later disputes, but the most significant characteristic of the years between 1910 and 1922 was not the raising of new issues but the resolution of older ones.

1.1 Old Issues Resolved by Legislation

1.1.1 Franchise Changes The pre-war franchise excluded women and men had to establish a right to vote. Quantitatively the most important franchise was the household and, apart from sex, the greatest restriction was the residence requirement. The best estimates suggest that in 1910 about three-fifths of adult males were entitled to vote.[1] Most of the restrictions tended to exclude the poorer classes and about 5%, all middle class, were entitled to more than one vote. Consequently Blewett has concluded that the middle class were almost twice as well represented on the register as in the population although they were still a minority of the electorate.

In 1918 all males over twenty one and most females over thirty received the vote. Apart from continuing the discrimination against women, major bias in the electorate was eliminated. The residence requirement was cut and plural voting was limited. As a result the 1918 electorate was almost three times the size of the 1910 electorate and when women gained equality with men in 1929 almost 90% of the adult population were on the register.[2]

The franchise was also changed by the settlement in Ireland. Between the elections of 1918 and 1922 Ireland was divided. The South received a parliament independent of Westminster and the North a parliament subordinate to Westminster. In spite of its subordinate status this northern parliament was used to justify a cut in the number of northern Irish M.P.s from twenty nine to twelve. Discrimination against Northern Ireland continued when the subordinate parliament was later abolished. The overall effect of the Irish settlement was to decrease Irish representation at Westminster from 15% of M.P.s in 1910 to 2% in 1922. Conversely English representation rose from 69% to 80%.

These franchise changes settled three specific issues of pre-war politics. The old Chartist and Radical demand for 'one man one vote' was conceded with only minor deviations from logical consistency. Secondly, the suffragettes won their fight. Thirdly, the Unionists lost.

Although in 1910 women had no votes, they played a violent part in the campaigns. If the 1918 reform had not occurred, especially if it had been blocked by one party, the election campaigns would probably have been much more violent and party votes might well have been affected. In the event women's suffrage was conceded by a vote of 385 to only 55 in Commons committee.

The Unionists failed to prevent the break up of the 'United Kingdom of Great Britain and Ireland'. In 1910 this issue had been in 80% of Unionist manifestos and in 40% of Liberal ones.[3] Just a month before Austria declared war on Serbia King George V summoned a conference on Ireland with the words 'civil war is on the lips of the most responsible and sober-minded of my people'. However by 1922 the question had been settled. The Irish, both in the North and the South, were outside British domestic politics and no one wanted them back. While the break up of the United Kingdom had been an issue big enough to form the basis of a party system what remained of the Irish question was not.The Unionists needed both a new name and a new policy to justify their continued existence.

Franchise changes had another important effect besides eliminating three of the most explosive pre-war issues: they altered the composition of the electorate. Loss of the Irish members was as significant as the loss of the Irish issue. Irish Nationalists in 1922 were reduced to just three M.P.s, one of whom represented an English constituency. So the system lost a party. Conversely the inclusion of women electors opened up the possibility of sexual divisions, even of sexual parties. It is much less clear whether increased numbers of working class electors increased the possibilities of class based party divisions. If the middle class constituted one-fifth of the pre-war population but two-fifths of the pre-war electorate, the post-1918 electorate must have been more homogeneous as well as more working class. Consequently the possibilities for a class based party system were much reduced. However the franchise extension necessarily increased the viability of any party that was unpopular with the middle classes even if it sharply reduced the viability of any party that was unpopular with the working class.

The two franchise extensions had one property in common: they gave the vote to people who had not voted before. Some women had voted in local government elections before 1918 but they were all new to parliamentary voting. The franchise extension for males was more complex. The old franchise had discriminated against lodgers, bachelors living with their parents, soldiers in barracks, living-in servants, but above all, the mobile and especially the propertyless mobile. These were characteristics of the young as well as the working class. The newly enfranchised males not only had the characteristics of leftist voters but of unstable, unattached voters.

A gap of eight years since the last of the pre-war elections also inflated the proportion of 1918 electors new to voting. Less than half the 1918 electorate voted and half of those who did vote opted for coalition candidates. This combination of factors meant that votes in the first few elections after 1918 were quite unusually there for the taking. Few electors could have developed any sense of identification with a party by voting for it in the past. No doubt it is possible to have a sense of party identification without a vote, but identification divorced from voting is likely to be weak.

Between November 1922 and October 1924 this new and generally very inexperienced electorate was asked to vote at three general elections. Turnout was high, similar to turnout in the elections of the sixties, for example. The pattern was set.

Rural and especially agricultural areas had particularly settled populations. Consequently they had high levels of pre-war enfranchisement. Matthew et. al. have shown that in 1911 the registered electorate formed 60% of the male population in the boroughs but 70% in the landward areas of the counties. Prosperous small town county boroughs had franchise rates equal to the rural average, but agricultural areas like Somerset, Devon, Cornwall and Lincolnshire averaged 81 %. In these counties the average franchise rate for males in 1918 only reached 95 %. So the change from pre-war levels was modest and the destabilising effect correspondingly small in these areas.[4]

1.1.2 Religious Confrontation The British state had long discriminated against all who would not conform to the rituals of the established Church. Although the practical effects were gradually reduced by measures such as annual Indemnity Acts, the Test and Corporation Acts remained law until 1828. Later in the century other non-conformist disabilities were gradually removed. Marriages in non-conformist chapels were legalised in 1836, compulsory church rates abolished in 1868, theological tests at the universities abolished in 1871 (though Anglican privileges remained) and in 1880 the Burials Act permitted burials in parish churchyards without the necessity of an Anglican ceremony.

However as legal disabilities were removed other religious issues arose. In the first place the non-conformists went over to the attack and demanded disestablishment of the Church. By 1910 Welsh disestablishment was opposed in a third of Unionist manifestos. Although official policy it was seldom mentioned in Liberal manifestos for 1910, but it was passed against the opposition of the Lords. It was put on the statute book in 1914 along with a deferment until the war ended, coming into effect in 1920. The established Churches in Scotland and England survived though not without threats.

Then there was the controversy over education. In 1870 elementary schooling was extended to the entire population by filling the gaps in the so-called voluntary system with state schools run by elected boards. Voluntary schools were sectarian, mainly Anglican and to a lesser extent Catholic. Non-conformists were so angry that Gladstone could only pass the bill with the help of Conservative votes, and then only after conceding an amendment that forbade teaching of the catechism in state schools. State grants to sectarian schools were doubled. An 1897 act increased state aid to church schools still further. In 1902 Balfour introduced a bill which gave the multipurpose local government agencies, the councils, financial responsibility for all schools, board and voluntary. Managers of sectarian schools were to hand over their buildings, but retained the right to appoint teachers; the councils were to pay all current expenditure from the rates. In the event they also paid for future capital expenditure. Anglicans and Catholics thus got the state to levy taxes to pay for their schools.

The Liberal government made four attempts between 1906 and 1908 to relieve non-conformist discontent. They eventually got the support of the Anglican episcopate but were defeated by the Anglican laity in the Lords. Passions subsided and the issue dropped out of national politics, although it remains an issue in some localities.

In Scotland, too, some old religious differences were coming to an end. In 1838 the mainly English and Anglican Lords had confirmed a ruling of the Scottish Court of Session that lay patrons had the right to impose ministers of their choice on Scottish congregations against the wishes of congregation, presbytery and General Assembly. Five years later, after unsuccessful appeals to the Crown, 395 ministers seceded and formed the Free Church of Scotland. The bulk of the two Scottish churches reunited in 1929 on Free Church terms.

So in the years around 1918 the political implications of old religious confrontations were greatly reduced. Most of the Catholic Irish left the Union. The Welsh non-conformists won their main objective. The English non-conformists came to accept the political impossibility of ending sectarian schools and the Scottish Disruption was over. Religion still structured personal contacts; religious attitudes and traditions continued to influence political attitudes on secular issues and the memory of direct religious confrontation remained. However after 1922 open quarrels about religion no longer figured prominently in national political debate.

1.1.3 The People versus the Peers: Democratic Confrontation   The central issue in 1910 was the power of the Lords. After 1906 the Liberals had 400 seats out of 670 in the Commons and only 157 of the remainder opposed them. But the Lord's right of veto hampered the passing of their legislation. Lloyd George, as Chancellor, attempted to ameliorate this situation with his 'People's Budget', designed to provoke the Lords but appeal to the electorate. Caught between demands for increased naval expenditures and his own wish to protect and extend social welfare spending, Lloyd George was forced to raise taxes, usually an unpopular activity. He burdened a tenth of the population with three-quarters of the increases and the least progressive measure, doubling the tax on alcohol, was aimed at inciting the Unionists. The Lords veto on finance bills had fallen into disuse: there was no precedent in the previous 250 years. So a veto on the Budget would be especially open to criticism. Nonetheless the trap worked. Although only 149 M.P.s opposed the Budget in the Commons, the Lords rejected it by 350 to 75. This veto provided Asquith with a pretext for the January 1910 election and he sought the King's assurance that an election victory would be followed by coercion of the Lords to accept a reduction in their powers. The King refused because he would not operate the 1832 precedent without two election victories by Asquith. Asquith's victory in January was narrow, only two seats more than the Unionists and he now relied on Labour and Nationalist support for a majority. Meanwhile the Lords passed the budget, leaving the December election as a referendum on the purely constitutional issue of the scope of their power and their specific fear that without a Lords veto the Liberals, dependent on Nationalist votes in the Commons, would be able to enact Irish Home Rule and unable to delay doing so.

The power of the Lords was clearly the dominant issue in January and more so in December. In January 96% of all candidates mentioned the issue. In December this rose to 99 per cent. In January it was treated as the most important issue by 82% of Liberals and 58% of Labour candidates, while Unionists tried to focus attention on other problems. By December Unionists were forced to shift ground, 74% gave the Lords greatest prominence in their manifestos compared with 98% of Liberals and 79% of Labour. The overall result in December was much the same as in January. A bill was passed abolishing the Lords veto and the King coerced them to accept it. Its passage removed from future politics the issue which had dominated both 1910 elections. It established the absolute power of the Commons and so of the party which won a general election. For thirty years after the fall of Asquith this was probably of little importance since the Conservatives dominated politics and the Lords did not obstruct Conservatives. However before he fell it allowed Welsh Disestablishment and Irish Home Rule Bills to succeed. Later it allowed Attlee to use his radical majority in the 1945 parliament unfettered by a constitutional crisis.

1.2 Old Issues Resolved by the War

1.2.1 The Drink Trade and the People's Budget
Liquor licensing was mentioned by 29% of Unionists, 38% of Liberals and a remarkable 61% of Labour candidates in January 1910, although interest was less in December. During the war Lloyd George described drink as a greater danger than the Kaiser. Opening hours were reduced from around sixteen hours per day to less than six. Penal taxation put spirits into the luxury class and beer was drastically reduced in specific gravity and heavily taxed. War put such burdens on the Trade that it ceased to be a major issue. Prohibition on American lines was not a major post-war issue, although a Prohibition candidate running with E. D. Morel for the two member seat of Dundee succeeded in ousting Winston Churchill at the 1922 election and held the seat until 1931.

Few candidates in 1910 claimed the People's Budget was the most important issue though many thought it vindictive. After the war taxpayers could have felt nothing but nostalgia for the low tax levels of 1910.

Yet the greatest effect of war was not on such specific issues but on party loyalties and party spirit.

1.2.2   The Issue of Party   On several occasions during the nineteenth century
radical changes were enacted by the party least in sympathy with them,
enthusiastically supported by the opposition. This arrangement very effectively
preserved civil peace and ensured permanence for the reform. Unfortunately for
the luckless governing party, civil peace within the nation came usually at the
price of civil war within the party.[5]

The effect of the First World War on the Liberals was in this tradition. They
survived the declaration of war, but later as doubts grew about its causes, were
forced to abandon one after another of their principles. They began totally
opposed to conscription. Then conscription was not to extend to Ireland and
conscientious objection was permitted. However before the war ended conscription was extended to Ireland, though not applied, and conscientious
objectors lost their right to vote for five years after the war. Private possession of
old pamphlets from the pre-1916 campaign against conscription had become
sufficient to secure conviction under the Defence of the Realm Act.

The behaviour of Liberals during the war arose from a much deeper division
than the one between Lloyd George's supporters and the Asquithians: the
division between Liberal principles and the measures needed to win the war; it
ran within individuals not just between them. Since at the same time Unionists
were conceding defeat over Ireland, the issue of party itself became much less
important than before the war. In 1919 Churchill, with Lloyd George's backing,
publicly advocated a new Centre Party since 'no deep division of principle' now
separated the two wings of the coalition.[6] Lloyd George, in his Criccieth
Memorandum had put forward a similar scheme to solve the 1910 crisis, but what
had been incredible in 1910 was reasonable after the war.[7] There had been deep
divisions of principle in 1910, but by 1922 both parties had so compromised their
principles that the old divisions no longer applied.

Before the war Labour was a junior partner in a Liberal led alliance. As early as
1886 there had been ten trade union M.P.s, all Liberals, and one had been a
minister. Before the war the motive behind Labour candidatures was to get
working men and the odd socialist into Parliament. These two objectives were
often in conflict and neither required a separate party. Some organisational
separation was implied by the decision of the TUC-backed Labour Representation Committee in 1903 not to connect any of its candidates with another
party. However in that same year the Committee's secretary concluded a secret
agreement with the Liberal Chief Whip.

In December 1910 Labour fought just fifty six seats, of the eleven in opposition
to the Liberals it won only two. This Liberal-Labour alliance was not just
imposed on the electorate by deals between party officials to restrict the voter's
choice of candidates. Until 1950 Britain retained a number of undivided
boroughs which elected two M.P.s. Each elector had two votes. He could vote for
one candidate and not use his second vote, or he could vote for two. He could not
give two votes to one candidate nor indicate a preference between two
candidates. The two candidates with the most votes were elected. In December
1910 Labour contested twelve two member boroughs. In each case Labour and

the Liberals put up one candidate each, continuing an old tradition in existence before the 1885 reforms of running a Whig and a Radical 'in harness'.

Detailed breakdowns are available of the cross-voting in the eleven undivided boroughs where Labour was successful.[8] These seats returned over a quarter of all Labour M.P.s. In six the Liberal and Labour candidates faced two Unionists. Only 2% of voters cross-voted between Unionist and non-Unionst and less than 5% plumped for just one non-Unionist, withholding their second vote. In four seats there were just three candidates, one from each party, and cross-voting with the Unionist might have been inflated by Unionists who did not want to waste their second vote. However 40% voted Unionist and withheld their second vote, only 6% plumped for a single non-Unionist and less than 3% cross-voted between Unionist and non-Unionist. In these ten constituencies spread from Dundee to Norwich over 189,000 people voted. The identity between Liberal and Labour voters was impressive. The only constituency that deviated from the pattern was Merthyr Tydfil where 8% cross-voted with the Unionist and 26% plumped for a single non-Unionist. Kier Hardie, the Labour candidate, had displaced a Liberal in 1900 and because Merthyr was not included in the original MacDonald/Gladstone pact he did it again in 1906. In December 1910 the Unionist stood as a Liberal Unionist. Despite this history of bitter rivalry few Merthyr voters could bring themselves to cross-vote even with a Liberal Unionist. At worst they voted just for one person. Before the war, whatever the difference of emphasis or the special interests represented, the electorate clearly perceived 'no deep division of principle' between Liberal and Labour.

During the war Labour became even less divided from important Liberal principles. Like Lloyd George the party opposed the war until the last moment; thereafter their paths diverged. Labour was never subject to quite the same pressures of government because it was a minor party and because its centre of gravity lay outside Parliament. Labour also had greater institutional contacts with the German people.

MacDonald lost the Labour leadership but joined with E. D. Morel to set up the Union of Democratic Control (UDC) to investigate pre-war diplomacy. The UDC made two demands: that the war should be ended by negotiation and that diplomacy should be open and subject to democratic control. Morel was imprisoned, but the UDC captured a part of Liberal principle for Labour and was a route for middle class Liberals defecting to Labour or, from another standpoint, infiltrating Labour.[9] Although all the Labour M.P.s in 1918 were of working class origin as soon as the party gained more seats its M.P.s included upper class UDC men like Trevelyan and Ponsonby, both ex-Liberal M.P.s. When the party moved on to form its first government the Cabinet included seven trade unionists and nine members of the UDC.

At the end of 1917 Labour and the TUC agreed a statement of war aims indistinguishable from those of the UDC. Labour ended the electoral truce at by-elections and as soon as the armistice was signed it withdrew from the coalition. It organised to fight the coming election as an independent contender for power with as many candidates as possible.

While some Liberals could no longer see any deep division of principle between them and the Unionists others felt even closer to Labour than before the war. If Labour had not been possessed so strongly by its limited, sectional, interest group tradition reinforced by its institutional links with the TUC, it might have been totally taken over by the wider Liberal party. However Labour was not a reincarnation of the old Liberal party: it had similar principles but different priorities. The old Liberal ideals which were damaged by the 1914–18 war were further damaged by two decades of 'peace' that followed. Labour opposed peace-time conscription before the outbreak of the 1939–45 war but the Churchill-Attlee coalition enforced more extensive conscription than in 1914–18. A Labour minister, Bevin, even used conscription to man the coal mines. Total military victory was official policy. If there was no electoral cry in 1945 to 'hang the Kaiser', the actions taken were far more deadly. Lloyd George did *not* hang the Kaiser. The next generation operated the Nurenberg trials and hung such relative nonentities as William Joyce.

1.3 Issues that Survived the First War

Elements of 1910 politics survived both the war and the legislative revolutions of the next twelve years.

1.3.1 Unemployment and Social Reform

In 1910 unemployment was almost exclusively the concern of Labour candidates although all parties were interested in some aspects of social reform. The war ended unemployment but it came back with a vengeance in the depression that followed. Detailed measures of social reform and the general question of 'taxation for social purposes' were as important after the war as before.

1.3.2 Trade Union Powers

Three other topics besides unemployment were almost exclusively mentioned by Labour candidates in January 1910.They were state control of industry, salaries for M. P.s and the Osborne Judgement. By December 81% of Labour candidates mentioned Osborne in their manifestos.

State salaries for M. P.s were considered necessary for working class M. P.s partly because of the Osborne Judgement: a railwayman named Osborne had succeeded in a legal action to stop his union using funds for political purposes. Earlier the Taff Vale Judgement had decided that trade unions were legally liable for any damage done to a company by a strike of their members, whether or not the union had approved the strike. These judgements attacked both the industrial and political activity of trade unions. Labour's national manifesto in December 1910 described the Osborne Judgement as 'only the latest example of Judge-made law from which you have already suffered so much'.[10]

The immediate problems were solved by a 1911 resolution awarding M.P.s £400 per annum and a 1913 act authorising unions to set up special funds for political purposes. Other issues of trade union power remained and were intensified by the pressures, particularly on skilled workers, of war.

1.3.3 Socialisation   War also put nationalisation more firmly on the political agenda. Apart from numerous 'controlled establishments' subject to the Ministry of Munitions, the State took over the railways and coal mines, insured wartime shipping, controlled food, rents and mortgages and by the end of the war was the direct purchaser of nine-tenths of all imports. Afterwards Churchill admitted he was 'very nearly' convinced that socialism was possible and wrote in the Liberal Magazine for 1919 that 'the achievements of the Ministry of Munitions constitute the greatest argument for State Socialism that has ever been produced'.[11]

1.3.4 Defence and Tariff Reform   The war evidently was not a war to end all wars and defence remained an issue after it. However economic defence was as significant as military defence. Chamberlain had launched his campaign for tariff reform, imperial preference and industrial protection in 1903. Every Unionist discussed tariffs in January 1910 and 74% made it the most important issue in their manifesto. Few others gave it such prominence but 88% of Liberals and 82% of Labour candidates discussed it. Tariff reform, although challenging economic orthodoxy, was, in essence, not new. It symbolised British nationalism in the same way that free trade did internationalism. It would benefit both of Disraeli's 'two nations', rich and poor, at the expense of the foreigner. It was the alternative to a drift towards class politics which would aid the British poor to the detriment of the British rich.

Before the war tariff reform was a minority view dividing Unionists but uniting their opponents. However reform had three great advantages in the longer term. Although divisive it was in keeping with the basic patriotic stance of Unionism. Secondly, it provided a core policy when Unionism became outdated by the secession of Ireland. Thirdly, it prospered in the nationalistic atmosphere of war and the economically depressed 'peace' that followed.

The first moves towards protection came in 1915 when McKenna, Liberal Chancellor in Asquith's coalition, a strong opponent of conscription and an equally strong advocate of free trade, felt compelled to introduce a 33% duty on luxuries. The McKenna Duties supposedly saved wartime shipping space but were retained as simple protection after the war. Lloyd George noted at the time 'the old system goes destroyed by its own advocates'.[12] McKenna's Duties helped to end the 'deep divisions of Principle' between Liberals and Unionists. Nevertheless tariffs remained an important issue after the war.

2   The Course of Party Appeals Since 1918

2.1 Opposition Status

In 1918 Labour won fifty seven seats, only fifteen more than in 1910 and a vote share of 21%, much the same as the Liberals obtained in 1974. Of the major groups elected to the Commons it was fourth in size out of five. However the Lloyd George Liberals were allied to the Unionists and Sinn Fein never came to

Westminster. So Labour claimed the status of Opposition.

During the next four years the Liberals failed to reunite. At by-elections Labour improved on its 1918 performance by an average of 11 % in 1919, only 4% in 1920, but 8 % in 1921 and 12 % in 1922. Consequently Labour was treated as the Opposition. Indeed the scale of its by-election successes, rather than the 1918 result, inspired something close to panic among non-Labour politicians.

2.2 Candidate Profiles

In 1910 92 % of Irish Nationalists were Catholic and 90 % of Unionists were Anglicans. Although 56 % of Liberals and 53 % of Labour were Anglicans they were the only parties to field large numbers of Protestant non-conformist candidates.[13]

Occupation distinguished Labour candidates even better than religion: 84 % had been manual workers, almost half in the mining industry. Occupation also distinguished other parties although less than 2 % were manual workers. Landowners, country gentlemen, military men and civil servants made up a third of Unionists but only an eighth of Liberals and a twentieth of Nationalists. The old Test and Corporation Acts, kept alive by family tradition long after their formal repeal, probably combined with Liberal anti-militarist principles to explain why there were six times as many military among Unionists as Liberals. Unionists included five times as many brewers and distillers. Liberals fielded more candidates from the talkative professions—publishers, academics, journalists and clergy. These accounted for 13 % of Liberal candidates but a mere 3 % of Unionists.

After the war, when Labour tried to assume the full role of the pre-war Liberal-Labour alliance, its candidates became less like those of pre-war Labour, resembling more those of the progressive alliance.

By 1974 only 19 % of Labour candidates had manual working class backgrounds compared with 14 % for the full Liberal-Labour alliance in 1910.[14] However in 1974 Labour still had ten times as many academics as the Conservatives who had thirteen times as many military men.

Labour was unique in giving its candidates an institutionally defined social class. From 1918 candidates could be sponsored by local parties, socialist organisations or trade unions. In 1918, 45 % were trade union sponsored. This dropped to 24 % in 1929 and thereafter stayed within the range 22 % to 27 %.

The social profile of the party elite reflected the interests which would be favoured. Nationalists might claim they would not favour Catholics, but had they not been Catholics the question would not have arisen. The same was true for non-conformist Liberals or trade union Labour.

Secondly, the social profile determined what social groups could be represented by the party, not as a lawyer represents clients, but as a painting represents a scene. Middle class candidates could articulate working class needs but not represent them in this strict sense. Strict social representation was the official objective of the pre-war Labour party. It had the virtues that it was both possible and visible.

After 1918 the appeal of social profiles changed dramatically because the pattern of party competition changed too much to be immediately offset by compensating changes in party profiles. The pre-war religious division between the two leading parties gave way to a combination of class and religious differences as Labour replaced the Liberals as one of the two main parties. Purely on the basis of candidates' characteristics, divisions between employers and workers should have been more significant determinants of post-1918 Labour versus Conservative support than of pre-war Liberal versus Unionist support. Similarly military versus anti-military feelings should have had more impact and sectarian religion should have remained constant. On the same basis class should have had a steadily decreasing effect after 1918 on Labour versus Conservative support as Labour's candidates became less working class.

2.3 Manifestos

2.3.1 Starting Positions: the 1918 and 1922 Manifestos   National manifestos provide a convenient, authoritative and standardised summary of the parties' explicit policy appeals to the electorate.[15]

In 1918 the Coalition, and Asquith's ambivalence towards it, meant there were no separate Conservative and Coalition Liberal manifestos and Asquith's was obscure. However the Labour manifesto was full of sharply defined policy. It began with the headline 'A PEACE OF RECONCILIATION' and denounced 'secret diplomacy' or 'any form of economic war'. Subsequent sections then demanded, in order, the immediate withdrawal of allied forces from Russia, self government for Ireland and India, a return to civil liberties including the repeal of the Defence of the Realm Act, abolition of conscription and the release of political prisoners. Only then did it move on to class issues, starting with land nationalisation, a million state-built houses for rent, a capital levy to pay off war debts, heavily graduated direct taxes and no indirect taxes such as tariffs. Next came more specifically socialist measures like nationalisation of mines, railways, shipping, armaments and electricity. Then a national minimum wage and recognition of the right to 'work or maintenance'. Labour also demanded equal pay for women, a single union movement including both sexes and full suffrage for women. Labour maintained that 'there must be no sex party: the Labour Party is the Women's Party'. Finally it emphasised that its programme was 'comprehensive, constructive' and to be achieved 'by constitutional means'.

The Coalition campaign was memorable for the hysterical demands by Lloyd George and others that Germany should pay 'the whole cost of the war'. Three days before the election he added 'we shall search their pockets for it'. By the eve of the election he was denouncing Labour as a 'Bolshevik group' not just because they opposed intervention in Russia but because 'what they really believe in is Bolshevism'.[16] Labour did well to emphasise its commitment to constitutional methods. The Coalition manifesto exulted in the 'brilliant and conclusive triumph of the Allied Armies'. It warned that Ireland must not be 'severed from the British Empire' or Ulster coerced: two restrictions that were 'in accordance with the declared views of all *English* political leaders'. Responsible government for India 'by gradual stages' was only a 'goal'. Tariffs would be needed to 'safeguard' industry from unfair competition and Imperial preference would be applied. Agriculture would get state aid, partly for defence reasons. In addition to these essentially Unionist policies it expressed concern for ex-soldiers, and working class unemployment, even proposing to adapt 'to peace conditions the experience gained in regard to the traffic in drink'.

By 1922 Unionism was out of date and the party reverted to its earlier titles of Conservative or Tory. Coalition was also over but Lloyd George fought the election with 144 National Liberals who wanted coalition even if the Conservatives did not.

Between 1918 and 1922 almost everything that could go wrong for a government had done so. At home rapid growth and inflation up to 1920 was succeeded by economic collapse. Unemployment which had never reached 8% in any year of the century before the war averaged 15% for the whole of 1921 and 1922, and reached a monthly peak in June 1921 of 21%, partly because of a coal strike. Industrial relations were bad generally. More workers, went on strike in 1919 than in any other year of the century until 1962, except in the General Strike of 1926. There were more stoppages in 1920 than in any year until 1943 in mining and until 1967 outside mining. Taxation reached 32% af National Income in 1921 compared with 8% in 1913 and around 20% from 1924 to 1930. However worst of all, the Government visibly failed to make peace abroad. Faced with another foreign crisis the Coalition decided to seek a renewed mandate in a general election. Conservative backbenchers met in the Carlton Club and voted 187 to 87 to fight as a separate party. The coalition was ousted. Austen Chamberlain lost the Conservative leadership. Bonar Law, his predecessor, took over to head what Churchill, then a Coalition minister, called a 'government of the second eleven'. He was right; but it was an asset since it made them a government of relatively unsoiled hands. Law held an immediate election.

All parties except the National Liberals denounced Lloyd George and the Coalition. Again Labour's manifesto began with issues of peace. It demanded a revision of the Versailles Treaties 'which have caused greater international wrongs than they removed'. German reparations were to be reduced and armaments limited by agreement; there were to be no military adventures in Turkey; Egypt and India were to get 'real independence' and every effort was to be made to help Ireland become 'united, prosperous and contented'. It was signlficant that Labour's manifesto should start in this way despite the economic disasters and industrial confrontations of the preceding years.

The Coalition was a convenient scapegoat for the Asquithian Liberals and especially for the Conservatives. The Liberals devoted the opening fifth of their manifesto to an attack on Lloyd George while the Conservatives took credit for ending a government which had only existed at their pleasure. Both joined Labour in denouncing Lloyd George's alleged inclination towards military adventures. Both denounced the high level of post-war taxation. Labour, by contrast, wanted to increase taxes on those with over £500 per annum and impose a capital levy on 'fortunes exceeding £5,000'.

Outside of their attacks on Lloyd George the Liberals and Conservatives differed. Liberals denounced Versailles and attacked indiscipline among the forces policing Ireland. They gave a little space to working class interests but more to their claim to be a classless party. They called for liquor reform and proportional representation. Conservatives pledged help for agriculture and cuts in government activities. 'Tranquillity' at home, non-interference in industry, was essential to restore trade. Unemployment relief was a mere 'palliative'. Conservatives emphasised the importance of the Empire and Empire Free Trade, that is tariffs, while Liberals advocated free trade. Fearing defeat Bonar Law revived the 1910 referendum pledge by promising that tariffs would not be introduced without a special election on the issue. Labour remained 'opposed in principle to indirect taxation' including tariffs.

2.3.2 The Tariff Election The Conservatives won an overall majority of seventy three seats. Baldwin succeeded Law as Prime Minister and decided to introduce tariffs. Despite his large majority he held an election in 1923 to get a mandate for tariffs since both Balfour in 1910 and Bonar Law in 1922 had specifically pledged no tariff reform without such a move. His unique manifesto of sixteen numbered paragraphs set out the details of his case for protective tariffs. He lost and renounced protection without even a conditional threat to revive it.

Labour's 1923 manifesto opened with the classic Liberal attack on tariffs stressing the international, not the class, implications:

Labour challenges the Tariff policy and the whole conception of economic relations underlying it. They are an impediment to the free interchange of goods and services upon which civilised society rests. They foster a spirit of profiteering, materialism and selfishness, poison the life of nations, lead to corruption in politics, promote trusts and monopolies, and impoverish the people. They perpetuate inequalities in the distribution of the world's wealth won by the labour of hands and brain. These inequalities the Labour Party means to remove.

2.3.3 Continuities in Labour Manifestos – Internationalism, Socialism, Class Interests and Trade Union Powers Many statements in these early manifestos were repeated as long as the issues were relevant. Labour's internationalism was expressed in attacks on Versailles in the twenties; later in its proposals for disarmament and opposition to rearmament; in its opposition to tariffs and in its insistence on self government for the Empire. Attlee's performance in government showed ruthless determination to decolonise the Empire, but his decision to manufacture nuclear weapons to deter Soviet aggression hardly matched the manifestos' support for Russia and opposition to arms. Still by 1955 the party was again proposing to encourage disarmament by 'the immediate cessation of H-bomb tests. . . . as a first step'.

Over time Labour diluted its original land nationalisation proposals but extended its programme of industrial nationalisation. The 1918 demands for nationalisation of mines, transport and power were dropped only when they had been achieved. Shipping and arms, also on the 1918 list, had to wait until the seventies but steel and the Bank of England, first listed in 1931, were nationalised by Attlee. As industries were taken over more were added to the party's shopping list.

Labour had the same attitude towards housing. It consistently favoured socialised ownership whether by state corporations or municipalities, public control of private landlords or occasionally, the compulsory socialisation of private rented housing.

Distinct from socialism it had a number of policies designed to favour the poor, the working class or both. In 1918, 1922 and 1923 it advocated a capital levy. At intervals it proposed to tax land values and capital gains from all sources. In the seventies it proposed a recurrent capital levy, a wealth tax. Throughout the interwar years it attacked all indirect taxes, including tariffs, that spread the burden of taxation. Generally it supported cheap food policies brought about either by subsidy or by abolishing tariffs. Between the wars it advocated public works to reduce unemployment and repeated the pre-war slogan that workers had a right to 'work or maintenance'. Usually it called for an extension of the Welfare State or attacked welfare cuts. The *non-socialist* justification for all these policies was never put more brutally than in October 1974:
'Our objective is to bring about a fundamental and irreversible shift in the balance of wealth and power in favour of working people'.

This constant commitment to redistribution like the constant commitment to socialisation implied ever more extreme policies. Despite semantic problems of discussing wealth and income, some clear trends emerge from the report of the Royal Commission on Income and Wealth. Labour was right to attack indirect taxes. Their regressive effect all but cancelled the progressive effect of direct taxes even as late as 1972.[17] And Labour was right to stress social welfare, for welfare benefits, not taxation, were the cause of income redistribution after it had been earned. Indeed welfare had over three and a half times the redistributive effect of direct taxes even if their effect had not been cancelled by indirect taxes. However over time there was a redistribution of gross income independent of the transfers made once income had been earned. The distribution of gross income within the working class was remarkably stable, virtually identical in 1886 and 1974.[18] Nevertheless there were gains by working people as a whole and an enormous redistribution of wealth and income within the middle class. The top percentile had 23% of the top half's total income in 1938–9 but only 8% in 1972–3. The top percentile had 75% of the total wealth of the top decile in 1911–13 and 64% in 1937–9 but only 51% in 1960 using comparable unofficial figures. On Inland Revenue estimates their share was 45% in 1960 and 43% in 1973. Perhaps the most telling statistic is that by 1972–3 over 58% of the tax units in the top decile, units that together earned 25% of total income, were units that included working wives. Castles and grouse moors were no longer an appropriate image of the wealthy.[19]

The political consequence was that as time passed redistribution could no longer be a policy that set the very few against the many as Lloyd George had done in 1910. There was still perhaps more scope for an attack on pockets of wealth than on high income, but Labour's 1974 pledge, if honoured, had to hurt a large percentage of the electorate.

Labour frequently demanded an increase in trade union and employees' rights though Conservatives seldom used manifestos to advocate a reduction. The classic Taff Vale and Osborne Judgements were indeed 'examples of Judge-made law'. After the General Strike of 1926 they passed an act outlawing general or sympathetic strikes and replacing 'contracting out' of the political levy with 'contracting in'. This was pure reaction, not planned policy. They had no electoral mandate for the act.

The General Strike was the culmination of a period of bad industrial relations that began shortly before the First War and was at its worst just after it.[20] Widespread unrest under the Coalition coincided with severe wage cuts when the post-war boom ended. Industrial relations next took a major turn for the worse around 1959, whether just before or after that year depends on the choice of measure. Coinciding with the rising industrial unrest came the new concept of a statutory incomes policy. With full employment after the Second War came the wish to restrain wage demands sufficiently to control inflation. In 1948 Cripps succeeded in persuading the unions to operate a voluntary wage restraint in return for government concessions and voluntary dividend restraint. It worked well until the effects of the 1949 sterling devaluation were felt in wage packets. Unfortunately the Conservatives were less able to coax the unions and more inclined to compel them. During the sixties strikes became more numerous and more workers were involved. In 1970 the Conservative manifesto promised a variety of anti-union and anti-council tenant legislation. Government versus union confrontation ended in the greatest lockout of the century, the three day week, and the defeat of the Conservatives in a crisis election.

However Labour proposals to curb strikes and wage rises by compulsion were no more welcome. The 1966–70 Labour government was the first with an industrial relations record worse than its Conservative predecessors. In 1969 only a humiliating government capitulation ended confrontation with the unions. Later Labour and the unions made common cause once again, formalising their renewed co-operation in the Social Contract, a series of documents setting out the pact between the unions and a future Labour government. It was an attempt to end two decades of escalating confrontation between the Government and unions and facilitate a return to the methods of Cripps.

2.3.4. Continuities in Conservative Manifestos—Patriotism, Resistance to Socialism, and Support for the Property Owning Democracy   After Ireland's secession Conservatives could no longer base their party on Unionism. Yet if Labour felt the need to break away from being a purely working class party the Conservatives had even more reason, in an era of universal suffrage, to avoid becoming a purely middle class party.

Tariff reform provided the first major plank in their post-war policy.

Protective industrial tariffs against the foreigner, lower tariffs against the Empire and home preference for agriculture were to unite the classes within Britain. Unemployment at home and economic nationalism in foreign countries justified tariffs. Coupled with Imperial Preference the Conservatives wanted more integration of the Empire in non-economic ways, such as a common defence policy, and they were consistently less enthusiastic than Labour about colonial independence.

Labour's anti-militarism was balanced on the Conservative side by patriotism not extreme militarism. The 1922 revolt had been partly a response to what Conservative backbenchers saw as military adventures. However there was no hint of pacifism in Conservative ranks. They were more willing to rearm before the Second War and afterwards linked their desire for disarmament with warnings about the dangers of unilateral disarmament. When Labour proposed in 1955 various initiatives to reduce the 'menace' of the 'hydrogen bomb' which 'looms over all mankind' it was the Conservatives who recalled that Attlee had authorised the atomic bomb and 'the Socialist Opposition has said it shares our view that the possession of the hydrogen bomb is necessary'.

Tariffs only ceased to be a major part of Conservative policy when they had been imposed. The 1931 manifesto asked for a mandate to do whatever was required, thus escaping a referendum on tariffs. The following year Neville Chamberlain introduced his Import Duties bill with proud references to his father. Although Labour voted solidly against it, it was passed with a large majority.

The enormous post-1914 increase in taxation provided the Conservatives with their second basic policy. They attacked the increased scale of civil government, opposed intervention in industry and demanded lower taxes. In 1950, for example, they denounced the 'swarms of full-time officers and supervisors like those who have sprung up in the health services. Many new Commissions or Committees outside the Ministries must be reviewed to see if they are wanted. There is also plenty of scope for retrenchment – to give only a few examples – in public relations, information services, excessive control over local authorities, the country agricultural committees, government travelling, etc.' When they created a National Economic Development Council in 1964 they seemed to concede their opponents case and lost the election. However Conservative attacks on taxation and controls did not end in 1964. Even when their 1970–74 government extended the nationalisation of industry they remained as bitterly opposed to the principle as ever.

After Labour's major extension of the Welfare State the Conservatives claimed, in 1950, that they 'and the Liberals' had invented it. However they generally favoured selective benefits being given only to those in need and not to all as part of a socialist process of demonetarisation. Their 'household means test' defended in the 1935 manifesto is the classic example, but not the only one.

They had a good record on two of the worst social evils: bad housing and unemployment. Interwar unemployment rose to its first peak under the Coalition and neared its second under Labour. The second American depression in

1937–38, which included the most rapid decline in American economic history, caused only a minor interruption in Britain's diminishing unemployment trend. From 1929 onwards the Conservatives repeatedly proclaimed their achievements in reducing the high levels of unemployment which they had inherited from others. With a free hand to impose tariffs they claimed they could have done even better. When Labour maintained full employment after 1945, Conservatives gave the credit to American and Empire loans, not socialist policies. They gave no similar credit to Hitler and interwar rearmament for their own success.[21]

Labour's 1918 manifesto demanded a million houses, built by the State, to be let at 'fair rents'. Until the late sixties Conservatives always managed to build houses faster than the preceding government. For five years in the mid thirties they built over 300,000 a year. In 1951 they pledged they could do it again and did so. Between the wars they built for purchase, not rent. In the fifties they not only built more houses than Labour but reversed Labour's policy of publicly owned houses for rent, prefering their own interwar policy.[22]

The 'property owning democracy' of their 1950 manifesto was a natural extension of their house building programme. People who knew the joys and responsibilities of ownership would instinctively side with the owners of land and industry to oppose nationalisation. In reality the man with a car on hire purchase, a mortgage and life insurance on monthly instalments owned more debts than property. Property owning increased only slowly. Between 1953 and 1968 the percentage of households owning their own home rose by only 4%, from 16% to 20%. However if mortgagors could be grouped with the owners they added up to over half the households in Britain by the sixties; if house tenure rather than occupation could be made the defining characteristic of class, Labour, not the Conservatives, was in danger of representing the minority class.

The campaign for a property owning democracy was broadened in 1959 until it became little more than the claim that the Conservatives were the party of prosperity, a dangerous claim so easily destroyed by events beyond any party's control.

'While we have been in charge of the nation's affairs, many more of the good things of life have been enjoyed by families large and small and so long as we remain in charge they will be able to fulfil many more of their hopes and ambitions'. Thus Macmillan devalued the concept of a property owning democracy. Expenditure on consumer durables, even in 1959, was remarkable for its insignificance.[23] They were a great help with daily chores but represented technological advances and almost no stake at all in established patterns of ownership. If the property owning concept was to realise its potential for determining party allegiance it needed development in a different direction, from mass house ownership to mass ownership of industry, the means not the fruits of production.

2.3.5 Continuities in Liberal Manifestos – Interest-free, Innovative and Anti-bureaucratic   Liberals justified their existence by stressing a range of classless principles and policies. They opposed 'waste' and high taxes, military adventures and large armaments. They advocated free trade, proportional representation and devolution of power to Scotland, Wales and England. Between the wars they continued to propose liquor reform. After the Second War they supported European integration and all its institutions.

Liberals claimed they had originated important policies. The Welfare State was 'pioneered by two great Liberals – Lloyd George and Beveridge' (1964). They also claimed to have invented the Commonwealth as distinct from the Empire (1950, 1951); the policies that produced full employment after the second war (1951) – here Lloyd George got the credit for his 1929 manifesto rather than his Coalition government; regional aid (1966) and European integration–
'The Council of Europe is a Liberal conception. It is the realisation of a dream of European Liberals for two centuries. . . . In this sphere, the Liberal Party can justly claim to have been the pioneer. It is the only truly international party of the three' (1951).

They were ambivalent on nationalisation. They opposed it at intervals, but in 1945 listed industries ripe for it and gave general criteria for further extensions. They soon returned to the anti-nationalisation side. Liberals wanted to defend or extend the social services and opposed the means test in the thirties. They proposed a major public works programme to reduce interwar unemployment. However any social provisions were subject to Liberal opposition to high taxes, tariffs and subsidies on food and council housing.

It was easy to be 'classless' in theory, but while issues like proportional representation, liquor reform, devolution and anti-militarism were genuinely 'classless', anything that involved the balance of taxation or benefit between classes necessarily had a class content.

It was more feasible to be a 'radical non-socialist party' – another Liberal claim. This meant it rejected state control of industry or housing but favoured legislation to help the poor. In as much as radical meant more than this, the Liberals were a party of new ideas which could somehow find better ways of doing what everybody wanted. Hence the stress on policy innovation. This mix of anti-bureaucracy, social concern and technical innovation is illustrated in one short quotation from their 1951 manifesto: 'The Social Services must be safeguarded. Food subsidies must remain until the increased productivity campaign has brought down the cost of living. Extravagance and waste have constantly occurred in public administration. We demand the setting up of a House of Commons Committee on National Expenditure'.

For Liberals politics was not a zero sum game at home or abroad.

2.3.6 Special Industries   Both Labour and Conservative had a client industry. Miners had been elected to Parliament before the Labour Party had existed; they continued as a separate body until 1908 when the Miners Federation decided to affiliate to the Labour Party. The Miners Federation supplied 44% of Labour M.P.s in 1918. The Conservatives had a similar link with agriculture, but after 1918 it was expressed primarily in the manifestos as candidates were drawn increasingly from business and commerce. Despite their general dislike of government intervention and subsidies Conservatives usually advocated aid to agriculture, often in surprising detail. In 1929 Baldwin listed sixteen specific actions by his government to help agriculture, ranging from rates relief, special freight charges, protection, credit, subsidies, telephone and electrical provisions for rural areas to directives that school teachers co-operate with the agricultural industry.

2.3.7 National Areas   Interwar unemployment fluctuated according to industry and area as well as over time. It remained relatively low in transport, in new industries like electrical engineering and in the drink trade. Steel and shipbuilding were worst affected.[24] These industrial variations meant that unemployment was concentrated in Scotland, Wales and the industrial north of England, while rising living standards were concentrated in the south.

After the Second War unemployment remained low and politicians argued over whether 2% or 3% should be regarded as 'full employment'. While the annual average never exceeded $2\frac{1}{2}\%$ in England up to 1971, in Scotland and Wales it was never less than $2\frac{1}{2}\%$ except in the two years 1955–6 when it averaged 2.4% in Scotland and 1.9% in Wales.[25] So on a reasonable definition England enjoyed full employment for a quarter of a century after the Second War, but Scotland and Wales did not.

Ireland had shown how economic grievances and religious differences could generate support for nationalist parties. Scotland, in addition, had a well developed set of separate political, economic and legal institutions. The British parties competed with each other, and collectively, against nationalists to show concern for national problems. European wars helped to strengthen British unity as did the personalities of leading politicians. At the first election after the end of the interwar boom no leader of a great party was an Englishman representing an English constituency.

The nature of interwar problems also weighed against nationalism. The Irish had wanted to disposess the English landlords and the Anglican church. However these were not the problems of interwar Scotland and Wales. The Anglican church had been beaten and separation would only have made their industrial economies even more biased than Britain's towards products which could not be sold. As long as they remained worse off than England, and the cause was clearly international economic forces not English villany, they could only cling to the Union hoping for British standards of welfare and perhaps prosperity.

All three parties promised to use Westminster to focus British resources onto Scottish and Welsh problems. From the thirties manifestos usually contained a section on Scotland and Wales; latterly the parties began to issue separate national manifestos and television advertisements. Liberals were consistently in favour of constitutional change – 'home rule all round'. Labour also promised national assemblies in 1929 but never took action to create them until the Scottish National Party's (SNP) 1974 election victories. More frequently Labour promised selective and discriminatory economic measures to cut unemployment

in Scotland and Wales. Conservatives promised more than economic discrimination controlled from London. In 1950, for example, they promised Scotland an
additional minister 'with Cabinet rank' and separate Boards for coal, electricity,
railways and gas 'in no way subordinate' to the English ones.

The Conservatives maintained that 'Centralised control which ignores
national characteristics is an essential part of Socialism. Until the Socialist
Government is removed neither Scotland nor Wales will be able to strike away
the fetters of centralisation and be free to develop their own way of life'.

The Unionists had a policy of killing Irish nationalism with kindness at the
turn of the century. The Conservatives inherited that tradition. They would
probably make concessions more willingly than any other party provided the
essential unity of the state was preserved. On that they would stick more firmly
than anyone else.

3   Review

3.1 General Issues

Although there were dozens of specific issues after 1918, they can be seen as the
concrete embodiments of a very few general issues. It was these latter issues that
formed the basis for policy decisions. However the connection between broad
principle and specific policy could often be so ambiguous as to make reasonable
men disagree on the policy implied by the principle.

Three general issues were very important just prior to 1918 but not afterwards:
sex, democracy and explicit religious confrontation. Universal male suffrage and
the fight for supremacy between Lords and Commons were two embodiments of
the democratic issue but other factors were present in both, especially in the
Parliamentary battle. Women's suffrage embodied the sex issue. The most recent
expressions of explicit religious confrontation had been the battles over religious
education and Welsh disestablishment.

After 1918 five general issues survived from pre-war days: trade union power,
class interests, socialisation, the scale of civil government and the patriotic versus
internationalist issue. For good historical reasons the first four of these issues are
often confused, but they were logically distinct. The first two need no definition.
Socialisation here denotes public ownership and control of industries and
services by the State or its subordinate agencies. The scale of civil government
means state control of how individuals spend their earnings, the extent to which
decisions about what they consume (not how much) is taken away from
individuals and placed in the hands of politicians or civil servants. Some idealised
examples may be useful.

A pure policy of trade union power would be legislation to put trade union
representatives on the board of all companies, public and private, or into the
Lords on terms similar to the Anglican episcopate. A pure class policy would seek
to equalise wages before payment so that no redistribution through taxation or
social services would be necessary. Purely socialised enterprises would be state

owned and controlled, but operate without subsidy or social conscience. It is more difficult to picture a pure policy of large scale government because government policies of forced collective purchasing and consumption were usually intended to extract more resources from the rich and confer more benefits on the poor. So the use of a progressive income tax to buy a national health service would be a bad example. A better example would be taxation to buy higher education. Since universities are, in theory, private bodies that would not be socialisation. Since middle class children consumed more of the benefits it might not redistribute income between classes even if the taxation were progressive. But it would still be a form of forced consumption.

The fifth general issue was easier to recognise in its concrete manifestations than to define. Internationalism was not, fundamentally, about international affairs. It was a view about the nature of the State, an assertion that existing States, including Britain, had no mystical qualities, no right to a life of their own as distinct from the lives of their citizens. At various times this issue assumed very different outward forms: in economic guise it was free trade versus protection; in imperial it was Empire versus Commonwealth; in military form it opposed all shades of British nationalists from patriot to jingo against all types of anti-militarist, from those who demanded a peace of reconciliation and careful restrictions on arms expenditure to those who campaigned against conscription or were uncompromising pacifists. Internally it distinguished those who wished to preserve the British state for mystical reasons from those who would dismantle it if there seemed any likely practical advantages. For some electors questions affecting the national areas were just another facet of the internationalist or British nationalism issue. No doubt some Scots supported devolution for Scotland because they were nationalists not internationalists while some Englishmen opposed it because they were internationalists not British patriots.

Finally, if nothing else was active to motivate party choice, there remained the residual issue of government competence, the choice between party elites as rival teams of managers. The Liberals claims to innovation implied that they would be most competent across the whole range of government, not just on economic matters. Macmillan's 1959 manifesto explicitly claimed that Conservatives were the most competent at ensuring a supply of consumer durables. However the question of competence was most obviously relevant in 1922 and 1931 when the collapse of government policies precipitated the fall of the Government itself.

During the fifties Labour and Conservatives were accused of convergence because disputes on three of the five general issues seemed less acute than before. Attlee's government had greatly extended socialisation in industry, the health services and housing; Conservatives accepted that the deed was done and contented themselves with a token denationalisation. For a time Labour pledged that beyond renationalisation of the denationalised industries 'we have no other plans for further nationalisation' (1959). By 1974 Labour's manifesto had a list of socialisation proposals worthy of 1918 or 1945 and the Conservatives were bitterly opposed to them.

Labour was institutionally linked to the trade unions. Consequently the trade union issue could never disappear entirely although there was little reference to it in the manifestos during the fifties. A sharp decline in industrial relations at the end of the decade put trade unions back into the manifestos. In 1966 the Conservatives promised to repeal Labour's recent pro-union legislation and substitute some anti-union legislation of their own. After its 1969 confrontation with the unions Labour quickly recanted and the issue still remains a major point of difference between the parties.

The internationalist issue suffered a secular decline from which it has not yet completely recovered. The First World War, the lack of international economic co-operation between the wars, the threat from Hitler and then from Stalin all combined to make the British more uniformly patriotic and reduce the importance of the internationalist issue. Interwar unemployment turned even principled internationalists into tariff reformers. Hitler made the concept of total victory in war respectable and Stalin did the same for peace time conscription and massive armaments. Conservatives grudgingly accepted Labour's de-colonisation as they had its socialisation and even went on to continue the process. All the old tendencies and inclinations persisted, but events in the outside world reduced the scope for alternative policies. Yet the longer peace in Europe continued, the greater the chance that disagreement over British nationalism would recur. Specific post-war issues that again expressed the internationalist issue included controversies over nuclear disarmament, coloured immigration and devolution.

Finally two general issues never disappeared and always divided the major parties: the questions of class interest and the scale of civil government.

Historical accidents linked these issues in ways that were not logically necessary. There were indeed no logical connections between the five general issues and many electors disapproved of the links that history made. They have been described as non-ideologues for this. In 1900 the Labour Representation Committee brought together different organisations committed to socialisation, working class interests and trade union power. Some individuals had multiple membership and multiple objectives, but not all. It was a coalition of different bodies whose objectives would hopefully complement each other more than they conflicted. When Labour tried to take the full role of the pre-war progressive alliance it put great stress on internationalism. It also inherited the old radical commitment to big government – 'taxation for social purposes'. However all this was historical accident, not inescapable necessity.

3.2 Issues and Social Groups

Even if issues had only the slightest direct relevance to social groups we should expect the processes of social interaction to produce detectable differences of opinion and partisanship between social groups. However the great issues in British politics were either about social groups themselves or about matters which had logical or traditional connections with them.

The pre-1918 issues of sex and religious confrontation were directly linked to social groups. The democratic issue was strongly but less directly linked with class. Of the five general post-1918 issues, class was both a social group and an issue. Trade Union power and socialisation were likely to appeal more to workers than bosses. Because taxation was widely, if erroneously, thought to be progressive the middle class might be expected to oppose big government, confusing it with redistribution. Scottish, Welsh and English nationalism and appeals to particular industries were obviously directly related to social groups. Even within Wales the appeal of the nationalist party, Plaid Cymru, was to social groups defined partly by religion but above all by language. The only example of a general issue pertinent to party choice, but minimally related to social groups, was the issue of Scottish nationalism within Scotland. In a British context the SNPs appeal was wholly group orientated, but within Scotland it did not appeal specially to class, religious or linguistic groups.

Internationalism was associated with religious non-conformity as patriotism was with Anglicanism. Since Anglicans revered the Monarch as head of their church and accepted that the State had the right to determine the details of their faith, it could hardly be otherwise. Less obviously, we might expect links between religion and other issues. Before the First War the party of the non-conformists had been most sympathetic to working class aspirations. They used the term 'social gospel' to describe pre-war welfare reforms. Socialist speakers were frequent at the secular sessions held in pre-war non-conformist chapels. If anything of this link survived beyond 1918 we should expect religion to structure political attitudes on the issues of the social gospel: class, social welfare, perhaps even high taxation.

Attitude groups are clearly not synonymous with social groups. It would be false to pretend that all non-conformists were internationalists or all workers socialists. That is not the intention. What is suggested is that social groups tended towards political parties for both direct and indirect reasons: directly because the parties appealed to obvious group interest; indirectly because the parties appealed to attitudes that were more common in some social groups than others. Because group antagonisms in Britain were so low and party appeals so diffuse, we should not expect whole social groups to support particular parties, rather a bias within a group towards a party. Conversely the same lack of inter-group antagonism meant that a high local density of members of one group could bias the political attitudes of those outside the group towards the group norm. Thus a local non-conformist or working class tradition might apply even to those in the locality who were themselves Anglican, agnostic or middle class.

Summary

1 Around 1918 several important pre-war issues were eliminated by legislation.
2 Southern Ireland left the Union and Northern Ireland had its representation in Parliament sharply reduced.
3 The franchise was extended to most males and many females, so that women made up 40% of the 1918 electorate.

4 The power of the Lords to veto Commons legislation was ended.

5 Religious confrontation was reduced by disestablishment of the Anglican church in Wales, acceptance of the Education Acts and the secession of Ireland.

6 Generally these changes were fundamental defeats for the Unionists whose very name was irrelevant to post-1918 politics.

7 Several other important issues were eliminated by the 1914–18 war.

8 The Drink Trade was so reformed during the war that after 1918 liquor reform was not an important issue, in sharp contrast to other countries and pre-war Britain.

9 Taxes rose so high during wartime that there could never again be controversy over tax levels as low as those in the People's Budget of 1910.

10 The war destroyed Liberal versus Unionist party identification; war waged by the Liberals was as anachronistic as Unionism without Ireland.

11 The young Labour party, small, weak and formerly dependent on Liberal indulgence, attempted to fill the political vacuum by replacing its pre-war class appeal with a continuation of the classic Liberal appeals to internationalist sentiment.

12 Some important pre-war issues survived.

13 Unemployment returned soon after the war at a much worse level. The war and lack of a meaningful peace afterwards were considered the main causes.

14 War pressures increased the significance of trade union powers as a potential source of controversy.

15 War brought a vast extension of socialisation in industry and commerce and put nationalisation firmly on the political agenda.

16 Attitudes to the foreigner, symbolised by defence and tariff reform policies, provided a continued basis for the Unionist party along its traditional lines.

17 Party appeals to the electorate can be divided into the appeal of status, of candidates and of manifestos. From 1918 to 1974 these appeals were as follows.

18 Opposition status went to Labour by default in 1918. The benefits showed in the by-elections of the 1918–22 Parliament.

19 In 1910 candidates were divided on religion, not class; Irish Nationalists were Catholics, Unionists Anglicans, while Liberal and Labour were about equally divided between Anglicans and non-conformists. Most of the small number of Labour candidates had a manual working class background, but even including Labour only 6% of all candidates came from such a background.

20 As Labour assumed the role of the pre-war Liberal-Labour alliance so its candidates resembled those of the alliance in class composition.

21 The class appeal of candidates differed in 1918 from 1910 because the pattern of party competition changed more rapidly than the compensating changes in candidate characteristics within parties.

22 Labour manifestos had four recurrent themes: internationalism, socialisation, class interest and trade union power.

23 In 1918 and immediately afterwards Labour put most stress on internationalism. At the quasi referendum Tariff Election of 1923 Labour put the classic Liberal internationalist case against tariffs rather than narrow class interest.

24 There were some changes and trends. Labour manifestos became even more extreme on socialisation and class interest as previous demands were met. Its internationalism was weakest during the Cold War and its support for ever greater trade union power was temporarily reversed in 1969.

25 The Conservatives were patriotic, anti-socialist and advocates of the property owning democracy. Tariffs and defence replaced Unionism as the patriotic issues. They were also less keen on colonial independence and legislative devolution.

26 The property owning democracy concept came from the success of their interwar house building programme. In the fifties it was broadened to include consumer durables rather than developed to include the means of production.

27 Liberals were radical non-socialists. They claimed to be anti-bureaucratic, non-partisan, socially concerned and administratively innovative.

28 There were special appeals to two industries. Conservative manifestos gave long detailed lists of aid by them to agriculture, Labour M.P.s were biased towards miners especially in Labour's unsuccessful years.

29 The national areas, Scotland and Wales, suffered especially high unemployment between the wars and never enjoyed the standard definition of full employment even after the Second War. All parties, even the Unionists made nationalistic appeals to the Scottish and Welsh electorates.

30 Competence to govern was always a residual issue. It was specially important in 1922 and 1931. Luckily for all the parties they could all evade responsibility for the post-1918 economic and international collapse. Lloyd George's Coalition was the scapegoat.

31 We can distinguish five general issues after 1918: trade union power, class interests, socialisation of industry and housing, the scale of civil government and the patriotic versus internationalist issues. They were logically independent though linked by the accidents of party history.

Electoral Implications of Issues and Party Appeals

1 Class issues were obviously relevant to class groups, religious issues to religious groups, but the other issues also appealed to specific social groups. Trade union powers and socialisation were specially relevant to employers, managers and trade unionists; internationalist issues to religious traditions.

2 Because the pre-war politics of the social gospel linked social issues with religious groups, we should expect weaker links between religious groups and the trade union issue and class interests. On the scale of civil government it is not obvious whether class or religious groups should be more affected.

43595

3 Trends in party appeals might be expected to produce the following effects on social alignments.

4 Settlement of the democratic issue by extension of the franchise created a large proportion of inexperienced voters whose initial party committment must have been low. This opened up the possibility of rapid change.

5 A working class dominated electorate increased the viability of working class parties but decreased the viability of middle class parties and made pure class politics incompatible with the alternation of parties in government.

6 Prospects for new parties were less in rural areas since the franchise had already included the vast majority of the working class before 1918.

7 The decline in sectarian confrontation would tend to produce a decline in sectarian effects on voting.

8 Loss of opposition status by Liberals in 1918 should have damaged future Liberal prospects.

9 Sudden, large, but declining, class differences between candidates would tend to produce a corresponding class polarisation in votes. Candidate changes should have had little, if any, effect on religious polarisation.

10 The course of the trade union issue would imply political polarisation between employers and managers versus trade unionists, steady or increasing in size, but with a temporary drop in 1970.

11 Labour's commitment to ever more redistribution to its favoured classes would tend to increase class polarisation over time. This class effect might not be so closely tied to the managers versus trade unionists division.

12 Labour's commitment to ever more socialisation would tend to increase polarisation along managers versus trade unionists lines.

13 The increasing scale of government would at least tend to maintain broader class divisions and possibly religious divisions also.

14 The patriotic versus internationalist issue was manifested in various forms, from Unionism and jingoism, to tariffs, to rearmament against Germany, to arguments about post-war armaments, decolonisation, Commonwealth immigration and devolution. Such issues were weakest during the Hitler-Stalin period and have only partially recovered their intensity since then. We should expect the internationalist issues to produce a substantial religious alignment in the twenties, declining to a minimum at the start of the fifties and only partially recovering afterwards.

CHAPTER 2
Basic Voting Patterns at a Post-War Election: 1966

1 Why 1966?

1.1 A Simple Party System

The British party system was at its simplest in 1951 and little had changed by 1966 when over 90 % of voters chose Labour or Conservative. 76 % of the register at this election voted out of a possible 93 % for an election in March. So while something must be said about Liberal voting and turnout it is reasonable to simplify our analysis by concentrating on the Labour versus Conservative division of the vote.

Nationalists gained 5 % of the Scottish vote and less than that in Wales. The Labour vote was 13 % higher in Wales and 2 % higher in Scotland than in England. There were some national differences but on nothing like the scale of 1974. Britain-wide analyses were still a reasonable approximation to reality.

1.2 The First Census Data on Parliamentary Constituencies

A parliamentary constituency volume of the 1966 Census gave data on class, the property owning democracy, immigration and other social variables relevant to party appeals.[1] Table 1 lists forty two such variables used in the analyses reported here. Before 1966 almost all census information was only available for national, regional or local government areas. Unfortunately the 1966 tables contained nothing on religion.

1.2.1 Preliminary Analysis of Available Census Data

When these census variables were used to predict Labour versus Conservative votes in the constituencies, the occupation variables were by far the most effective. The percent employers and managers, EMPL, explained two-thirds of the variation in Labour versus Conservative voting in 1966. It did even better at predicting the Labour share of the total vote in each constituency but, though the best predictor, it explained only half the variation in Conservative shares of the vote.

Table 1
Social Variables from the 1966 Census used in Constituency Analyses

Class subdivisions (% of economically active males)

EMPL	% employers and managers
PROF	% professional
CLERK	% other non-manual
MID	% non-manual = EMPL + PROF + CLERK
SKIL	% skilled manual including foremen and non-professional own-account workers
SEMI	% semi-skilled manual including agricultural and personal service workers
UNSK	% unskilled manual

In the Census there was also an 'armed forces and inadequately described' category; for analysis we repercentaged EMPL, PROF, CLERK, SKIL, SEMI, UNSK to sum to 100 % without the inadequately described and armed forces.

Property owning democracy (% of tenures, etc.)

COUN	% public authority housing
OWN	% houses owned or on a mortgage
RENT	% privately rented = 100 % − COUN − OWN
TENURE	bipolar tenure = OWN − COUN
AMEN	% with 'full amenities' (i.e. fixed bath, etc.)
GPHS	estimated % good private houses = AMEN − COUN (council houses usually had high rates of officially defined amenities)
CARS	% cars per household

Immigration (% of population)

NI	% born in Northern Ireland
EIRE	% born in Eire
CIMM	% born in colonies or 'New' Commonwealth
TIMM	total immigrants = NI + EIRE + CIMM
IRISH	total Irish = NI + EIRE

Rurality

AGRI	% economically active males in agriculture

Unemployment (% of economically active males)

UNEML	% unemployed with no job in last year
UNEMS	% unemployed but who had worked in last year

UNEM   % unemployed = UNEML + UNEMS

Age and Sex (% of population)
  MALE   % male
  OLD   % aged over 65

Special Industries (% economically active males)
  AGRI   % in agriculture
  FORCES   % in armed forces and inadequately described
  GOVT   % employed by national and local government
  CIVIL   GOVT − FORCES

Nations and Regions (dummy variables)
  SCOT   Scotland
  WALES   Wales
  ENG   England
  N   North and North East England
  YH   Yorkshire/Humberside
  EM   East Midlands
  EA   East Anglia
  SE   South East
  SW   South West
  WM   West Midlands
  NW   North West
  LCC   Inner London (old London County Council area)
  CENT   Central   England,   or   Middle   England =
                        WM + EM + EA + SE + LCC

  PERI   Peripheral England = ENG − CENT

Note: all forty two social and regional variables are described and their effect on partisanship discussed in Chapter Three.

Political Measures
  TWOCON   Conservative share of Conservative plus Labour vote
  VCON, VLAB,
    VLIB   Party shares of three party vote
  TURN   Turnout rate as a percent of registered electorate

1.3 The First Comprehensive Survey Study of a British Election
  The first major sample survey of the British electorate for academic purposes was carried out by Butler and Stokes in 1964.[2] They continued their study with more interviews in 1966. Before this there had been many local surveys by

academics and many national surveys by commercial pollsters. The Butler/Stokes study provides a wealth of data for comparison with census based analyses. We distinguish their published findings from our reanalysis of their data by using 'Butler/Stokes' for their findings and '1966 Election Study' when reanalysing their data.

1.3.1 An Empirical Check on the Relationship between Issues and Social Groups　The 1966 Election Study provides an empirical check on the conclusions in the previous chapter about the relationship between issues, social groups and parties. The data shows that, in 1966 at least, survey respondents associated issues with parties in the expected ways. Secondly, respondents did not themselves accept or reject the complete packages of issues which they recognised the parties were offering. Thirdly, the patterns of political attitudes across social groups had the expected signs and the relative magnitudes.

Butler and Stokes themselves have already shown how sharp a public image Labour and Conservative had on the five general issues of class, socialisation, trade union power, internationalism and the scale of civil government. When asked to place the parties on a scale running from middle class to working class 90% put the Conservatives towards the middle class end and 83% put Labour nearer the opposite end.[3] There was no question on which party favoured the unions, but a question on whether Labour should have close ties with the unions was based on the presumption that all respondents already knew that it did have such links. The low level of 'don't know' responses, less than 12%, suggests the link was a familiar idea.[4] There were more specific questions on the other three issues. In 1964, 90% of respondents thought Labour more likely than the Conservatives to nationalise more industries.[5] By a majority of 64% to 7% in 1966 they thought Labour more likely than the Conservatives to increase social service expenditure.[6] There were questions on two specific issues which were at least partly representative of the general internationalist issue. By a majority of 72% to 8% in 1964 respondents thought the Conservatives the more likely to retain an independent nuclear force.[7] On immigration they always felt the Conservatives were more likely than Labour to keep immigrants out.[8] In 1970 they chose the Conservatives as the anti-immigration party by a majority of 57% to 4%. Events modified the perceived distinctions between the parties. When the Labour government kept the bomb and ran into financial difficulties the perceived distinction between the parties declined, although it still remained large. Conversely the distinction on immigration was not large until Powell's crude summary measures because class and religion may interact, but they are sufficient for our present purpose.[10]

Clearly there was a well defined structure to the electorate's perception of party policy. Butler and Stokes then sought to show that there was very little ideological structure to respondents' own policy choices. Since the packages of policies proposed by the parties were formed by a sequence of historical accidents, not logic, this finding is evidence of free-will rather than intellectual disorganisation on the part of the electorate. Purely technical factors also contributed to the failure to find generally accepted correlations between positions on different issues. Popular issues could not correlate highly with issues on which opinion was divided. Thus, while it is true that 46 % wanted either more nationalisation or an end to an independent nuclear role, but not both, it is also true to say that 35 % only supported the more popular issue and 11 % only supported the less popular.[9] Consequently the correlations between some issues were depressed by technical factors.

Ideological structure is not the only possible structure for opinions. Opinions had a social structure which helps to explain why some of the ideological structure was so weak. For easily understood reasons, working class individuals were more likely than middle class individuals to favour some Labour policies but less likely than middle class individuals to favour other Labour policies. The interests of social groups produced different issue packages than those offered by the parties. Ten questions chosen from the 1966 Election Study as more or less imperfect representatives of the five general issues are shown in Table 2. Socialisation is represented by the percent wanting more nationalisation; trade union power by the per cent saying trade unions had too much power. The scale of civil government is represented by a soft question on whether social service spending should be increased or not, and a hard question on whether respondents would chose a tax cut or an increase in social spending. The internationalist issue is the most subtle and is represented by answers to five questions: the percentages who would give up the bomb completely ('unilateralists'); who felt very strongly that too many immigrants had been let in; who felt Britain had relinquished the Empire too fast; who would accept Smith's terms on Rhodesian UDI or at least negotiate with him; and who felt the Queen and Royal Family were very important. Obviously each of these questions touched on other issues besides the general internationalist issue. Finally class is represented by the percent feeling close to their own class.

Eight social groups are used, defined by whether the head of the respondent's household had a manual or non-manual occupation and whether the respondent was a non-conformist (excluding Presbyterians), a Catholic, an active Anglican attending at least once a year or a purely nominal Anglican. In the 1966 Election Study survey only 5 % of respondents refused to state a religious preference. So the nominal Anglicans probably included a large measure of the irreligious.

On all questions except the class question, the class structure of opinion can be measured by the average within-religion class difference of percentages and the religious structure of opinion by the average within-class difference. These are crude summary measures because class and religion may interact, but they are sufficient for our present purpose.[10]

Irrespective of religion almost 60 % of the working class felt close to their own class. About the same percentage of middle class non-conformists felt close to their class though other middle class respondents showed less class feeling, Catholics very much less. This question is difficult to compare with the others but it shows at least a 20 % difference between the classes in their attitude to their own class.

Table 2
The Social Structure of Public Opinion 1966

General issues and specific questions	Class	Non-Conformist	Active Anglican	Nominal C of E	Catholic	Religion	Class
			Religion			Social Effects of	
Class							
% feeling close to own class	M	59	50	44	43	NA	NA
	W	57	60	63	59		
Socialisation							
% wanting more nationalisation	M	20	13	21	19	−3	−11
	W	26	28	29	31		
Trade Union Power							
% feeling TUs have too much power	M	73	81	74	71	11	21
	W	49	63	58	56		
Internationalism							
% unilateralist	M	22	9	9	6	−12	−4
	W	25	14	15	19		
% feeling very strongly that too many immigrants have been let in	M	29	41	51	42	13	−8
	W	36	49	53	46		
% feeling Britain relinquished Empire too fast	M	47	50	49	45	7	10
	W	33	44	40	36		
% willing to accept UDI or negotiate with Smith	M	53	61	53	56	7	20
	W	35	40	37	44		
% feeling Queen and Royal Family very important	M	47	62	52	73	12	−9
	W	59	67	55	60		
Scale of Civil Government							
% wanting no increase in social service spending	M	58	58	51	45	−4	18
	W	44	36	33	41		
% preferring tax cut to more social spending	M	52	63	61	58	10	6
	W	48	56	51	51		

The other questions can be directly compared. Social differences were relatively small on socialisation. The working class was only 11% more favourable to nationalisation than the middle class. On trade union power the middle class were 21% less favourable to the unions and Anglicans were 11% less favourable than non-conformists. The relative sizes of these effects, both between issues and between class and religion, match expectations. The only surprise is the relative strength, secondary though it is, of the religious effect on attitudes to trade unions. On the scale of government, class had the greatest effect on answers to the soft question, religion on answers to the hard question. It seems plausible to interpret the soft question as evoking working class feelings of self interest and the hard question, tax cuts versus social spending, as evoking the social gospel feelings associated with non-conformity.

One of the five questions selected to represent internationalism, the Rhodesia question, displayed a pattern similar to the trade union question: a 20% class effect and a 7% religious effect, with the middle class and Anglicans being pro-Smith. On the broader Empire question the religious effect was close to the class effect in size and on the other three questions the religious effect was the larger. Anglicans were more than 12% more anti-immigration, anti-unilateralist and pro-royalty than non-conformists. Overall the data confirm that non-conformity was associated with internationalist issues but not to the extent that class was associated with class and trade union issues.

On six questions the direction of Anglican tendencies was the same as the direction of middle class tendencies. These were: socialisation; trade union power; the hard question on public spending; unilateralism; the Empire; and Rhodesia. However on three questions Anglican tendencies coincided with working class tendencies: immigration; royalty; and the soft question on public spending. The working class were more anti-immigration and pro-royalty and the non-conformists more opposed to increases in public spending. If we accepted a combination of internationalism with pro-working class policies as a definition of the expected general ideology these three questions were exceptions, but they are easy enough to explain. Immigration involved more economic dangers for the working class than for the middle class. Extreme social distance gave the working class a more romantic notion of royalty and less of a conflict of economic interest. Given the substance of the issues it would have been surprising if the working class had always taken the same side as the non-conformists.

Across the whole range of ten questions there was no consistent evidence of interaction between class and religion. On some questions religious differences were larger in the middle class, on others in the working class, and on two important questions, unilateralism and immigration, religious effects were almost the same in the two classes.

None of the social differences on issues could be described as extreme issue polarisation. Indeed the differences on individual issue questions were less than the voting differences between class groups, although much the same as the voting differences between religious groups. Applying the same measures of social effects to voting in 1966 shows the class effect on the Conservative vote was

	Test of Model					Estimates of Effects in Model:		
	Social Groups → Votes → Attitudes					Social Groups → Votes ← Attitudes		
	Religious Effect on Attitudes with no control for party (average of within Labour and within Conservative effects)		Class Effect on Attitudes with no control for party (average of within Labour and within Conservative effects)		Issue	Effects of three variables, each with a control for both the others, on Conservative vote		
	with no control for party	average of within Labour and within Conservative effects	with no control for party	average of within Labour and within Conservative effects		Religion	Class	Attitude
	− 3	+ 1	− 11	+ 1	Nationalisation	+ 11	+ 29	− 44
	+ 11	+ 5	+ 21	+ 12	TU power	+ 3	+ 33	+ 34
	− 12	− 6	− 4	+ 1	Unilateralists	+ 7	+ 37	− 24
	+ 13	+ 7	− 8	− 5	Immigration	+ 11	+ 40	− 4
	+ 7	+ 8	+ 10	+ 8	Empire	+ 9	+ 40	+ 23
	+ 7	+ 7	+ 20	+ 10	Rhodesia	+ 5	+ 34	+ 32
	+ 12	+ 9	− 9	− 11	Queen	+ 8	+ 44	+ 15
	− 4	− 6	+ 18	+ 13	Social spending	+ 11	+ 41	+ 14
	+ 10	+ 9	+ 6	− 3	Tax Cut	+ 11	+ 44	+ 22

R² using attitudes only = 42%
R² using groups and attitudes = 46%

Multiple Regression Equation to Predict Votes from Groups and Attitudes

% CON = 2+20 Class+5 Religion
−23 Nationalisation
+17 TU Power
−5 Unilateralist
−8 Immigration
+14 Empire
+28 Rhodesia
+7 Queen
+6 Social Spending
+6 Tax Cut

Note: (1) Class effect = average class difference among non-conformists and active Anglicans.
(2) Religious effect = the average difference between active Anglicans and non-conformists in the two classes.
(3) Positive effects imply higher response percentages for active Anglicans or for the middle class.
(4) M = respondent's head of household had non-manual occupation, W = manual.

33%, on Labour 42%, on Liberal 10%; the religious effects were 11% on Conservative, 7% on Labour and 4% on Liberal. Labour and Liberal were favoured by non-conformists, Conservative and Liberal by the middle class. This suggests that class, if not religion, had a direct effect on voting and did not operate purely through its effect on the tabulated issues. Indeed it is sometimes suggested that voting depends directly on social divisions alone, while issue polarisation is dependent upon voting choice. If that were true the match between social groups and issues would be weaker than between social groups and voting – as it is for class divisions – and the correlation between issue positions and social groups would disappear altogether when party choice was controlled. Controls for Labour and Conservative voting do indeed destroy the relationship between some issues and social groups. On nationalisation, for example, after control for party, the middle class and Anglicans were each half a per cent more pro-nationalisation than the opposite social groups. Viewed in isolation it would be plausible to interpret differences on nationalisation as a consequence, not a cause, of party choice. However on trade union power, a control for party only reduced the class effect from 21% to 12% and the religious effect from 11% to 5%. This was a more typical effect. Table 2 shows that only nationalisation attitudes could be considered totally dependent on partisanship.

If we accept as a very rough approximation the model in which social divisions affect votes both directly and via political attitudes, then the last part of Table 2 provides estimates of the power of these three links. On average class had twice the effect on partisanship of any single attitude; religion had one quarter the effect of class. Neglecting nationalisation attitudes as possibly dependent on voting, attitudes to trade unions were almost as powerful as class. The weak link in the causal chain from social groups to party votes via attitudes was the relatively low dependence of attitudes on social groups. Even so, and taking only trade union attitude into account, the indirect link between groups and voting via attitudes was responsible for a fifth of the overall class effect and over half the overall religious effect. However it is almost inevitable that any calculation of indirect effects via attitudes is an underestimation since there were so many issues differentially appealing to social groups; the overlap between supporters of different issues was so weak that there was a multitude of independent indirect paths. Even if we only take account of the nine attitudes listed in Table 2, measured as crudely as they are, the estimate of the direct effects of class and religion drop to 20% and 5% respectively; that is to about half the overall effect in each case. These estimates could be lowered with the adoption of more subtle measures of attitudes, the inclusion of other specific issues current in 1966 and, more important, the addition of the particular issues which, although not contemperaneous, had contributed to socio-political patterns through their influence on previous partisan choices.

2 The Meanings of Class

Up to now we have not given a precise meaning to class, although it was important in the party debate and was a powerful predictor of the voting choices made by individuals and constituency electorates.

2.1 Characteristics that Define Class

The definition of class depends upon the use we make of the concept, in this case the explanation of voting behaviour. The 1966 Election Study included two occupational breakdowns: the Registrar General's seventeen socio-economic groups and a set of six occupational grades based upon the Market Research Society's classification. The Registrar General's socio-economic grouping was simplified in the parliamentary volume of the census to provide the class categories shown in Table 1 plus the 'inadequately described and armed forces' category. The six occupational grades used in the survey were: (1) higher managerial; (2) lower managerial; (3) skilled or supervisory non-manual; (4) other non-manual; (5) skilled manual; and (6) unskilled manual. There was also a category for pensioners and welfare recipients.

For most purposes survey analysts in Britain have used a very simple class distinction: class is defined by the occupational of the respondent's head of household, divided into manual versus non-manual occupations i.e. grades one to four against five and six.[11] In their early analyses Butler and Stokes split grades one to three against four to six, but later reverted to the more usual manual/non-manual distinction.[12] Both their original choice and their decision to change stemmed from a comparison of the class labels respondents chose for themselves, their class identification, with the six objective grades.[13] Although the percent identifying with the middle class dropped steadily from grade one to grade six, the largest drop between two adjacent grades was between grades three and four in 1963 and four and five in 1970. This was chiefly the result of a sharp rise in middle class identification in grade four between 1963 and 1970. Similarly Rose decided on a grouping of social grades, in his case a trichotomy not a dichotomy, on the basis of the distribution of party support within each of the six grades.[14]

These approaches have several common properties. Both were justified by their empirical predictive power not by some external sociological theory and both assigned almost all individuals to classes. Most obviously they were both based on workplace-defined occupational grades. All three properties need examination.

Although other surveys have not always produced the same result, Butler and Stokes found that the great majority of their respondents were familiar with the term class and 74% described the 'working class' in occupational terms. However there was less agreement on 'middle class' characteristics: 61% used occupational descriptions and 21% referred to income or wealth. Manners, morals, education or other characteristics received few mentions. To the electorate class was familiar, dichotomous and mainly based on the workplace.[15]

However there is an alternative view of class which was not directly contradicted by the survey respondents, even if they did not express it sufficiently articulately for it to register in the survey report. This is the notion of core classes, ideal or typical classes. Rose has defined an ideal type working class by five characteristics: minimum education; trade union family; council house; working class identification; and manual occupation. In his 1970 Gallup sample only 9% were ideal type working class and only 12% ideal type middle class.[16] It seems likely that the broad mass of the electorate were familiar with this concept. It was enshrined in at least one best selling popular song of the period. The essence of this view of class is that very few people can be considered 'members' of the class, most are outside both core classes but linked more or less strongly to each.

Core classes were more evident in political debate than total population class breakdowns. Lloyd George was reputed to feel that in the 1918 parliament he 'had the Trade Union Congress in front of him and the Association of Chambers of Commerce at his back', not the manuals in front and the non-manuals behind.[17] Labour made the most explicit class appeals. It did not restrict its sympathy to an ideal type working class but it was careful to restrict its attacks to a very idealised opposing class. It frequently reiterated the slogan from its 1918 constitution that it stood for 'the workers by hand and by brain'. It attacked the landowners, big businessmen, profiteers and the rich while it defended wage earners, 'the average citizen' (1966), the 'ordinary man' (1945), and even the 'lower middle classes' (1929). The party's socialist policies constituted an attack on employers and existing management while its institutional links with the unions necessarily associated it with another core group. Core classes made up of those who controlled the workforce and those who most resisted that control were, like Rose's ideal types, only a small subset of society; unlike his ideal types they were still defined by a single workplace characteristic.

2.2 Controls for Correlated Attributes

Some attributes correlate empirically with occupational grades but are unambiguously distinct from class: region, nation, rurality, religion, for example. There is a case for measuring class effects only after controls to remove the effects of these other attributes. Controls were applied in Table 2 for this reason. However there are other attributes which correlate highly with occupational grades and appear to have an independent effect on party choice which are conceptually less distinct from class. Possession of a telephone is a clear example. In 1970 manual workers renting a telephone were 20% more Conservative than manual workers without telephones and managers with telephones were 18% more Conservative than those without one. In the 1970 Gallup survey the difference in Conservatism between manuals and managers was 32%, but controlling for telephones reduced that difference to only 22%.[18] Both figures are equally correct measures of class differences, but which should be preferred?

The habits of multivariate analysis incline us towards the controlled figure of 22% or at least a multiple statement of a 22% grade difference and a 19%

telephone difference. This involves comparisons of highly deviant working class telephone renters with normal upper class telephone renters. Moreover we know that one-fifth of households rented a telephone in 1964 and two-fifths a decade later, without these being a gross partisan shift towards the Conservatives. So telephones were not direct causes of partisanship, nor, by defining a social group, does it seem likely that they were an indirect cause. It is much more likely that those elements within the manual working class who had most in common with the upper class were the keenest to rent a telephone. It seems reasonable to avoid controls for such selective rather than causative attributes when measuring party differences between classes.

It is less easy to decide whether to impose controls for education, car ownership and especially, house tenure. These are on the borderline between 'normal' occupational correlates and genuinely different attributes.

2.3 Multiple Links to Class

Whether we view classes as all inclusive or as core classes, it makes more sense to view individuals as linked to classes rather than belonging to a class. Between a third and a half of the electorate do not have paid occupations; those that do, have had previous occupations and anticipate future ones. They all have parents and most have brothers, sisters, children or spouses with jobs of their own. Their neighbours and associates also have jobs. There is evidence that these other occupations also affect partisanship. Butler and Stokes found that non-manual respondents with non-manual fathers and grandfathers were 31% more Conservative than other non-manuals. Their findings on the influence of house tenure could be interpreted as an effect of the occupational mix in the neighbourhood rather than of tenure itself.[19]

It is unusual to measure class differences only within comparable family traditions or local environments. This would appear to compare normal members of one class with deviants in the other. However lack of control means that the observed partisan differences may owe something to occupations other than the respondents' own.

3   The Meanings of Polarisation

The rise of a class alignment or an increase in class polarisation does not mean victory for a class party.

3.1 Fit or Slope

Two reasonable definitions of a social alignment are: that party support should vary sharply with social divisions—the slope definition; or that party support should not vary much, either systematically or randomly, except across social divisions—the fit definition. These two definitions do not contradict each other, but it is logically possible for one to show a high level of alignment when the other indicates a low level. In the language of data analysis, one definition implies a high correlation coefficient between party and society, the other a high regression slope coefficient.

Butler and Stokes measured a class alignment by taking the difference between levels of Conservative support among manuals and non-manuals.[20] It is easy to show that this measure must equal the regression slope in a dummy variable regression in which Conservatives and non-manuals are coded 1 and others 0. The correlation coefficient associated with that regression is

$$r = (\text{slope}) \times \sqrt{\frac{M(1-M)}{C(1-C)}}$$

where M is the proportion non-manual middle class and C is the proportion Conservative in the sample. According to Butler and Stokes $M = 40\%$ and, since the Second War, C ranged between 45% and 53% (taking percent of the two party vote). So r ranged from a minimum of 0.9798 times the slope to a maximum of 0.9847 times the slope. For all practical purposes the measure of slope and fit were identical.

However this identity depended upon the particular class and party dichotomies. Slope and fit would be very different if the same class dichotomy were used to predict Liberal voting. Perhaps more important, the slope and fit were very different if other class dichotomies were used to predict Conservative versus Labour voting. Table 3 shows how slope and fit measures varied under alternative dichotomisations of the six occupational grades. A division into managers versus the rest produced a slope only a little smaller than the manual/non-manual dichotomy, but a far worse fit. Managers and supervisors versus the rest gave the sharpest slope, but manuals versus non-manuals the best fit.

Although discussion usually focuses on measures of slope, the much better fit achieved by contrasting two large classes, manual versus non-manual, is one reason why survey analysts have favoured this split.

3.2 The Effect of Simple Spatial Aggregation on Measures of Polarisation

As we shall see, the problem with spatial aggregates is that they are not simple aggregations of individuals. For the moment let us assume that they are.

Suppose that fraction a of the middle class and b of the working class are Conservative. The Butler/Stokes measure of class polarisation, the slope measure, is $(a - b)$. If these rates of class partisanship applied to all constituencies then in any constituency with a fraction M of the electors middle class, the proportion Conservative would be

$$\begin{aligned} \text{CON} &= a\,M + b\,(1 - M) \\ &= b + (a - b)\,M \end{aligned}$$

A plot of data from several constituencies would show all the data points lying on a straight line with a slope of $(a - b)$. Thus the aggregate data slope would equal the survey data slope but the aggregate data would fit the relationship perfectly, irrespective of the size of the survey data fit. In particular the aggregate data fit would be equally good whichever class dichotomy was employed.

By similar reasoning it can be shown that aggregate data and survey data would show identical slopes even if partisanship were predicted from several social variables. This is provided that the form of the relationship was a linear additive model and the social variables did not produce interactive political effects.

The only possible cause of a less than perfect fit between aggregate partisanship and aggregate social characteristics is that partisan rates in social groups may vary from constituency to constituency. It has been shown that if such variations are random, in the sense that rate variations are not systematically related to concentrations of the social groups themselves, a regression through the aggregate data would give the same slopes as found in the survey data, but the fit would, of course, be less than perfect.[21]

The survey fit is almost a statistical artefact depending as it does on the sizes of the classes. The aggregate data fit is a measure of the political effects of cross-cutting cleavages, both the systematic ones related to variables excluded from the

Table 3
Slope and Fit for Three Alternative Class Dichotomies

Basic Data

		Occupational Grade of Head of Household					
		1	2	3	4	5	6
No. of respondents in each grade		96	166	170	122	568	358
% of grade Conservative (of two party partisans in 1963)		86	81	77	61	29	25

Calculations

Class Dichotomy		% *Conservative*		*Slope*	*Fit*
Middle Class	*Working Class*	*in middle class*	*in working class*		
Managers (1, 2)	rest (3, 4, 5, 6)	83	38	45	0.35
Managers and supervisors (1, 2, 3)	rest (4, 5, 6)	81	31	50	0.46
Non-manuals (1, 2, 3, 4)	Manuals (5, 6)	76	28	49	0.48
Middle class identifiers	Working class identifiers	79	28	51	0.49

prediction scheme and the random ones associated with the incidence of particular candidates, local events and traditions and the like.

3.3 Party Symmetry

Over a very short period of British electoral history there is perhaps some value in a symmetric concept of polarisation, one party's gain being another's loss. However a symmetric concept is less useful for analyses of elections when three parties gained sizeable shares of the vote; or for long term trend analysis when, on different occasions, the two party system existed but comprised different pairs of parties. Moreover appeals to social groups in British politics were not in fact symmetric between the parties. Labour had a special appeal for the working class, but that did not single out one of its opponents as the middle class party. Similarly there was a link between Anglicanism and the Conservatives which did not single out one party as the party of non-conformists.

If a symmetric measure is used there are two variants which show very different values depending upon the size of the third party vote. As third party votes fluctuate the two symmetric measures of polarisation follow different trends. As an extreme example from recent British politics Table 4 shows some calculations based on a survey of Scottish electors in October 1974. Using the Butler/Stokes approach, excluding those who did not vote Labour or Conservative, gives a class polarization of 48%. However averaging the class differences in Labour and Conservative shares of the all voters gives a value of less than 32%. If the Liberals and SNP were to disappear at some subsequent election and class polarisation using the Butler/Stokes measure showed a zero trend, then the other symmetric measure would show a 16.5% trend. Conversely if the second measure showed no trend, the Butler/Stokes measure would show a sharp change.

Table 4
Two Alternative Symmetric Measures of Class Polarisation

Basic Data from October 1974 Election Study in Scotland

% of votes for

	CON	LAB	LIB	SNP	
Among middle class identifiers	39	21	13	28	100%
working class identifiers	12	57	4	27	100%

Butler/Stokes measure	= difference between middle and working class on Conservative share of Conservative plus Labour votes
	= 48%
Alternative measure	= average of differences between middle and working class on Conservative and Labour shares of total vote
	= [(39−12)−(21−57)]/2
	= 31.5%

4   The Z Model: A Simple Two Level Model of Class Polarisation

4.1 Empirical Contradictions in a Single level Model

The 1966 Election Study found that out of those who voted Labour or Conservative about 73.4% of non-manuals and 30.0% of manuals voted Conservative (after correcting for a 3.4% pro-Labour bias in the survey). Simple aggregation would imply that in a constituency where a fraction M were non-manual middle class, the fraction Conservative of the two party vote would be

$$CON = 0.734M + 0.300(1 - M)$$
$$= 0.300 + 0.434M$$

But a regression on constituency data using the census measure of non-manuals gave

$$CON = 0.16 + 0.93M$$

The actual slope in the pattern of constituency data was over twice that implied by a simple aggregation of survey data.

The contradiction between these empirical results can be avoided by postulating a two level model in which individuals of both occupational groups respond to the occupational mix in their constituency.[22] Specifically we might approximate their response to environmental class by letting partisanship in each class be a linear function of the local class mix. The probability of an individual voting Conservative in a constituency where a fraction M of electors were middle class would then be $(a_0 + a_1 M)$ for middle class individuals and $(b_0 + b_1 M)$ for working class individuals. Summing over all individuals in the constituency, typically some 57,000 people, would give the statistically expected fraction Conservative as

$$CON = (a_0 + a_1 M)M + (b_0 + b_1 M)(1 - M)$$
$$= b_0 + (a_0 - b_0 + b_1)M + (a_1 - b_1)M^2$$

and the scatter around these statistically expected values should be very slight since the summation is over so many individuals.

If both classes were equally responsive to the local class mix then $a_1 = b_1$ and

$$CON = b_0 + (a_0 - b_0 + b_1)M$$

which implies a linear relationship between voting and class at the constituency level. However the slope is the sum of two components

$(a_0 - b_0)$ = the slope due to differences between middle and working class individuals in the same environment, the 'individual level' effect

and b_1 = the slope due to environmental differences alone, the 'ecological' or 'environmental' effect

If the two classes were not equally responsive to the class mix in the environment a $\neq$ b, the original formula would indicate a quadratic relationship between voting and class, humped if the working class were more responsive to the environment, dished if the middle class were more responsive. Linear and quadratic regressions explained 47% and 52% of the variation in Conservative votes. So the quadratic gave only a little better predictive fit; over the range of actual data, from about 15% non-manual to 55% non-manual, the quadratic gave case by case predictions·very similar to those of the linear formula. Therefore as a first approximation we might accept $a_1 = b_1$ and the linear model. Nonetheless there was some evidence that the real relationship was humped which means that working class partisanship was more sensitive than middle class partisanship to the mix of classes in the locality.

4.2 Size of Area Spanned by Environmental Influences of Different Kinds.

Over very small areas few doubt the influence of one person's social characteristics on other people's political behaviour. Hence the use of the head of household's social characteristics in survey analysis. The question is how much further beyond the household does the social character of the area affect the political behaviour of individuals within it. We can expand the two level model to become a multi level model in which an individual's partisanship depends upon his own class and on the class mix in his neighbourhood, constituency, borough, county and region. Specifically the probability that a non-manual votes Conservative becomes

$$a_0 + a_1 M_n + a_2 M_c + a_3 M_b + a_4 M_t + a_5 M_r$$

where each M is the proportion non-manual at one of these five levels of environment. If we write a similar expression for working class individuals, sum over areas as before and assume both classes are equally responsive as before, then the multi level model implies:

(1) for constituencies $CON = b_0 + (a_0 - b_0 + b_1 + b_2)M_c + b_3 M_b + b_4 M_t + b_5 M_r$

(2) for boroughs $CON = b_0 + (a_0 - b_0 + b_1 + b_2 + b_3)M_c + b_4 M_t + b_5 M_r$

(3) for counties $CON = b_0 + (a_0 - b_0 + b_1 + b_2 + b_3 + b_4)M_t + b_5 M_r$

(4) for regions $CON = b_0 + (a_0 - b_0 + b_1 + b_2 + b_3 + b_4 + b_5)M_r$

From these expressions it is impossible to disentangle the effects b_1 and b_2 of neighbourhood and constituency, but various tests can be applied to check the higher level effects. Regressions using different levels of aggregated data suggested that the higher level terms could be neglected. The fit was not improved by adding higher level terms; regressions using all levels in one multiple regression showed that the constituency class term was highly significant (by the F test) but the others were not. Bivariate regressions performed at different levels of aggregation produced very similar slopes. This indicates that the widest span of area whose class mix affected its inhabitants' partisanship was less than or equal to a constituency, in extent perhaps as small as a neighbourhood.

If only individual class and area class mix affected voting probabilities the fit around some aggregate data relationship, perhaps non-linear, would be perfect. However scatterplots show a scatter of partisan values associated with each value of class. Cross-cutting influences from non-class variables or purely local factors explained between a quarter and a third of the variation in Conservative support. Although the borough class mix added nothing to the class explanation of partisanship, residuals from constituency regressions were correlated over constituencies within the same borough. About half the residual variation could be attributed to unknown but borough-wide influences. This result remained true even for multiple regressions using a seven category occupational division, house tenure and unemployment rates to predict partisanship. In as much as these borough-wide and even county-wide influences on residuals cannot be attributed to excluded variables like religion or rurality, they indicate another sort of environmental effect operating over a wider area than the class concentration effect.

Different kinds of environmental influence operating over different spans of area suggests that they may be caused by different mechanisms. Personal contact has been put forward as an explanation of environmental influence. This explanation would fit the class concentration effect best. The wider effects unrelated to class composition, might be attributed to pure area causes such as local newspapers, television stations and political parties organised at borough or regional level.

4.3 Power of Environmental Influences

Since a multi level model is unnecessary we can retain the simple two level model

$$\text{CON} = b_0 + (a_0 - b_0 + b_1)M$$

Constituency regression can estimate the sum of the individual level effect $(a_0 - b_0)$ and the environmental effect b_1, but it cannot separate them. A crude method that works quite well in practice is to estimate the individual level effect $(a_0 - b_0)$ from a sample survey whence b_1 is the difference between survey and aggregate data slopes. However it is easy to show that individual level data, that is survey data, does not give unbiased estimates of individual level effects. Survey variations between classes result mainly from the differences between middle and working class individuals but also, to some extent, on the logically necessary fact that middle class individuals tend to live in relatively middle class areas and vice versa. For example, a country of three constituencies, one 50% middle class, one 33% and one 17% middle class, in which both classes were 60% Conservative in the first constituency, 50% in the second and 40% in the third would be entirely free from any individual level class effects. However a sample survey would show middle class individuals 5% more Conservative than working class individuals.

A theoretically justifiable procedure is to divide a sample survey according to the constituency class mix in each respondent's constituency. Then the average partisan difference between individuals of different class in similar environments, averaged over all environments, gives an unbiased measure of the individual effect $(a_0 - b_0)$; two scatterplots of partisanship by environmental class one for middle class respondents and one for working class respondents give two estimates of the environmental effect b_1. These two estimates can be pooled or their difference used as a check on the assumption that middle and working class respondents are equally responsive to environmental class. There are practical difficulties with this method since the survey sample must be divided into a large number of subsamples which may be particularly inaccurate if respondents in each constituency have not been chosen at random throughout the complete constituency: for example, if cluster sampling has been used to cut costs. The 1966 Election Study was unclustered in urban areas but heavily clustered in rural areas. Butler and Stokes did produce within-class scatterplots of partisanship by the area class mix. For this purpose they used a sample of 120,000 respondents interviewed between 1963 and 1966 by the commercial pollsters, National Opinion Polls; they used the sample itself to estimate the local class mix. Clearly this variant also has its disadvantages, not least the fact that the Conservative share of the two party support in regular monthly polls varied from 39% to 56% in this three year period. The method is necessarily unspecific in time and cannot be applied to a particular election result.[23]

A third possibility is to use the overall class difference found in a sample survey without assuming that it equals the individual level effect. First we apply the model

$$CON = b_0 + (a_0 - b_0 + b_1)M$$

to find the proportions of middle and working class individuals in the national electorate who are Conservative. The total number of middle class individuals is

$\sum_c E_c M_c$ where E_c and M_c are the electorate size and the proportion middle class

in constituency c. So the proportion of the middle class living in a specific constituency q is

$$\frac{E_q M_q}{\sum_c E_c M_c}$$

and of these the model predicts that a fraction $(a_0 + a_1 M_q)$ are Conservative. Since $a_1 = b_1$ by assumption, this equals $(a_0 + b_1 M_q)$. Thus the proportion of all middle class individuals who are Conservative is

$$\sum_q \left[\frac{E_q M_q (a_0 + b_1 M_q)}{\sum_c E_c M_c} \right] = a_0 + b_1 \left(\frac{\sum_q E_q M_q^2}{\sum_c E_c M_c} \right)$$

By similar reasoning the proportion Conservative among working class individuals is

$$b_0 + b_1 \dfrac{\sum\limits_q E_q M_q (1 - M_q)}{\sum\limits_c E_c (1 - M_c)}$$

These are the proportions estimated by the survey data proportions Conservative within the classes. A perfect survey sample would give, as a measure of class difference

$$(a_0 - b_0) + b_1 \left(\dfrac{\sum\limits_q E_q M_q^2}{\sum\limits_c E_c M_c} - \dfrac{\sum\limits_q E_q M_q (1 - M_q)}{\sum\limits_c E_c (1 - M_c)} \right)$$

$$= \text{individual level effect} + b_1 (\ )$$

It can be shown that the term in brackets is a perfect square and hence is always positive. This proves that if the basic model is correct the survey difference of proportions will always overestimate the true individual level class effect, provided b_1, the environmental effect, is positive (i.e. individuals tend towards the majority response in their environment). Similarly if b_1 is negative the survey difference must be negatively biased.

   These formulae also allow us to separate the individual and environmental influences of class and check the adequacy of the model since now our estimates of the two class effects are not merely determined but overdetermined. From an aggregate data regression we have

$$b_0 = \text{constituency regression intercept} = 0.16$$
$$a_0 - b_0 + b_1 = \text{constituency regression slope} = 0.93$$

$$a_0 + b_1 \left(\dfrac{\sum\limits_q E_q M_q^2}{\sum\limits_c E_c M_c} \right) = \begin{array}{l} \text{survey estimate of proportion CON} \\ \text{in middle class} \end{array}$$

$$= 0.734$$

$$b_0 + b_1 \left(\dfrac{\sum\limits_q E_q M_q (1 - M_q)}{\sum\limits_c E_c (1 - M_c)} \right) = \begin{array}{l} \text{survey estimate of proportion} \\ \text{CON in working class} \end{array}$$

$$= 0.300$$

The expressions in brackets can be computed from the census data. They come to 0.36 and 0.31 respectively. We can now solve any three of these equations for a_0, b_0, b_1 and use the fourth as a check for consistency. Solving the first three gives $a_0 = 0.53$ and $b_1 = 0.56$ while substitution of these values in the last equation gives

$$0.16 + (0.31)(0.56) = 0.33 \text{ which is close to } 0.30$$

By these calculations the individual level effect is $(a_0 - b_0) = (0.53 - 0.16) = 0.37$, only 6% less than the 0.43 given by the raw difference of survey proportions. Without these calculations there would be no justification for using the survey difference since, although knowing it was a biased overestimate, we would have no guide to the degree of overestimation.

These calculations produce a model comprising two equations

for middle class individuals $CON = 0.53 + 0.56M$
for working class individuals $CON = 0.16 + 0.56M$

which can be displayed in a Z shaped diagram like Figure 1. The lines predicting the proportions Conservative in each class are parallel but slope up to the right. The empirical regression line through a constituency data scatter is the cross member of the Z shape. The diagram also shows the prediction equations derived by Butler and Stokes from the 120,000 National Opinion Polls sample spread

Figure 1. Diagram of Z model estimates

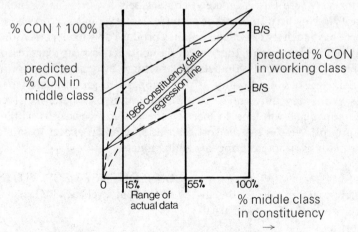

Notes:
(1) Z model predictions derived from 1966 constituency regression plus national survey estimates of class partisanship in 1966.
(2) B/S=Butler/Stokes estimates obtained from breakdown of 120,000 respondents to NOP surveys between 1963 and 1966.

from 1963 to 1966. Over the actual range of the data there is a remarkably close agreement between the purely empirical scheme based on the Polls and the predictions of the Z model.

Therefore calculations based on the Z model fit both constituency data, the 1966 Election Study data and the 1963–66 National Opinion Polls data very well. They permit easy estimation of the separate individual and environmental effects and they are time specific.

They indicate that in 1966 class polarisation of constituency partisanship depended more on environmental effects than on individual level effects, the relative power of these two effects being in the ratio fifty six to thirty seven.

5   Some Theoretical Explanations of Environmental Effects

Putnam has examined three theories explaining the environmental effect on voting.[24] First, a locally well supported party might fight a particularly good campaign and so further increase its support. He found that in America, and the same is almost certainly true in Britain, there was little correlation between the strength of the local campaign and the prior strength of the party. Second, a sense of local identity might make people vote with their perception of the local norm. Putnam's evidence appeared to refute this. Third, the environmental effect might be simply a special case of the general effect of social contact. A classic statement of the contact theory was given by Berelson et. al. in their study of the 1948 American Presidential election.[25]

The basic tenet of this theory is that contact produces consensus, or at least in Berelson's words 'contact is a condition for consensus'. It is easy to think of circumstances where this is unlikely: contact between extreme Catholics and Protestants in Northern Ireland, for example. However in societies where social differences have such a weak effect that they produce only tendencies rather than definitive political responses, the basis of the contact theory appears reasonable. It also maintains that social contacts are structured by family, choice of friends, social characteristics and locality. If party appeals to group interest or group attitudes evoke any differential political responses, the patterns of contact between individuals will tend to increase the political consensus within high-contact groups. We can list the sort of effects we might expect to result from different patterns of interest appeals and contacts:

CAUSE	CONSEQUENCES FOR VOTING
1 differential appeals to the interests or attitudes of social categories.	1 individual level social effects.
2 socially structured contacts.	2 individual level social effects $(a_0 - b_0)$ larger than caused by 1 alone.

3 differential appeals to area interests.

3 constituency deviation from general socio-political pattern (including borough-wide correlated residuals, etc.).

4 area structured contacts.

4 environmental social effects (b_1).

5 family structured contacts.

5 intergenerational persistence.

6 self-chosen contacts, friends, etc.

6 individual persistence.

In essence the theory is extremely simple; in application it can explain a large variety of phenomena. Putnam found strong empirical support for this theory. In particular he found that the partisanship of respondent's friends varied with constituency partisanship; this variation was only half as extreme as would have resulted from randomly selected friends, which indicated some degree of partisan selection. Individuals whose friends had the same partisanship voted much the same way irrespective of area, but higher proportions of individuals had Republican friends in Republican areas. Although all Putnam's data was American, findings from various survey studies in Britain suggest that the same processes were at work.

5.1 Survey Evidence of Environmental Influences on Political Attitudes, Class Consciousness and Voting

The contact theory indicates that contact somehow produces political consensus on voting. However voting preferences could be transmitted with or without the range of political attitudes generally accompanying voting. In particular Przeworski and Soares have put forward a range of theoretical models in which high concentrations of the working class increase class consciousness in the working class; in some models high concentrations of workers cause a reactive increase in class consciousness within the middle class as well.[26]

The 1966 Election Study can be used to check the other factors which vary with the social environment besides party choice. For this purpose respondents were divided into four subsamples according to whether their constituency fell into the first, second, third or fourth quartile on percentage employers and managers in the Census. The percents non-manual among respondents in these four subsamples were twenty three, thirty two, forty two and fifty two which suggests they were reasonable samples of different environments. Since they were necessarily quite small samples, subject to high sampling error, we should not expect further breakdowns to produce such neat patterns. So as a convenient summary of the environmental effect on attitudes we can compute the regression slope for a four point regression through attitude levels in the four subsamples. This slope is given by $0.3 \ (3A_4 + A_3 - A_2 - 3A_1)$ where A is the percent of respondents in the most middle class environment who hold the attitude and A_1 is the corresponding percentage in the least middle class environments. It is a smoothed approximation to the difference between attitudes in the most and least middle class areas.

We need some measure of what is a large and what is a small environmental effect. Since the non-manuals in the full sample were 44% more Conservative than the manuals and the subsample from the top quartile of middle class environments contained 29% more non-manuals than the subsample from the bottom quartile, simple class substitution would make the top quartile 13% ($=44\% \times 0.29$) more Conservative than the bottom quartile. Any environmental effect greater than 13% would indicate an environmental effect greater than the individual effect. Table 5 shows that the environmental effect on the partisan identification of middle class individuals was 1.3 ($=17/13$) times the individual effect; for working class individuals the ratio was 2.5 ($=32/13$) times. This is further evidence that working class partisanship was more sensitive to the social environment than middle class partisanship. However it also suggests that the ecological division by employers and managers was much more powerful than the division by the level of non-manuals which we used in earlier sections of this chapter (which implied a ratio of 1.5 between environmental and individual effects).

Class identification also varied sharply with the social environment but not in the same way as partisanship. There was no evidence of a reactive increase in middle class identification in working class areas. Both manuals and non-manuals tended more towards middle class identification in middle class areas. Indeed it was the non-manuals whose class identification varied most with the social environment, particularly the lower managers and supervisors. Consequently variations in class identification did not explain variations in party support. Among middle class identifiers party choice varied with the social environment almost as much as it varied among non-manuals, similarly for working class identifiers and manuals.

Our set of basic political attitudes can also be related to the social environment. Table 6 shows the results and gives, for each attitude, the effect of a simple class substitution of 29% non-manuals for manuals. Although the absolute scale of variation was lower for attitudes than class identification, the environmental effect was many times higher than the class substitution effect and the working class were more sensitive to the environment. On nationalisation, for example, the environment had no effect on the middle class but had a large effect on the working class, five times as powerful as the individual class effect. Generally there was a tendency towards more middle class attitudes in more middle class areas but there were two strong exceptions. On attitudes towards the Queen, the working class were more favourable in middle class areas despite the middle class being generally less favourable to royalty. The most dramatic exception was on attitudes to trade unions which was a perfect example of a reactive pattern. Overall, the middle class were less favourable to trade unions, but in middle class areas this difference was relatively small; in working class areas the workers were much more pro-union and the middle classes much more anti-union. Although this was the one issue which divided the classes the most, the environmental effects, in opposite directions within the two classes, were 2.7 times as powerful as the overall class difference. The effects within classes were

Table 5
Party Identification, Class Identification and Voting
by Environmental Class 1966

*Social environment measured
by % employers and
managers in Census*

	Bottom quartile	2nd	3rd	top quartile	Smoothed Slope
Check: % respondents non-manual	23	32	42	52	29
% Conservative party identification 1966					
among non-manuals	61	61	78	74	17
among manuals	15	21	36	46	32
% Middle Class identification 1966					
among non-manuals	33	48	61	61	29
among manuals	9	15	21	22	14
among social grades:—					
1 higher managerial and professional	(100)	64	81	82	(−11)
2 lower managerial and administrative	58	48	82	78	28
3 skilled or supervisory non-manual	27	53	53	59	29
4 lower non-manual	11	36	37	24	12
5 skilled manual	9	15	22	24	16
6 unskilled manual	9	15	17	18	9
5a skilled manual (TU only)	9	18	18	20	10
6a unskilled manual (TU only)	9	11	19	(0)	(−6)
Among Middle Class identifiers					
% CON of two party	74	63	79	83	13
% CON of total vote	64	59	65	72	9
% LAB of total vote	22	34	17	15	−11
% LIB of total vote	14	7	18	13	2
Among Working Class identifiers					
% CON of two party	17	22	38	42	27
% CON of total vote	16	21	34	36	22
% LAB of total vote	77	73	56	50	−29
% LIB of total vote	7	7	10	14	7

Note: ( ) indicates percents based on less than ten respondents.

equal in size though opposite in direction; the data fitted the pattern so well that identical results were obtained whether the smoothing procedure was used or not. These attitudes towards trade unions help to explain the greater correlation between partisanship and the environment within the working class; within the middle class trade union attitudes operated not merely to reduce but to reverse the environmental response. The fact that they did not do so completely may be attributed to the high variation of class consciousness within the middle class. This is illustrated in figure 2.

Figure 2. Environmental effects within classes on attitudes towards Trade Unions, class identification and party identification.

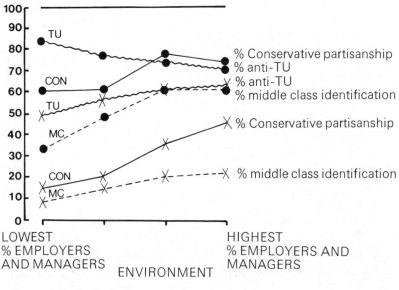

6   Curvilinear Models: Some More Advanced Two Level Models of Class Polarisation

The simple Z model had three features some, or all, of which could be improved. It distinguished two social classes, manuals and non-manuals; it let partisanship within each class depend on the local concentration of non-manuals; it represented this dependence by a linear relationship with the same slope for both classes. The evidence to be given in this section suggests that a linear relationship between within class partisanship and some measure of the social environment is acceptable. However it is useful to distinguish at least three classes, each with a different sensitivity to the environment. The critical characteristic of the environment is not the local concentration of some large class but the local concentration of what we have called core classes.

The relationship between constituency partisanship and constituency class

Table 6
Political Attitudes by Environmental Class 1966

Respondents class	All respondents	Social Environment measured by % employers and managers in Census				For comparison the effect of class substitution on overall attitudes in environments = 0.29 × class difference in col. a	Smoothed slope estimate of environmental effects (from cols. b, c, d, e) + indicates tendency to middle class attitudes in middle class areas
		bottom quartile	2nd	3rd	top quartile		
	a	b	c	d	e		
Socialisation: % for more nationalisation							
M	19	15	25	17	17	3	+1
W	29	34	32	27	19		+15
TU power: % saying TU have too much power							
M	75	84	77	74	71	5	−13
W	57	49	56	61	63		+14
Internationalism							
% unilateralist							
M	11	10	13	11	11	2	0
W	17	20	17	14	16		+5
% very strongly against immigration							
M	41	46	36	42	42	2	+2
W	47	47	47	49	41		+5
% gave up Empire too fast							
M	48	47	51	45	50	2	+1
W	40	34	38	40	51		+16
% accept UDI or negotiate							
M	56	47	57	57	57	5	+9
W	39	33	40	41	42		+8
% feel Queen and Royal Family very important							
M	55	59	50	57	56	1	+1
W	59	53	61	59	64		−9
Scale of Government							
% no increase in social services							
M	53	58	47	55	53	5	−2
W	36	36	30	39	36		+3
% prefer tax cut to more social services							
M	60	59	55	61	65	2	+7
W	53	52	46	55	59		+9

Note: M = non-manual respondents.
W = manual respondents.

was not grossly non-linear, but it was sufficiently so as to justify some consideration of models that would reproduce that non-linearity. There are many possibilities, of which four will be discussed here. They are:—

(1) The Split Vote Charge: One reason why electors chose a Labour or Conservative vote was to defeat the opposite party. Such 'anti' feelings helped to minimise defections to third parties like the Liberals. However wherever the Conservatives had twice the amount of Labour support, or vice versa, voters for the locally dominant party were entirely free to switch to a third option since no amount of defection could let the main, nationally defined, enemy win the seat. So in very 'safe' Labour or Conservative areas the dominant party might do much worse than a linear class to party prediction scheme would indicate. Whether the curve was J, S or Γ (capital gamma) shaped would depend on whether Liberals hit safe Labour, all safe seats, or just safe Conservative seats. The effect would only be apparent if the Liberals took more than twice as many votes from the locally dominant party as from its opponent.

(2) Semi-random Contacts: In any locality individuals tend to associate more with people like themselves, people within the same class, religious, industrial or partisan groups. In as much as the locality does influence contacts, its effect is likely to be non-linear. Putnam showed that contact groups had characteristics half way between the characteristics that would result from random contacts within an area and contacts with people similar to the respondents themselves. The majority social characteristic within a random contact group varies with the character of the area, but as a power function, not as a linear function. This is illustrated in Figure 3. The degree of the power function, the degree of S-shapedness, increases rapidly with the size of the contact group.[27] If individuals had only eleven randomly chosen contacts in a constituency the probability that a majority of these would be non-manuals would be 0% where there were 0% non-manuals, only 15% where there were 35% non-manual, as much as 85% where there were 65% non-manual and, of course, 100% where there were 100% non-manual. So the contact model itself might suggest that environmental effects would make large differences to partisanship in the middle range of class environments but make little difference at the extremes.

(3) Declining Returns: As a general rule it may be more plausible to construct predictive schemes for logits, the logarithms of the odds ratio, rather than probabilities. Since the logarithm of the odds can range from minus infinity to plus infinity no predicted value is ever logically impossible. This is not so for probabilities which must lie between 0% and 100%. If the logit of the environmental effect depended linearly upon class, the environmental effect itself would be something like an S shape: steep for intermediate class values; less steep, but never quite flat, nearer the extremes. The general rationale for logit models, that it takes a greater influence to make people 5% more Conservative if they are already 90% Conservative than if they are only 50% Conservative, would apply here.[28]

(4) Class Specific Sensitivities: One explanation of non-linearities has already been discussed in a simple form. If working class people were more

Figure 3. Probability that a randomly selected group contains more middle class than working class individuals.

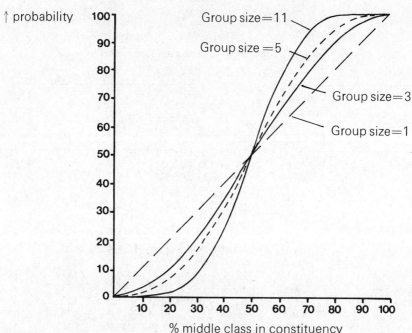

↑ probability   **100**

Group size=11

Group size =5

Group size=3

Group size=1

% middle class in constituency

responsive to their environment than middle class people, then even though the environmental effect was linear within each class, the overall constituency partisanship would not be linearly related to constituency class. The relationship would be a quadratic: humped if the middle class were less responsive; dished if they were more responsive. This notion of class specific sensitivities could be expanded to include more than two classes, each with a different sensitivity to the social environment.

These four explanations can be tested empirically using the census data for constituencies. The split vote explanation can be checked by performing all regression analyses for all seats and for seats without a Liberal candidate. The others can be tested by removing the class substitution or individual effect from the data and then checking whether a power function of odd degree, a logistic or a quadratic, best explained the remaining partisan variation.

Regression results are shown in Table 7. A linear prediction showed an environmental slope of 0.55, as before; this was not altered by excluding contests with Liberals, although the fit was very slightly improved. However excluding Liberals did not improve the fit of curvilinear models. Of these, the quadratic did as well as any and the odd degree power functions used to model S shapes had positive coefficients on the highest powered term, indicating that they were modelling gamma shapes not, in fact, S shapes.

Table 7
Some Tests of Alternative Explanations of Curvilinearity

Model	All British Constituencies or Two Party Contests only	Regression Equation	R^2 %
linear	ALL	$EF = 0.35 + 0.55M$	25
	TWO	$EF = 0.33 + 0.55M$	27
logistic	ALL	$\text{logit}\left(\dfrac{EF - 0.2}{0.6}\right) = -1.2 + 4.2M$	24
	TWO	$\text{logit}\left(\dfrac{EF - 0.2}{0.6}\right) = -1.2 + 4.1M$	24
cubic power function	ALL	$EF = -0.11 + 4.0M - 7.4M^2 + 4.6M^3$	33
	TWO	$EF = 0.08 + 2.7M - 4.9M^2 + 3.0M^3$	32
quintic power function	ALL	$EF = -0.05 + 3.1M - 4.1M^2 + 2.9M^5$	33
	TWO	$EF = 0.09 + 2.4M - 3.4M^2 + 3.7M^5$	32
quadratic	ALL	$EF = 0.10 + 2.0M - 2.0M^2$	32
	TWO	$EF = 0.16 + 1.8M - 2.0M^2$	32

Note: (1) EF = environmental effect = Conservative percent minus Conservative per cent predicted by applying survey estimates of individual level class differences.
(2) Before we can test the logit formula we have to specify minima and maxima. In this test the specifications were that working class Conservatism could sink to zero but not below zero and middle class Conservatism rise to 100 % but not above. With a constant 40 % class difference this implied middle class Conservatism could range 40 % to 100 % with the environment and working class Conservatism 0 % to 60 %, although the data analysis might indicate a smaller range.

So we return to the possibility of class specific environmental effects. Both constituency and survey data have already suggested greater sensitivity among the workers, but this result may be too simple. One surprise in the constituency analyses was that the percent employers and managers, EMPL, was by far the best predictor of constituency partisanship. Table 8 shows that it explained 39 % more variation in the Conservative share of the two party vote than any one of the other five census classes. The dichotomy of EMPL versus the rest explained more than any other dichotomy, in particular 29 % more than a manual versus non-manual split, and only 1 % less than a multiple regression using all the class variables simultaneously. It was also the best class predictor of Conservative, Labour and Liberal shares of the total vote and never explained more than 2 % less than all the class variables together. Since Scottish and Welsh seats included

Table 8
Comparative Predictive Power of Nine Measures of Occupation

| | Partisan measures | | | | | | | |
| | TWOCON | | VCON | | VLAB | | VLIB | |
All Britain or England alone	B	E	B	E	B	E	B	E
Occupational class measures	Proportion of Partisan Variation Explained by Each Measure (= squared correlations with signs indicating direction of effect)							
EMPL	68	70	50	53	−70	−71	31	36
PROF	37	41	33	35	−35	−40	10	16
CLERK	19	19	21	19	−16	−18	2	5
SKIL	−35	−35	−28	−27	34	34	−12	−16
SEMI	−15	−19	−16	−18	13	19	−2	−6
UNSK	−36	−37	−29	−32	36	38	−14	−16
EMPL + PROF	63	64	48	51	−63	−65	25	30
EMPL + PROF + CLERK	50	51	43	43	−48	−50	14	21
EMPL + PROF + CLERK + SKIL	34	38	32	34	−33	−38	9	14
	Proportion of Residual Variation Explained After Control for EMPL (= squared partial correlations)							
PROF	−1	−1	1	0	2	2	−5	−3
CLERK	0	−1	2	0	1	1	−5	−3
SKIL	0	1	0	0	−2	−2	2	1
SEMI	0	0	−2	0	0	0	2	1
UNSK	0	0	0	−1	0	0	0	0
EMPL + PROF	−1	−1	1	0	2	2	−5	−3
EMPL + PROF + CLERK	0	−1	2	0	1	2	−6	−3
EMPL + PROF + CLERK + SKIL	0	0	2	1	0	0	−3	−1
Multiple regression	Proportion of Variation Explained by a Multiple Regression using all the Occupation Measures							
	69	71	51	53	71	72	35	38

Note: (1) All mnemonics are defined in Table 1.
(2) Signs attached to squared correlations apply strictly to the unsquared correlations.
(3) Any class or sum of classes is equivalent to the sum of all the excluded classes, except for a reversal of signs.

extremes of class the analyses were repeated for England alone, but the results were little changed.

In the section on the effect of simple spatial aggregation on measures of polarisation, we noted that simple aggregation of the employers and managers versus the rest dichotomy would produce a constituency data slope only slightly smaller than the one for a manual/non-manual dichotomy; there was no reason to expect the fit to be either better or worse since fit does not aggregate. However the regression equation predicting constituency Conservatism from EMPL had a slope that was not smaller than the one for the regression on non-manuals, but almost three times as large. The numbers of employers and managers never exceeded 25 %. So their own votes could not explain the power of this variable; nor could the accidental co-occurrence of non-occupational influences towards Conservatism. A multiple regression using non-manuals and house owners as predictors divided the explanatory load between these two variables, but EMPL still explained 25 % more of the variation by itself; its coefficient was 2.7 times the sum of the non-manual and house owner coefficients in the multiple regression.

One possibility is that core classes are the critical ingredient of the social environment. Concentrations of employers and managers, the controllers, on the one hand or manual trade unionists, the anti-controllers on the other, were far more significant than variations in the ratio of skilled manuals to junior clerks. Of these two core classes only one was measured in the census. EMPL also correlated at-0.72 with the unskilled manuals; this was a higher correlation than any of the other classes had with this category. So variations in the one core class recorded probably coincided to a considerable extent with variations in the other.

If this explanation is correct we should expect that the core classes themselves would be the least responsive to the social environment, while those at the margin between controllers and anti-controllers would be the most responsive. To test this hypothesis we need at least three class groupings.

6.1 Survey Evidence

In Table 9 respondents to the 1966 Election Study have been divided into their seventeen 'socio-economic groups' and, alternatively, into the six 'social grades' used by Butler and Stokes. Each occupational category was then subdivided into four subsamples according to the social environment. The Conservative share of the 1966 two party vote was computed for each occupation and social environment; smoothed estimates of the environmental effects in each occupational group were calculated by the method used for Table 5. Where the multiple subdivisions meant that partisanship was being calculated for a set of less than ten respondents, the four social environments were grouped into two sets of two and the environmental effect re-estimated using these larger samples. If one of these larger samples still contained less than ten respondents, no estimate was made; if not the new estimate was averaged with the estimate based on the original four categories of environment was used. Only two occupations in the Table were exceptions to this rule.
Neither farming employers and managers nor self-employed professionals provided large enough samples. Since no one in these occupations voted Labour, regardless of the environment, they have been included with an environmental effect of zero.

Despite the attempts to smooth estimates all the samples were small, particularly for non-manuals in working class areas and for manuals in non-working class areas. So no great weight should be put on any single entry.

Nonetheless there is a clear pattern in the Table. The groups whose partisanship varied most with the environment were those who were on the boundary between controllers and controlled, not, for example, those at the margin between manuals and non-manuals. The most sensitive were: manual foremen; intermediate non-manuals who had supervisor functions but were below university degree standard; the lower managerial and administrative grade; and those employers and managers who must inevitably have been, on average, insignificant individuals in large organisations. The least variable non-manuals were those with most and least freedom of control: the higher managers and professionals; self-employed professionals; farming and small establishment employers and managers; and the junior non-manuals. Although the manuals were generally more sensitive to the environment, the most sensitive were the foremen and the most skilled workers; the least sensitive were the least skilled, especially if they had trade union connections.

6.2 Comparative Analyses of Constituency Evidence

If we can accept that the percentage employers and managers is the best measure of the critical features of the class environment it becomes possible to estimate from constituency data analyses a two or even three class model with class-specific sensitivities to the environment. The logic of the three class model, for example, is as follows:—

$$\text{proportion CON in class } 1 = a_1 + b_1 E$$
$$\text{proportion CON in class } 2 = a_2 + b_2 E$$
$$\text{proportion CON in class } 3 = a_3 + b_3 E$$

Where the a s and b s are constants and E is the percent employers and managers in the locality. If the classes make up proportions C_1, C_2 and $C_3 = 1 - C_1 - C_2$ of the local electorate then the constituency proportion Conservative becomes

$$CON = a_3 + b_3 E + (a_1 - a_3)C_1 + (a_2 - a_3)C_2$$
$$+ (b_1 - b_3)C_1 E + (b_2 - b_3)C_2 E$$

and a regression using the five predictor variables is sufficient to extimate the six parameters of the model. One problem is that these five predictors, E, C_1, C_2, $C_1 E$ and $C_2 E$ are inevitably very highly intercorrelated and the regression estimates are somewhat indeterminate since other values of the parameters would predict the dependent variable, CON, almost as well.

To overcome this problem of multi-colinearity we can use the technique known as 'ridge regression' in which all intercorrelations are uniformly reduced by multiplication by some constant fraction, before the regression calculations begin. There is an elegant justification for this relatively little used procedure.[29] It introduces bias into the estimates, but as the correlations are reduced the bias increases slowly while the indeterminacy declines very rapidly. Intuitively it may

Table 9
Estimated Environmental Effect on Partisanship within Occupational Grades and socio-Economic Groups.
(Effect is on 1966 vote for Conservative rather than Labour)

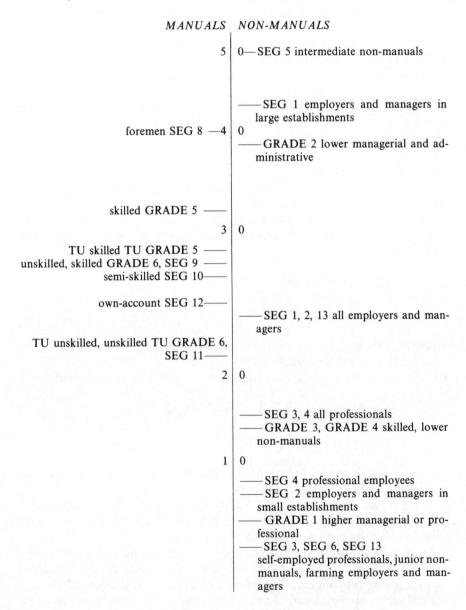

MANUALS   *NON-MANUALS*

5 | 0—SEG 5 intermediate non-manuals

——SEG 1 employers and managers in large establishments

foremen SEG 8 —4 | 0

——GRADE 2 lower managerial and administrative

skilled GRADE 5 ——

3 | 0

TU skilled **TU GRADE 5** ——
unskilled, skilled **GRADE 6, SEG 9** ——
semi-skilled SEG 10——

own-account SEG 12——

——SEG 1, 2, 13 all employers and managers

TU unskilled, unskilled **TU GRADE 6, SEG 11**——

2 | 0

——SEG 3, 4 all professionals
——GRADE 3, GRADE 4 skilled, lower non-manuals

1 | 0

——SEG 4 professional employees
——SEG 2 employers and managers in small establishments
—— GRADE 1 higher managerial or professional
——SEG 3, SEG 6, SEG 13 self-employed professionals, junior non-manuals, farming employers and managers

be justified by noting that it is the exact inverse of the standard procedure used by factor analysts who increase correlations to focus their analyses on the 'communal' parts of their variables. In regression we wish to focus on the unique characteristics of each variable.

Two models were estimated, in each case using no ridging, then ridging by factors of 0.95, 0.90 and 0.80. The results are shown in Table 10. Two classes, manuals and non-manuals were used in the first model; three classes EMPL + PROF versus CLERK + SKIL versus SEMI + UNSK were used in the second. The Registrar General's socio-economic groups five and eight, the two groups which appeared from the survey data to be most sensitive to the environment were included in CLERK + SKIL along with nine and twelve which were moderately sensitive, the small category fourteen of own-account farmers and group six which was the least variable. Unfortunately no better separation of groups could be achieved on the basis of the six broad categories given in the parliamentary volume of the census. Despite the imperfections we should expect the intermediate class to be the most sensitive, the working class next and the professionals and managerials the least, if the survey data was accurate.

Using no ridging, results for the first model indicated far greater sensitivity in the working class, as expected. However it estimated a slight negative sensitivity for the middle class and made logically impossible predictions even within the range of data. Ridging by 0.95 produced plausible predictions, gave a data fit only 2% worse than the best possible, and estimated an environmental effect of 1.67 in the middle class and 2.55 in the working class. For anyone who is unfamiliar with, or suspicious of, ridge regression this solution could be justified in simulation terms. The parameters have values which conform to the theory and match the survey analysis results while predicting constituency voting almost as well as is possible even with totally implausible parameter values. Further application of ridging eventually produced higher sensitivities for the middle class, but only when the fit had been considerably reduced and the predictions again reached implausible values.

The same techniques and judgements applied to the second model produced estimated environmental effects of 0.46 among professionals and managers, 2.67 in the intermediate class and 1.93 in the working class. These confirm the conclusions obtained from the survey data.

7 Political Alternatives to Labour and Conservative Voting: Basic Social Patterns

7.1 Liberal Voting

In 1966 only about 70% of the English electorate voted Labour or Conservative, slightly more if we take account of the aging of the register, slightly less otherwise. Table 11 shows some results taken from stepwise regressions using all the social variables defined in Table 1 to predict Conservative, Labour and Liberal shares of the total vote and also the level of turnout. Although

Table 10
Ridge Regression Estimates of Parameters
in Models with Class-specific
Environmental Sensitivities

Estimation Method	Model and Parameter Estimates	Fit check $(R^2\%)$	Plausibility Check (predicted within-class $CON\%$ at extremes of range of actual data i.e. $EMPL = 0\%$ and 25%)	
	Two classes EMPL + PROF + CLERK/SKIL + SEMI + UNSK			
no ridging	prop $CON_1 = 0.57 - 0.27$ E	72	57*	50*
	prop $CON_2 = 0.00 + 4.10$ E		0	103**
ridge × 0.95	prop $CON_1 = 0.37 + 1.67$ E	70	37	79
	prop $CON_2 = 0.14 + 2.55$ E		14	78
ridge × 0.90	prop $CON_1 = 0.37 + 2.00$ E	68	37	87
	prop $CON_2 = 0.18 + 2.00$ E		18	68
ridge × 0.80	prop $CON_1 = 0.42 + 2.05$ E	65	42	93*
	prop $CON_2 = 0.21 + 1.48$ E		21	58
	Three classes EMPL + PROF/CLERK + SKIL/SEMI + UNSK			
no ridging	prop $CON_1 = 0.67 - 0.52$ E		67	80
	prop $CON_2 = 0.30 + 1.34$ E	72	30	64
	prop $CON_3 = -0 31 + 6.81$ E		−31**	139**
ridge × 0.95	prop $CON_1 = 0.65 + 0.46$ E		65	77
	prop $CON_2 = 0.15 + 2.67$ E	69	15	82
	prop $CON_3 = 0.15 + 1.93$ E		15	63
ridge × 0.90	prop $CON_1 = 0.63 + 1.36$ E		63	97*
	prop $CON_2 = 0.19 + 2.17$ E	68	19	73
	prop $CON_3 = 0.16 + 1.43$ E		16	52
ridge × 0.80	prop $CON_1 = 0.64 + 1.97$ E		64	113**
	prop $CON_2 = 0.25 + 1.71$ E	66	25	68
	prop $CON_3 = 0.16 + 1.02$ E		16	42

Note: (1) prop CON_1, etc. = proportion Conservative in class 1, etc.
(2) *predicted per cent implausibly high or pattern implausible.
(3) **predicted per cent logically impossible since over 100% or less than 0%.
(4) E = proportion employers and managers = EMPL.

Conservative and Labour candidates stood in almost all seats the Liberals only contested 49 % of them in 1966. So Liberal votes have been analysed four ways using: (1) all seats and setting the Liberal vote at zero where they had no candidate; (2) all seats which they contested in 1966; (3) all seats which they contested throughout the sequence of five elections between 1955 and 1970; and (4) all the seats within the South West region of England, a traditional Liberal stronghold.

EMPL was the best predictor of Conservative, Labour and, over all seats, Liberal voting. It explained two-thirds of Labour variation, half of Conservative and over a quarter of Liberal. This does not imply that support for some parties was more predictable than for others since the standard error of prediction was similar for all three parties. However in addition to similar amounts of random variation, there was a much larger systematic, class-related variation for Labour than for the other parties caused by the simple fact that Labour's disadvantage in middle class areas equalled the sum of the Conservative and Liberal advantages there.

Analyses restricted to seats with Liberal candidates or to the South West region showed that AGRI, the percent employed in agriculture, was the best predictor of Liberal voting. So the overall superiority of EMPL was partly due to the low incidence of Liberal candidates in working class areas.

7.2 Turnout

The best predictor of turnout was AMEN, the percent of houses with full 'amenities', a bath, hot water and an indoor toilet. It explained over a third of turnout variation. The standard deviation, after allowing for the electorate being larger than the total vote, showed that turnout was about as unpredictable as party votes.

Since class, as measured by EMPL, has been so central to the analysis of Conservative, Labour and even Liberal voting we might want to ask how turnout was related to class. There was very little evidence of a linear relationship between turnout and EMPL which explained only 14 % of turnout variation in 1966, 9 % in 1964 and 1970 and only 1 % in 1955 and 1959, but there was evidence of a stronger and developing non-linear relationship. Class in Britain was related to turnout in two ways. Middle class individuals and areas were more prone to vote because they possessed many amenities making voting easier; this made other problems less pressing, made the voters feel less alienated and encouraged them to get out and support the established order in the widest sense. However the partisan battle also had its effects on turnout.[30] Where majorities were low each elector who stayed at home had to consider his potential feelings if the party he disliked won the seat with only a handful of votes. The party machines also tended to increase turnout where they saw that a differential turnout could decide the result. Most marginal seats were between Labour and Conservative; since EMPL was such a good predictor of Labour versus Conservative voting, marginal seats tended to have intermediate values of EMPL centered round $EMPL_0$: the value of EMPL predicting a 50:50 split between Labour and

Conservative. Therefore two simple models of the relationship between EMPL and turnout are

$$\text{quadratic} \quad \text{TURN} = a + b\,\text{EMPL} + c\,(\text{EMPL} - \text{EMPL}_0)^2$$

$$\text{or double linear} \quad \text{TURN} = a + b\,\text{EMPL} + c\,|\text{EMPL} - \text{EMPL}_0|$$

where the vertical bars indicate the positive or 'absolute' value of the difference. In both these models the parameter b estimates the 'pure class' effect and c the 'class marginality' effect. The models can be estimated by first regressing the Conservative share of the two party vote on EMPL to find the value EMPL_0 which predicts $\text{CON} = 50\%$.

Table 11
Basic Social Patterns in Constituency Partisanship 1966

Partisan Measure of 1966 Vote	Best Social Predictor	Proportion of Partisan Variation Explained by Best Predictor Alone (R^2)	Standard Error of Prediction (% of votes)
TWOCON	EMPL	68	*
VCON	EMPL	50	7·9
VLAB	EMPL	−70	8·6
VLIB (all seats)	EMPL	31	8·9
VLIB (where stood 1966)	AGRI	31	7·0
VLIB (where stood at all five elections 1955–70)	AGRI	56	*
VLIB (South West England)	AGRI	34	*
TURN	AMEN	36	5·3

Note: (1) All mnemonics are defined in Table 1.
     (2) * denotes standard error not relevant to discussion.
     (3) See text for non-linear relationship between TURN and EMPL.

Over several elections these two models performed about equally well. In 1966 the estimates were

$$\text{TURN} = 0.73 + 0.51 \quad \text{EMPL} - 0.11(\text{EMPL} - \text{EMPL}_0)^2$$
$$(R^2 = 33\%)$$
$$\text{and TURN} = 0.75 + 0.43 \quad \text{EMPL} - 1.11\,|\text{EMPL} - \text{EMPL}_0|$$
$$(R^2 = 32\%)$$

It is easiest to compare pure class and class marginality effects by using the coefficients in the double linear model since they are directly comparable with each other, while those in the quadratic are not. By this test class marginality was over two and a half times as powerful as pure class.

8 Summary

1 The links between issues and social groups suggested by the history of party appeals did exist, at least in 1966.
2 The strongest links involved class and class related issues.
3 Class polarisation can be measured by fit or slope.
4 Fit for individuals has no implications for fit at aggregate levels.
5 Individual slopes contribute to aggregate slopes.
6 At a minimum, the class characteristics of the social environment have more effect on constituency partisanship than class differences themselves, perhaps much more. The partisanship of individuals is influenced more by where they live than what they do.
7 A simple two level model of class polarisation in which there are two classes, each equally responsive to the social environment, fits both survey and constituency data quite well.
8 Although some area effects span quite wide areas, the effect of the social characteristics of the environment depends upon the social mix in a narrow area, certainly as small as a constituency perhaps even as small as a neighbourhood.
9 The effect of the social environment may be explained by contact models: those who speak together vote together. However class consciousness and political attitudes on issues vary with the social environment in ways distinct from each other and from voting. In particular there was evidence that on one important issue contact prompted a reaction rather than a consensus.
10 Models involving a curvilinear response to the environment did not perform well.
11 One more complex model did fit both survey and constituency data especially well. Its elements were:—
  (a) The critical feature of the social environment is the local concentration of core classes, the controllers and anti-controllers.
  (b) All classes are more Conservative in environments with high densities of controllers, but class sensitivities vary.
  (c) The most sensitive to the environment are those at the margin between controller and controlled irrespective of whether they are manuals or non-manuals. The least sensitive are the controllers themselves, but since they were easier to define and measure than the opposite core, it is likely that both sets of core classes were themselves insensitive to the environment.
12 Class, as measured by the concentration of employers and managers, was the best predictor of constituency votes for Conservative, Labour and over all

seats, Liberal. In an appropriate non-linear model it rivalled the best social predictor of turnout.

13 In seats where the Liberals had candidates the best predictor of their votes was the percent in agriculture.

14 The best linear predictor of turnout was a measure of housing amenity.

CHAPTER 3

Variations and Trends in Post-War Voting Patterns

1 Why 1955–70?

From 1955 to 1970 there was no general redistribution of constituency boundaries. So for the five elections in that period the 1966 Census gives a guide to the social characteristics of constituencies. Obviously it is likely to be less accurate for 1955 than 1966, but there are advantages as well as disadvantages in using a single census as a consistent measure of social patterns.

The standard error of regression predictions of constituency partisanship from class was around 8 %; the prediction formula approximated to

$$\% \, CON = 17 + 2.6 \, \% \, EMPL$$

So the deviance of individual constituencies from the general class alignment was quite large compared to the political effect of small changes in class. Moreover these deviances may have been random in respect to social predictors or other general explanations at any one moment but they were presistent over time. They were local deviations rather than random shocks. In this situation there would be some advantage in using a single census rather than a sequence of censuses even if such were available. Where real change is small, or the analysis depends upon a small subset of constituencies, small changes in social measures may bias any analysis of trends by changing social positions of large persistent local deviances.

2 Classification of Variations from Socio-Political Patterns

Table 1 sets out the hierarchy of variations to be discussed in this chapter. First, variations from basic social alignments may be social, that is dependent upon some other social divisions whose political significance is secondary, or spatial such as regional or national differences, or temporal.

Both spatial and temporal variations can affect the levels of party support or the patterns linking partisanship and social divisions. Changes or spatial variations in social alignments may be variations of degree or, more fundamentally, may link partisanship to different social divisions in different times and places. The main religious division, between Anglicans and non-conformists, stops at the Scottish border, for example. In Table 1 trends in support between elections have not been subdivided into levels versus patterns. So far most research on mid-term trends has concentrated on variations in levels; even that is beyond the scope of this study. Preliminary results suggest that mid-term popularity is qualitatively different from voting support on election day.[1]

The methods used in this chapter to describe each of these forms of partisan variation are as follows:–

A   Multiple regressions and squared partial correlations between partisanship and social variables after controls for the basic social alignments. These squared partials show what proportion of the residual variation in partisanship, unexplained by the basic alignments, can be explained separately by each secondary predictor.

B   Regional dummy variables in a Britian-wide regression.

C, D Within-region regressions.

E   Chart of trends by time.

F, G Compare coefficients in regressions for different elections.

H   No results are reported here: the principal methods, however, have been time-series regression and spectral analysis.

3   The Limits on Temporal Change

The most striking feature of British voting trends between 1955 and 1970 was continuity, not variation. Labour's share of the vote stayed within a 5 % range, Conservative and Liberal within 9 %. Qualifications for voting were changed in 1970, but until 1966 turnout had stayed in a 3 % range or, if allowance is made for varying election months, within 8 %. (see Table 2)

Only the SNP enjoyed an unvarying trend. All the other party votes and turnout showed both increases and decreases at different times in the period.

Stable levels of support might mask large scale changes in the patterns of support, but it did not. We can show this without reference to any specific pattern by correlating constituency votes at different times. On average the Conservative share of the two party vote at consecutive elections correlated at 0.97, turnout at 0.90; Liberal's share in the seats regularly contested averaged a 0.93 correlation for consecutive elections. Stable national levels and high correlations between constituency support at different time points still does not guarantee stability at the constituency level since both these facts are consistent with polarising and depolarising trends. However constituency stability was implied if, in addition, the standard deviations remained constant over time, as they did for the Conservative share of the vote in regularly contested seats. (Table 3)

Table 1
Classification of Voting Variations

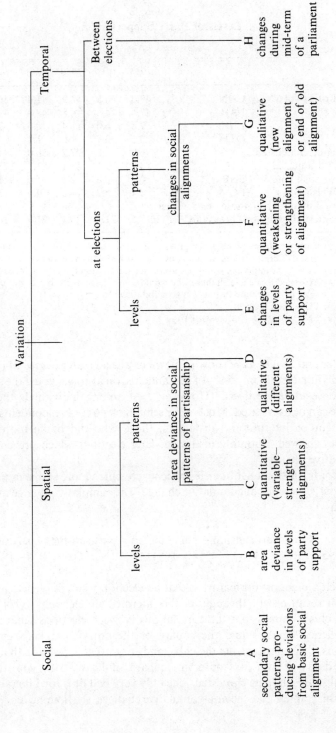

Note: 'Voting', 'party support', 'partisanship' here include minor parties and abstentions.

ELECTORAL DYNAMICS

Table 2
Levels of Party Support 1955–70

		1955	1959	1964	1966	1970	Range
% of British votes	CON	49.3	48.8	42.9	41.4	46.2	7.9
	LAB	47.4	44.6	44.8	48.8	43.9	4.9
	LIB	2.8	6.0	11.4	8.6	7.6	8.6
	OTH	0.5	0.7	1.0	1.1	2.2	1.7
% turnout unadjusted		76.9	79.0	77.2	76.0	(71.9)	3.0
%turnout adjusted		83.9	89.1	87.1	81.7	(78.7)	7.4
% of Scottish votes	SNP	0.5	0.8	2.4	5.0	11.4	10.9
% of Welsh votes	PC	3.1	5.2	4.8	4.3	11.5	8.4
Average Liberal % in those seats which were contested on all five occasions		17.5	21.1	25.2	21.9	18.4	7.7

Note: (1) Turnout adjusted for age of register by assuming only 94% of names available to vote on first day of operation, declining by 0.6% per month thereafter.
(2) In 1970 the minimum voting age was lowered from twentyone to eighteen and the register expanded to include all those who would come of age by the last day of operation of the register. Hence the turnout range is for 1955–66 only.
(3) PC = Plaid Cymru.
(4) SNP = Scottish Nationalist Party.

Butler and Stokes have shown that there was a greater degree of instability at the individual level: only 54% of respondents, on average, voted the same way at two consecutive elections.[2] However even among individuals the degree of change can be overstated. Most of the remaining 46% of respondents were either consistent or intermittent abstainers; those who did make more important switches showed a homing instinct at later elections which prevented a rapid cumulative change.

By contrast, the constituencies which were much more stable in the short run did show some signs of cumulative change. The cumulative change model can be written

partisanship → partisanship → partisanship → partisanship → partisanship
　　1955　　　　　1959　　　　　1964　　　　　　1966　　　　　　1970

in which the important feature is that no election result influences a succeeding election result except through all the intermediate elections. This elementary causal chain implies that the correlations between elections separated by two parliaments should equal the square of the correlation between successive elections, three parliaments the cube, and so on. Table 6 shows that this model fits the data quite well for Conservative shares of the two party vote, turnout, and Liberal shares in seats contested. The only very bad fit is for Liberal votes in all seats: this implies that the non-cumulative changes, the homing tendencies, were

Table 3
Partisan Correlations 1955–70

	Conservative share of two party vote						Liberal share of vote (all seats)					
	1955	59	64	66	70	DAV	1955	59	64	66	70	DAV
1955	100	96	92	91	89	–	100	62	49	49	48	–
1959		100	96	95	94	89.0		100	67	63	64	48.0
1964			100	98	97	92.5			100	81	74	56.5
1966				100	98	94.7				100	79	62.0
1970					100	97.0					100	72.3
St. Dev.	14	15	14	14	15			8	9	11	10	9

	Turnout						Liberal share (where stood)					
1955	100	93	84	81	65	–	100	92	73	68	62	–
1959		100	91	85	70	65.0		100	84	78	75	62.0
1964			100	94	81	75.5			100	92	84	71.5
1966				100	80	83.3				100	90	78.3
1970					100	89.5					100	89.5
St. Dev.	5	5	6	7	8		12	8	7	9	8	

	Liberal share (where stood five times)					
1955	100	94	79	77	77	–
1959		100	85	81	78	77.0
1964			100	97	93	77.5
1966				100	96	84.3
1970					100	93.0
St. Dev.	12	11	10	11	11	

Note: (1) DAV = diagonal average = average correlations between elections separated by four
parliaments, by three, by two and by one parliament.
(2) St. Dev. = standard deviation of partisan measure.

the result of intermittent candidatures by moderately active Liberal constituency
associations.

Overall these correlation tables suggest that trends in partisan patterns were
small; unlike the trends in levels they were cumulative and over the longer term
more substantial changes await explanation.

4 The Dynamics of Multi Level Class Polarisation

4.1 The Z Model

When the term polarisation is to be used in a dynamic sense, meaning
increasing or decreasing polarisation, the need for a multi level model becomes

Table 4
Tests of an Elementary Causal Chain 1955–70

		Average correlations between elections which were:			
		consecutive 1955–59 1959–64 1964–66 1966–70	*two apart* 1955–64 1959–66 1964–70	*three apart* 1955–66 1959–70	*four apart* 1955–70
TWOCON	actual	970	947	925	890
	predicted	–	941	913	885
Turnout	actual	895	833	755	650
	predicted	–	801	717	642
VLIB (all seats)	actual	723	620	565	480
	predicted	–	522	377	272
VLIB (where stood)	actual	895	783	715	620
	predicted	–	801	717	642
VLIB (core seats)	actual	930	843	775	770
	predicted	–	865	804	748

Note: (1) actual = diagonal average from Table 3.
(2) predicted = square, cube, and fourth power of the correlation for consecutive elections.

even more apparent than when simply measuring the quantity of polarisation. Figure 1 shows eight forms of dynamic polarisation or depolarisation using the Z model of the last chapter.

Increases in either individual or environmental effects would steepen the slope relating constituency class and constituency voting. If both had a tendency to happen together we could regard the environment effect as an amplifier of dynamic polarisation among individuals. Indeed when analysing only one election, the concept of the environment effect as an amplifier is natural. However, if over time the environmental effect tended to diminish as the individual effect increased, and vice versa, then what can be viewed as an amplifier in a static model would simultaneously be a dampener in the dynamic model.

The notion that environmental effects could act both as an amplifier of class polarisation and as a dampener on fluctuations in the degree of class polarisation is less paradoxical than it at first appears. If we accept that contacts within a spatial environment make all classes tend towards the partisanship of the locally dominant class, we need to explain why the contacts that produce political consensus fail to produce total consensus; why localities which should be, say

Figure 1. Types of dynamic polarization in the Z model.

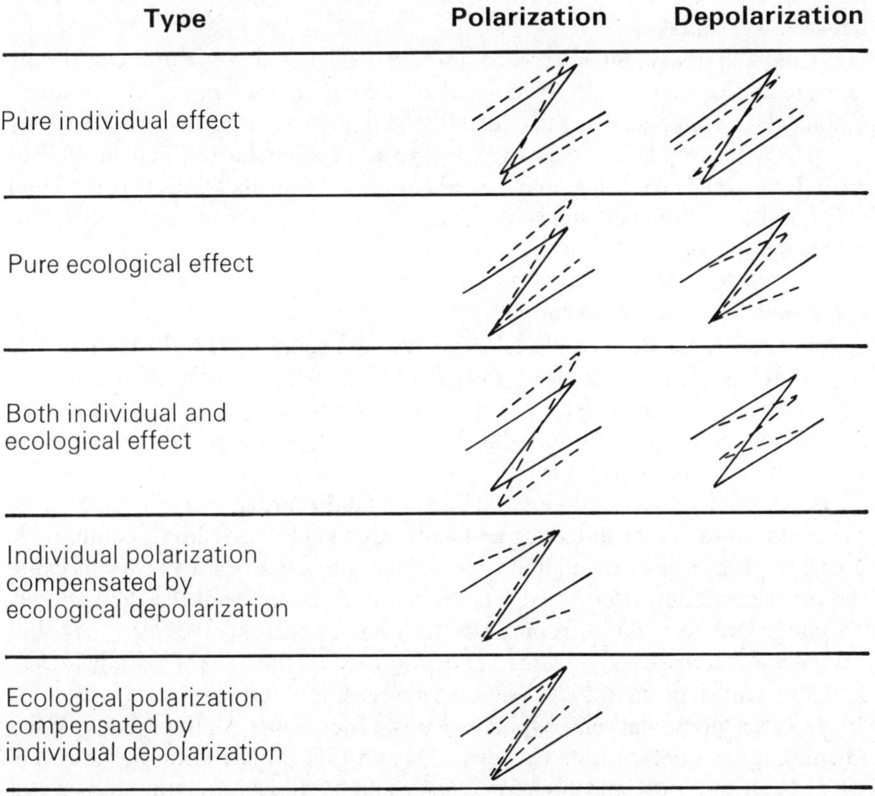

Type	Polarization	Depolarization
Pure individual effect		
Pure ecological effect		
Both individual and ecological effect		
Individual polarization compensated by ecological depolarization		
Ecological polarization compensated by individual depolarization		

Note:
Bold lines show first election, dotted lines show second.

60% Conservative on grounds of class composition alone, were 75% Conservative but not 100% Conservative. The answer must be that the consensus-generating effects of social contacts were in equilibrium with the divisive effects of individual characteristics. Thus the partisanship of middle class individuals in a working class constituency would be determined by the opposition of a pro-Labour environment and pro-Conservative individual characteristics. If individual reasons for choice between parties declined there would be less to oppose the consensus-generating effect of the environment which in working class areas would already be Labour dominated and vice versa. So the decline in individual effect would be offset by an increase in environmental effect and the slope relating constituency class and voting, rather than declining, could even increase. Conversely a sharp rise in individual level polarisation could well be offset by the resultant drop in environmental effect. For example, if individual level polarisation became total, with all the manuals voting Labour and all the non-manuals Conservative, the environmental effect would necessarily sink to zero and the constituency regression slope at 1.00 would only be marginally different from the 0.93 slope recorded in 1966 with only a 37% polarisation between individuals.

Finally individual and environmental effects might vary over time completely independent of each other. Whether they did so, or whether the environment amplified or dampened trends in individual polarisation, can be tested by comparing the trends in survey and constituency class polarisation from 1955 to 1970. If the trends were the same it would indicate an unchanging environmental effect, if the constituency trends were larger an amplifying tendency, if smaller or zero a dampening tendency.

4.2 Trends in Survey Polarisation

According to the Butler and Stokes analysis of the years 1963–70 'the evidence of a trend is remarkably clear. Indeed the declining strength of association between class and party is one of the most important aspects of political change during the decade'.[3] Their data did show such a decline especially between the non-election years 1963 and 1969. Their evidence and various other polarisation measures applied to the 1964–66–70 Election Studies are shown in Table 5. Since the point is an important one politically, the Table also shows comparable polarisation measures calculated from a variety of other survey series, because the empirical findings depended very much on the accuracy of the 1970 sample.

Gallup provides data from 1945 to 1966 and from 1970 to 1974 but comparisons across 1966–70 are not possible because the basis of Gallup's 'class' measurement changed in 1970. The academic election studies provide a series for 1964–74 as does National Opinion Polls. The earlier Gallup series shows fluctuating class polarisation between 1945 and 1966. Polarisation was lowest in 1945, 1951 and 1964 and highest in 1959 and 1966 whatever the measure of polarisation. Gallup does suggest that polarisation was also low in 1970 if only because it jumped up so much between 1970 and 1974.

Using the total vote measure, the Election Study series shows a drop in polarisation in 1970 that was maintained in 1974 while NOP indicates little change between 1964 and 1974 except for a slightly higher value in 1966. Using the Conservative share of the two party vote spuriously increases the measure of polarisation when third parties did well. Since 1974 was the Liberals' best year and 1970 their worst, between 1964 and 1974 the trends in this two party measure of polarisation follow a predictable course. Applied to the Election Study series it indicates a sharp fall between 1964 and 1970 followed by a sharp rise in 1974 and with NOP data it shows 1974 as the year of greatest class polarisation.

The survey evidence on trends in individual class polarisation is not completely consistent. A sharp drop between 1964 and 1970 can only be produced by selecting one survey series and applying a biased measure of polarisation. Nonetheless no survey series, and no polarisation measure, puts the 1970 polarisation as high as in 1964 or 1966 which is some evidence for a decline during the sixties.

Table 5
Survey Estimates of Class Polarisation 1945–74

Two party measure: Polarisation = CON share of two party vote in middle class minus CON share in working class

Survey	Year 1945	50	51	55	59	(63)	64	66	(69)	70	74	74
Gallup	38	44	36	39	45	–	39	43	–	23	33	33
Election Studies	–	–	–	–	–	–	44	43	–	33	41	38
NOP	–	–	–	–	–	–	38	39	–	35	41	43
Butler/Stokes	–	–	–	–	–	(47)	42	43	(29)	34	–	–

Note: Figures in brackets are for surveys at non-election times.

Total vote measure: Polarisation = average of CON lead over LAB in middle class and LAB lead over CON in working class

Survey	Year 1945	50	51	55	59	64	66	70	74	74
Gallup	33	38	35	38	41	34	40	22	27	27
Election Studies	–	–	–	–	–	38	39	30	33	31
NOP	–	–	–	–	–	33	35	32	31	33

Single party polarisation: Polarisation = party share of total in middle class minus party share in working class

Survey	Year	1945	50	51	55	59	64	66	70	74	74
Gallup	CON	32	37	34	38	40	34	39	22	27	24
	LAB	−35	−39	−35	−38	−42	−34	−40	−21	−28	−30
	LIB	3	3	1	0	2	0	1	−1	1	6
Election Studies	CON	–	–	–	–	–	35	36	29	29	28
	LAB	–	–	–	–	–	−42	−43	−31	−36	−33
	LIB	–	–	–	–	–	8	8	1	7	5
NOP	CON	–	–	–	–	–	31	34	32	30	31
	LAB	–	–	–	–	–	−35	−36	−32	−32	−34
	LIB	–	–	–	–	–	4	4	2	4	3
Alford	LAB	−37	−40	−42	−41	−40	–	–	–	–	–

Note: (1) As far as data permits, middle class means non-manual, working class manual.
(2) Gallup: see Durant in Rose (ed), *Studies in British Politics,* 3rd ed., 1976
(3) Election Studies: reanalysis by author using tapes of surveys conducted by Butler and Stokes (1964–70) and Sarlvik and Crewe (1974).
(4) NOP: see the Nuffield Election Studies by Butler et. al. for 1964, 1966, 1970. For February 1974 NOP. supplied comparable figures but in October 1974 none were available. The October 1974 figures come from the Harris Poll quoted in the October 1974 Nuffield Study.

(5) Butler/Stokes: from Butler and Stokes, *Political Change in Britain*. These figures differ slightly from those in the second row because Butler and Stokes used party identification, not vote, and respondent's occupation not head of household's occupation. The differences do not affect the conclusions.

(6) The 1963 and 1969 figures were for non-election years. Reanalysis showed that the breakdown of party identification by class for those years was

	middle class		*working class*	
	1963	*1969*	*1963*	*1969*
CON	63	66	25	41
LAB	21	20	66	51
LIB	16	15	8	8

This represents a Butler swing of 2% in the middle class and 15% in the working class. Over all five waves of the Butler/Stokes Election Study (1963–64–66–69–70) middle class support for the Conservatives never strayed outside the range 61% to 66% while working class support for Labour ranged between 51% and 69%. This evidence that the working class was more sensitive to the mood of the times matches the finding that they were more sensitive to the spatially distributed social environment.

4.3 Trends in Constituency Polarisation

Constituency class polarisation did not follow the same time trends as the survey class polarisation. Table 6 shows the same polarisation measures as Table 5 but with values calculated from constituency regressions. Since there were obvious national trends in the period, and Scotland and Wales were deviant in class composition, the Table shows some figures calculated for England alone. These check closely with the all-Britain trends.

Liberal voting had more effect on constituency class polarisation than on survey polarisation because the numbers of Liberal candidates varied and because they tended to contest the more middle class seats. In 1955 they contested only 17% of seats but by 1964 they had candidates in 58% of seats. These 58% were a class-biased subset. In terms of EMPL the seats contested by the Liberals were well over a full standard deviation more middle class than those they did not. Consequently the increased numbers of Liberal candidates and the larger votes gained by them in the mid-sixties reduced the degree of Conservative class polarisation and increased Labour's class polarisation by taking votes from the Conservatives in their best areas and from Labour in its worst.

The Table shows two symmetric measures of class polarisation between Labour and Conservative, and as with their survey equivalents, the two party version is biased upwards in the mid-sixties by Liberal successes. We might hope to completely eliminate the effects of Liberals on Conservative versus Labour polarisation measures by restricting analyses to seats without Liberal candidates. Unfortunately the estimated trends would then depend upon a changing collection of seats and a set that became rapidly more working class between 1955 and 1964, then somewhat less working class in 1966 and 1970. Since there was evidence that the relation between class and party was curvilinear, slightly humped, that would bias the trend towards higher slopes in the mid-sixties.

The slope between partisanship and the percent non-manuals, MID, declined from 1955 to 1964, went up sharply in 1966 and then fell back to about the 1959

Table 6
Constituency Class Polarisation 1955–70

Class Measure	Polarisation Measure	1955	1959	Year 1964	1966	1970
EMPL	two party	2.35	2.46	2.57	2.61	2.68
		(2.29)	(2.35)	(2.41)	(2.46)	(2.46)
	total vote	2.29	2.27	2.25	2.38	2.42
		(2.22)	(2.15)	(2.08)	(2.22)	(2.21)
	CON	2.10	1.86	1.54	1.73	1.92
	LAB	−2.47	−2.68	−2.96	−3.02	−2.91
	LIB+OTH	0.37	0.82	1.42	1.29	0.99
MID	two party	0.92	0.96	0.94	0.95	0.95
	total vote	0.96	0.90	0.84	0.97	0.89
	CON	0.98	0.78	0.62	0.73	0.75
	LAB	−0.94	−1.01	−1.06	−1.21	−1.03
	LIB+OTH	−0.04	0.23	0.44	0.48	0.28

Note: (1) Two party polarisation measure = regression slope when prediction CON share of two party vote.
(2) CON, LAB, LIB+OTH polarisation measures = regression slopes when prediction party shares of total vote. Note these must sum to zero.
(3) Total vote polarisation measure = regression slope when predicting CON lead over LAB as percent of total vote = (CON polarisation measure − LAB polarisation measure)/2.
(4) EMPL = employers and managers; MID = non-manuals.
(5) Figures in brackets for England only.

level. Using the two party measure of polarisation, the bias was just sufficient to offset this trend and give the appearance of stability for the whole period. However MID was never even close to being the best class predictor of partisanship; for both theoretical and empirical reasons it would be better to assess trends with respect to EMPL. Slopes on EMPL showed a combination of a steadily rising trend and a dip in the mid-sixties. Using the two party measure introduced enough bias to eliminate the dip without altering the rising trend.

4.4 Polarisation or Depolarisation between 1955 and 1970?

Given all the sampling problems of surveys and the lack of unanimity between rival survey series it is possible to argue that the survey evidence of depolarisation was not compelling. Since it is the best we have, the combination of survey and constituency trends suggest the following conclusions:–

(1)   There was a decline in the individual level class effect at the end of the sixties.

Table 7
Basic Multiple Regression Equations 1955–70

Partisan Measures		1955	1959	1964	1966	1970
Con v. Lab. TWOCON	R²	63	66	67	69	73
	Equn	2.37 (79) EMPL	2.48 (81) EMPL	2.58 (82) EMPL	2.61 (83) EMPL	2.59 (80) EMPL −0.14 (−23) WALES
LEAD	R²					
	Equn	2.30 (80) EMPL	2.28 (81) EMPL	2.50 (81) EMPL	2.37 (84) EMPL	2.34 (80) EMPL −0.13 (−23) WALES
Lib. Votes VLIB	R²	11	23	39	40	35
	Equn	0.30 (33) AGRI	0.76 (38) EMPL 0.09 (26) SW	1.20 (49) EMPL 0.41 (27) AGRI	1.04 (45) EMPL 0.45 (32) AGRI	0.79 (40) EMPL 0.40 (33) AGRI
System support TURN	R²	35	49	56	50	55
	Equn	−0.17 (−37) RENT −1.99 (−34) UNEMS	−0.13 (−30) RENT −0.47 (−36) TIMM −1.80 (−31) UNEMS	−0.86 (−55) TIMM −0.74 (−43) UNSK	0.28 (53) CARS −0.56 (−34) TIMM	−0.46 (−27) TIMM 0.32 (58) CARS −0.05 (−33) MID ENG
TWO	R²	30	27	32	20	32
	Equn	−3.01 (−38) UNEMS −0.35 (−34) AGRI −0.47 (−26) TIMM	−0.22 (−30) RENT −0.70 (−37) EMPL −2.42 (−26) UNEMS	−0.31 (20) SKIL −0.68 (−22) OLD −1.19 (−33) CIMM −0.37 (−30) AGRI	−0.26 (−34) RENT −0.31 (−26) AGRI	−2.89 (−31) UNEMS −0.14 (−19) RENT −0.96 (−52) EMPL 0.17 (40) GPHS

Table 7 [continued]

		1955	1959	1964	1966	1970
TURN	R²	41	54	63	57	54
	Equn	-0.57 (-29) EMAR	-0.51 (-27) EMAR	-0.71 (-30) EMAR	-0.83 (-34) EMAR	-1.12 (-42) EMAR
		0.10 (9) EMPL	0.10 (9) EMPL	0.27 (20) EMPL	0.35 (24) EMPL	0.59 (38) EMPL
		-0.15 (-33) RENT	-0.12 (-26) RENT	-0.83 (-54) TIMM	-0.18 (-32) RENT	-0.84 (-48) TIMM
		-1.78 (-30) UNEMS	-0.46 (-35) TIMM	-2.03 (-29) UNEMS	-0.45 (-27) TIMM	
			-1.65 (-28) UNEMS			
TWO	R²	37	24	31	39	29
	Equn	-0.69 (-26) EMAR	-0.51 (-17) EMAR	-0.47 (-14) EMAR	-0.93 (-28) EMAR	-1.00 (-32) EMAR
		0.02 (1) EMPL	-0.39 (-21) EMPL	-0.89 (-44) EMPL	-0.50 (-26) EMPL	-0.21 (-12) EMPL
		-2.80 (-36) UNEMS	-0.26 (-35) RENT	0.25 (40) AMEN	-0.49 (-41) AGRI	-3.55 (-38) UNEMS
		-0.35 (-35) AGRI		-0.31 (-25) AGRI	-0.76 (-34) TIMM	
		-0.44 (-25) TIMM			-1.47 (-29) UNEM	
Liberal Sympathy						
LIBCAND	R²	5	16	28	27	24
	Equn	1.93 EMPL	4.22 EMPL	5.76 EMPL	5.82 EMPL	5.41 EMPL
VLIB where stood	R²	56	42	40	41	31
	Equn	0.69 (70) AGRI	0.70 (81) AGRI	0.77 (81) AGRI	0.84 (82) AGRI	0.65 (69) AGRI
		-1.43 (-75) SEMI	-0.50 (-32) SEMI	-0.69 (-41) SEMI	-0.71 (-39) SEMI	-0.50 (-31) SEMI
		-0.84 (-50) CLERK				
		0.11 (26) SCOT				
VLIB core seats	R²	73	68	58	56	57
	Equn	0.51 (46) AGRI	0.58 (57) AGRI	0.86 (80) AGRI	0.84 (73) AGRI	0.79 (71) AGRI
		0.15 (32) SCOT	4.76 (40) UNEMS	-0.83 (-40) SEMI	0.18 (32) SCOT	0.19 (36) SCOT
		3.85 (30) UNEMS	-0.14 (-25) EA	0.14 (28) SCOT	-0.67 (-30) SEMI	-0.66 (-31) SEMI

Table 7 [continued]

		1955	1959	1964	1966	1970
SQLIB all seats	R^2	11	24	37	34	27
	Equn	0.11 (34) AGRI	0.22 (55) AGRI −0.16 (−28) SEMI	0.35 (68) AGRI −0.31 (−39) SEMI	0.32 (65) AGRI −0.24 (−32) SEMI	0.23 (58) AGRI −0.17 (−28) SEMI
SQLIB all seats	R^2	12	20	34	33	25
	Equn	0.04 (5) EMAR 0.02 (3) EMPL 0.11 (33) AGRI	0.04 (4) EMAR 0.08 (13) EMPL 0.15 (38) AGRI	0.05 (4) EMAR 0.26 (30) EMPL 0.21 (41) AGRI	0.14 (10) EMAR 0.22 (27) EMPL 0.22 (45) AGRI	0.11 (10) EMAR 0.12 (18) EMPL 0.16 (40) AGRI
Three Way contests						
VLIB where stood (see above)						
VCON where LIB stood	R^2	66	65	52	60	58
	Equn	0.38 (60) GPHS −0.13 (−28) WALES −0.61 (−29) SKIL	0.18 (7) EMPL 0.31 (46) GPHS −0.71 (−43) SKIL	1.56 (67) EMPL −0.13 (−25) WALES	0.93 (41) EMPL 0.21 (36) GPHS −0.12 (−24) WALES	1.62 (68) EMPL −0.12 (−28) WALES
VLAB where LIB stood	R^2	69	73	73	71	71
	Equn	−0.36 (−49) GPHS −0.67 (−47) AGRI −0.43 (−34) MID	−1.34 (−50) EMPL −0.39 (−29) AGRI −0.24 (−33) GPHS	−1.42 (−49) EMPL −0.44 (−30) AGRI −0.24 (−32) GPHS	−2.11 (−73) EMPL −0.49 (−34) AGRI	−1.98 (−68) EMPL −0.51 (−34) AGRI 0.13 (24) WALES

Note: (1) Coefficients without brackets are unstandardised multiple regression slopes. Constant terms have been omitted.

(2) Coefficients in brackets are standardised slopes ('path coefficients' in casual path analysis). They equal the regression slopes we would get if all variables, political and social, were measured in standard deviation units.

(3) For dummy variables – the nations, regions and LIBCAND – the unstandardised coefficients are easier to interpret.

(4) Because of the very steep slopes in regressions predicting LIBCAND it is clear that a curvilinear model, for example the logistic, would be more appropriate but the coefficients in this Table give a rough guide to the strong link between EMPL and LIBCAND.

(5) All regressions are for all seats, excluding the handful which lacked a Labour or Conservative candidate, except for those describing patterns of support in three-way contests. The number and characteristics of these seats varied.

Table 8
Within Region Analyses 1966

Best predictor and % of variation explained (R^2)

Region or Nation	Unstandardised slope on EMPL	TWOCON LEAD	TWOCON	LEAD	CON	LAB	LIB	TURN	LIB SQ	LIB CAND	% of turnout variation explained by EMAR
Britain	2.6	2.4	69 E	70 E	50 E	71 E	31 E	39 C	26 A	27 E	26
Scotland	3.0	2.8	75 E	77 E	49 SK	75 E	44 A	55 UN	42 A	21 A	30
Wales	3.4	3.5	65 E	74 E	65 M	73 E	62 A	41 G	66 A	31 A	28
England	2.5	2.2	71 E	72 E	54 E	72 E	36 E	45 C	21 E	28 E	27
N	3.7	3.5	84 E	83 E	76 E	81 E	47 G	32 OWN	50 OLD	44 G	15
YH	3.1	2.9	80 E	84 E	65 E	84 E	27 E	35 USK	12 G	26 E	35
EM	2.8	2.7	71 E	72 E	61 M	69 E	16 OWN	50 C	18 OWN	12 OWN	38
EA	2.2	2.1	69 E	70 E	60 G	54 UN	41 UNS	30 SK	36 UNS	37 UNS	13
SE	2.0	1.7	62 E	61 E	51 G	64 E	36 E	39 AM	28 E	13 E	10
SW	2.9	2.3	61 E	69 E	39 SK	66 E	59 A	37 C	52 A	38 E	35
WM	2.2	2.1	74 E	74 E	64 E	70 SK	30 SK	64 G	29 A	29 SK	33
NW	2.4	2.2	79 E	77 E	55 G	81 E	52 E	65 UN	48 P	35 E	39
LCC	2.2	2.1	91 M	90 M	87 M	88 M	30 ML	59 C	34 ML	23 USK	43

Note: (1) No signs are attached to R^2 values in this Table. The signs are the same as for Britain-wide analyses.
(2) Compressed mnemonics are:-
E = EMPL, M = MID, A = AGRI, G = GPHS, UN = UNEM, SK = SKIL, UNS = UNEMS, ML = MALE, C = CARS, USK = UNSK, AM = AMEN, P = PROF.
(3) See text for comments on other years.

(2)   The total class effect, the sum of the individual and environmental effects, went up at this time.

(3)   There can be little doubt that the environmental effects did not amplify trends in the individual level effects.

(4)   With less certainty it seems that the environmental effects totally dampened the individual level trends and even reversed their direction. Declining individual effects permitted more local consensus.

Apart from their details, these conclusions show that the term 'class polarisation' is almost meaningless unless it is qualified by a statement of what is polarised. In particular, surveys by themselves tell us nothing about trends in constituency polarisation.

5   Trends in Secondary Social Patterns 1955–70

To document both the minor social deviations and the changes over time, stepwise regressions were used to predict nine political measures from forty three census measures at each of the five elections between 1955 and 1970. The forty three social predictors were those listed in Table 1 of Chapter Two plus EMAR, class marginality. These measures are discussed in detail later in this chapter. The nine political measures were

VCON, VLAB, VLIB = the Conservative Labour and Liberal shares
                                of the total three party vote.
TWOCON = VCON/(VCON + VLAB).
LEAD   = (VCON − VLAB)/2.
TURN   = total vote as a percent of registered electors.
TWO   = Conservative plus Labour votes as a percent of registered
                  electors.
SQLIB   = (VLIB)^2.
LIBCAND = dummy variable indicating the presence of a Liberal
                  candidate.

VCON, VLAB, VLIB measured party votes. TWOCON and LEAD measured Conservative versus Labour polarisation. TURN and TWO were two measures of system support: one of support for the parliamentary system, the other of support for the two party system.

Our prime concern was to analyse voting patterns not patterns of sympathy. In seats without Liberal candidates sympathy and votes were likely to be two different things. A variety of methods were used to investigate the effects of candidature patterns on voting patterns. Firstly, by using LIBCAND as a dependent variable we could expose the social structure of Liberal candidatures. Secondly, we could compare the social patterns of Liberal votes within different subsets of constituencies: (1) all constituencies, setting the Liberal vote to zero where there was no candidate; (2) seats where the Liberals had a candidate; (3) seats which the Liberals contested in all five election years; (4) all seats in the South West region, an area where the party was particularly strong. A third method of analysing liberal support was to use SQLIB, the square of the Liberal vote as a dependent variable. The effect of this transformation was to make the difference between 20 % and 40 % twelve times the size of the difference between 0 % and 20 %. It was relatively easy for a party like the Liberals, which suffered from widespread indifference rather than specific antagonism, to raise its vote from 0 % to 10 % almost anywhere merely by putting up a candidate. A rise from 10 % to 20 % or 30 % was at once much more difficult and a more significant indicator of local support. On the assumption that the Liberals would have obtained relatively low votes in the constituencies they failed to contest if they had fielded candidates, an analysis using SQLIB would not be greatly affected if the Liberals had fought all seats.

5.1 Basic Multiple Regressions

As a standard criterion for presentation of the stepwise regression results we define a basic multiple regression as one whose predictive power (R^2) would not be increased by as much as 5 % by the inclusion of any single excluded predictor. Although forty three social predictors were available for inclusion this seemingly lax criterion produced very simple basic equations. Most of the partisan variation that could be explained by the forty three social predictors could be also explained by a very small subset of them. However the chosen subset varied with the type of partisanship. For Conservative and Labour class was all important; for Liberal votes agriculture was particularly significant and for turnout, a range of property owning democracy measures. Table 7 gives the details.

The multiple regressions for Conservative versus Labour partisanship used only one predictor, EMPL, at the first four elections and only supplemented it with WALES in 1970. Nonetheless they explained between 63 % and 73 % of the partisan variation.

EMPL was also the only predictor used in the equations predicting Liberal candidatures. Since LIBCAND was a dummy variable the R^2 values for these equations were spuriously depressed compared to those for voting predictions. The middle class bias in Liberal candidatures increased rapidly between 1955 and 1964 and then steadied. The slopes indicated that over the range of EMPL the Liberal candidature rate went from 0 % to 100 % at all elections in the sixties. This explains the patterns and trends in the difference between analyses of Liberal voting in all seats and in seats with candidates.

All methods of analysing Liberal votes concurred that the two basic predictors of Liberal votes were AGRI plus a class measure. They indicated that Liberals did well where EMPL was high or SEMI, which included agricultural labourers, was low. Additional predictors were only included in three of the twenty equations except where EMAR was forced into the equation. Restricting the analysis to seats with Liberal candidates gave greater weight to agriculture rather than class. Including all seats left agriculture as the sole basic predictor in 1955, but later the bias of candidatures helped to shift the predictive load firmly onto class. During the post-1959 Liberal revival, the Liberal vote became much more firmly associated with the middle class: this was largely the result of the party's own decisions. The predictive fit (R^2) was generally much better in analyses restricted to seats with Liberal candidates, and better still in the core areas which the party consistently contested and also within the South West region. (Full results for these areas are not shown in Table 7. Agriculture was the dominant predictor in them). Forcing EMAR into the equations showed only a small tendency for higher Liberal votes in 'safe' seats in 1955, but the effect increased.

Equations for TWO, the two party system, did not show a distinctive pattern, rather a mix of the patterns for Liberal voting and turnout. We shall not discuss them further.

Basic equations for turnout never included more than three predictors except when class and class marginality were forced in, when the equations still included up to three other predictors. Which set of predictors of turnout was used varied from election to election but the choice was always from a list comprising RENT, CARS, TIMM, UNSK, UNEMS plus in one equation only, CENT. Low turnout went with high levels of privately rented housing, unskilled workers, unemployment and immigration or low levels of car ownership. These consist partly of measures of deprivation and partly of technical influences on voting. Cars obviously facilitated getting out to vote. Privately rented housing indicated temporary accommodation, transient populations and an out of date register. Immigrants might be insufficiently integrated to get round to civic duties like voting. However the presence of unemployment and unskilled workers on the list must indicate something more than mere technicalities. Places where the electorate had done well out of the established order were more likely to show higher turnouts.

The last section of Table 7 shows equations for each party in constituencies where all three parties had candidates. These introduce a point that must be developed later: there was a clear lack of symmetry between the equations. The pattern was more complex than a class polarisation between Labour and Conservative plus a rural polarisation between Liberals and the rest.

5.2 Explanations of Deviations from the Alignments described by the Basic Equations

As a standard measure of the power other variables had to explain deviations from the basic equations we used squared partial correlations which equalled the proportions of residual variation (or deviance) explained by each one of the forty two predictors not in the basic equation. Almost from the definition of the basic equations these proportions had to be small. Almost, but not quite, for if the basic equation itself explained a very large proportion of partisan variation some further predictors might explain a lot of the small total of deviance without adding much to the explanation of partisanship. An extreme example which we shall consider later is voting patterns within Inner London. A single class predictor explained 90% of Labour versus Conservative partisan variation within London. So any further predictor would have to explain fully half the residual variation or it would be excluded from the basic equation. However that is an extreme example. No variable excluded from a basic equation ever explained more than about one-eighth of deviance when we were analysing Britain as a whole. For that reason, and also because we present a more extensive check on deviations from basic patterns in Chapter Six, we shall give only a brief summary of the findings here. They differ from those in Chapter Six in that they come from an analysis of constituency data and they are British in scope. In Chapter Six we cannot use constituency data and the results are for England only. Nonetheless there is considerable agreement between the two sets of findings.

5.2.1 The Classes

EMPL was a basic predictor of Conservative versus Labour partisanship, of Liberal candidatures in all years, Liberal votes in every year except 1955 and system support in all years. SEMI was always a basic predictor of Liberal votes in seats contested and of SQLIB in every year except 1955. With these controls the influence of other class measures was slight.

The highest residual correlations were between low turnouts and unskilled workers, correlations that increased steadily until they explained 10 % of turnout deviance in 1966, with a small reduction in 1970.

5.2.2 The Property Owning Democracy

We used seven measures of the property owning democracy. First, cars per household (CARS) and the percent with full housing amenities, bath, hot water, etc. (AMEN), measure the affluence or life-style version of the concept. Second, the percent of tenures which were rented from some socialised body (COUN), owned or mortgaged by the occupant (OWN) or rented from private landlords (RENT) measured the more genuinely property owning versus socialism version of the concept. Then two constructed variables measured affluence and tenure in a polarised way. GPHS, which stands for 'good private housing', equalled AMEN minus COUN. Since socialised housing often had what the State described as 'full amenities' this variable was intended to distinguish areas where residents owned good, affluent housing whose amenities probably went far beyond the state definition. Second, TENURE, equal to OWN minus COUN, measured the balance of owner-occupation and socialised housing. It was a pure tenure polarisation measure that took no account of affluence.

System support was most strongly linked to these measures. Privately rented housing was either in the basic equation for turnout or showed a relatively high negative partial correlation with it. This was the least politically significant of the property variables since high rates of private renting went with an unsettled, transitory life style and a more than usually inflated electoral register.

Council tenancies went with relatively low turnouts, though not so low as in private renting areas, and owner occupation with higher turnouts. It should be noted that this effect occurred even after stringent controls for class and class marginality. There was a growing tendency for high turnouts where the number of cars per capita was high. Thus both affluent areas and non-socialised areas showed relatively high turnouts, but of the two effects the link with affluence started weaker but ended stronger.

Private renting had a neutral effect on Conservative versus Labour partisanship. Socialised housing, even after the class controls, was bad for the Conservatives. As time passed socialised housing became even worse for the Conservatives and house ownership began to correlate with anti-Labour deviations. These effects intensified in 1970.

In car owning areas, the trend towards high turnout, was parallelled by a trend against Labour. The effect was larger, the trend much the same, when affluence was measured by GPHS which explained 13 % of anti-Labour deviations in 1970.

5.2.3 The Urban-Rural Dimension Only one measure, the percent in agriculture, was used to measure urban-rural differences. After some investigation it was decided not to transform this variable in any way although its distribution is strongly skewed. It was the best predictor of Liberal sympathy and usually in the basic equation for Liberal voting. Perhaps surprisingly it had little effect on where the Liberals put forward candidates. There was a steady trend towards a pro-Conservative anti-Labour bias in rural areas which was increased by a Welsh control, but still only explained 8 % of anti-Labour deviance in 1970.

5.2.4 Immigration Ethnic effects produce a special kind of political deviance, more individual than electoral. Within an electorate they tend to produce two cancelling effects: immigrants favouring one party and their indigenous neighbours reacting and favouring another. No matter how strong these effects they only produce constituency deviance if they fail to cancel perfectly and there is no theoretical reason why the net deviance should be in favour of one party or another. Anti-immigrant reaction favoured the Conservatives. So we can tell from the results which effect, if either, dominated.

Five measures of immigration were used: immigrants from Northern Ireland (NI); Eire; the New Commonwealth (CIMM); the total Irish = (NI + EIRE); the total of both Irish and New Commonwealth (TIMM), all as percents of the population.

From 1959 onward TIMM was in the basic equation for turnout and in 1955 it was the best immigration predictor of low turnouts. Its effect increased over time. Immigration measures had no effect on Liberal votes but the pattern linking immigration to Conservative versus Labour votes was the inverse of that for turnout. The best predictor of Conservative deviance was NI: the effect which was relatively large in 1955, explaining 12 % of deviance, declined to almost nothing by 1970.

5.2.5 Unemployment There were three measures of unemployment, each an unemployment rate as a percent of those males economically active: those with no job in the last year (UNEML); those currently out of work at the time of the 1966 Census but who had been employed within the last year (UNEMS); and the total of long and short term unemployment. Although both UNEML and UNEMS were biased towards traditional areas of unemployment, UNEML has a greater bias towards Scotland, Wales and the North while UNEMS had a greater bias towards London.

Unemployment was in the basic equation for turnout until 1964; then it continued to show a negative, declining partial correlation. The Liberals did relatively well in unemployment areas provided we impose controls for AGRI and candidature. This effect also declined in the late sixties. Meanwhile the Conservatives began to do relatively badly in unemployment areas. The Labour governments from 1964 to 1970 publicised their intentions and their achievements in using governmental power to switch economic resources away from the areas of traditional prosperity, although their record on the total quantity of unemployment was unimpressive. Unemployment never explained more than 5% of Conservative/Labour deviance.

5.2.6 Age and Sex Sex ratios varied very little from constituency to constituency. The percentage male had a mean of 48% and a standard deviation of 1.5%. So, however powerful sex might be as a predictor of voting in surveys, we should expect it to explain very little of the variation between constituencies. Analysis justified that expectation but it also showed that men were always detrimental to the Conservatives and Liberals and beneficial to Labour.

As a primitive measure of age we used OLD, the percent aged over 65 years. This age variable measured rather more than age, for people grow old everywhere. OLD took specially high values in places like Bournemouth, Hastings, Torquay, Worthing, Honiton, Harwich, Thanet, Morecambe, Eastbourne, Rye and West Sussex. Such places were all in England, mostly in the south, often described as 'seaside resorts', places where a special sort of elderly could afford to concentrate. Two influences might dispose them against Labour. They would be particularly hurt by inflation and they may have retained, individually and as a society, the political spirit of an earlier age. Areas with high rates of OLD also tended to have other anti-Labour characteristics. Class, of course, was controlled in the basic equations for most political variables, but the highest correlations with OLD were a 0.62 with the percent female, and 0.47 with the lack of socialised housing.

There was a consistent negative partial correlation between OLD and turnout, although it never explained more than 1% of residual variation. A larger positive link with Liberal voting was only partly explained by greater numbers of Liberal candidates in OLD areas. Larger still was a positive link with Conservative voting which was increased still further by a Welsh control. So in 1970 OLD explained 8% of pro-Conservative deviance.

5.2.7 Special Industries: Agriculture, Mining and Defence Correlations with the percent in agriculture have already been reported under the heading of an urban/rural dimension, but very few seats could be described as truly agricultural. We defined agricultural seats as those with over 20% in agriculture; mining seats had a similar percentage definition. The agricultural areas were all more middle class than any of the mining areas. So one group should have been more Conservative than the other on class grounds alone. However all the mining seats deviated to become even more Labour and three-quarters of the agricultural seats deviated to become even more Conservative. Of the three agricultural seats deviating strongly away from the Conservatives, two were Welsh, one Scottish. There were Liberal candidates in 80 % of agricultural seats in 1966; they scored an average vote of 31 % compared to the 1966 average of 17 % in all seats contested by Liberals.

There were two useful measures of another special case, defence. The census occupational breakdown included a category of 'armed forces and inadequately described' (FORCES). It was unfortunate that the inadequately described were included but it is reasonable to suppose that they varied relatively little across the country. Overall FORCES had a mean of just 2 % many of whom were, no doubt, 'inadequately described' but it went up to 21 % in West Portsmouth, 18 % in Moray, 16 % in Aldershot. The industrial breakdown included GOVT, the percent employed 'by national and local government'. This averaged under 5 % but was 25 % in Moray and in Aldershot and 41 % in West Portsmouth. It correlated at 0.86 with FORCES. Again it would seem that there were civil employees everywhere, but large concentrations of GOVT meant defence employment whether the individuals were classed as civil or military. No London constituency had over 14 % for GOVT despite being the centre of administration. Nonetheless GOVT must have had a slightly more civilian bias than FORCES and since it was larger a third variable, CIVIL, was defined equal to GOVT minus FORCES.

We should expect FORCES and GOVT to go with pro-Conservative deviations because the Conservatives were the most patriotic pro-military party. CIVIL might go with pro-Labour deviations since Labour favoured large scale, civil government. Analysis showed that all three variables went with pro-Conservative deviations and that the partial correlations increased steadily over time to explain 9 % of deviance by 1970. The highest correlations were with GOVT, the smallest with CIVIL. Clearly concentrations of civilian defence employees produced the same sort of pro-Conservative effects as concentrations of military personnel themselves. Either CIVIL failed to tap the variation in truly civil employees of government or they were no more pro-Labour than their occupational class would predict. Even where civil employees are concentrated for work it tends to be in large cities and they disperse to many different constituencies to live and vote. Defence establishments, by contrast, tend to be away from the largest cities and their workers disperse less at nightfall. Thus any measure of government employment concentrations based on residence may be inevitably a measure of military related work.

5.2.8 *Nations and Regions* An analysis of regions by name is the least satisfactory of any social analysis for it may point to the existence of deviance without saying much about it. This criticism may be less severe for an analysis by nation if only because we can usually distinguish the nations by important social characteristics and possibly recall some separate past existence.

To assess regional deviance we defined dummy variables for Scotland, Wales and each region of England and calculated squared partial correlations with dummy predictor variables. 'Squared' partials with regional and national dummies could be large if a large region deviated moderately or a small region extremely. The measure is justifiably biased against small regions: small regions that deviate only moderately are of little interest.

Wales deviated strongly against the Conservatives explaining over 12% of Conservative deviance at every election until it was included in the basic equation for 1970. Then the slope coefficient indicated that the Conservative share of the two party vote was 14% less for a Welsh constituency than its level of employers and managers would indicate. No other regional deviance was comparable in importance to this Welsh effect. Scottish constituencies in 1955 were more Conservative than average for their class but by 1964 they had begun to deviate against the Conservatives. They followed the same trend as the North West of England which had deviated strongly to the Conservatives in 1955 but only a little after 1964. The South West and the West Midlands deviated little in 1955 but both went more anti-Labour thereafter, the West Midlands deviation peaking in 1964. The South West was the only region to show a strong and persistent bias to the Liberals. This was partly due to a bias in candidatures. Liberals did particularly badly in the small East Anglian region.

Turnout was high in Wales, low in England. Within England it was always particularly low in London, especially in 1964 and 1970.

In addition to the national areas and the standard regions of England two further English variables were used: Central England (CENT) and Peripheral England (PERI). Central England comprised the West Midlands, East Anglia, London and the South East. Peripheral England was the North, North West, Yorkshire/Humberside and South West. This definition of Central England was primarily geographical. It was approximately the square bounded by the Welsh border, the south and east coasts of England and the 53° North latitude. Central England took in three-fifths of English constituencies. There were strong social biases in Central England towards high levels of employment, immigration, clerks, cars and professionals, and a small bias towards employers and managers; there was no bias towards or against defence, agriculture, housing amenity, any form of house tenure, age or sex. Central England was roughly that part of Britain outside the 'development areas'.

In most years turnout was low in Central England but about average in Peripheral England. There was little overall effect on Liberal votes, but among the seats where they had candidates the party did badly, especially from 1959 to 1966, in Central England, and well in Peripheral England. Between 1959 and 1964 they were more prone to field candidates in Central England. Over the years a small Conservative advantage in Peripheral England declined to zero. On class grounds the Conservatives should have done badly on the periphery. In 1955 they did not fare quite as badly as the peripheral class characteristics would have suggested. In that year the Conservatives, not Labour, had the regional advantage on the English periphery, especially in North West England; they also had the national advantage in Scotland.

Regions could differ not just in the levels of support for parties but also in the patterns relating society and politics. All the regression analyses were repeated on data sets restricted to constituencies within each particular region. This generated a vast amount of information. Some of the more striking results include the following:—

(1) In 1966 employers and managers (EMPL) was the best predictor of LEAD and TWOCON in ten of the eleven regions, and the best predictor of VLAB in eight (see Table 8). The uniform power of EMPL as a predictor of Labour voting in all years and regions was impressive. In eight of the eleven regions it was the best predictor in every year. The three exceptions were: Inner London were EMPL explained as much partisan variation as anywhere else, but the full non-manual middle class did even better every time; East Anglia where the number of constituencies was low and the best predictor varied between EMPL, housing amenity and unemployment; and the West Midlands where at four of the five elections Labour votes were best predicted from the percent of skilled workers.

(2) When and where EMPL was not the best predictor it was not far behind. This was true even in the West Midlands.

(3) The West Midlands result was significant in that the best predictor there, unlike everywhere else, was in no sense a stratification variable. It put the skilled workers on one side and everyone else, from captains of industry to unskilled manuals, were lumped together on the other. Nor was there evidence that Labour benefited greatly from concentrations of skilled workers who might be strongly unionised. The TUC included powerful unions representing the unskilled and throughout England Labour votes correlated with unskilled workers as well as with skilled. Indeed the trend was towards better correlations with the unskilled than with the skilled. However in the West Midlands Labours votes correlated badly with semi-skilled and unskilled workers. It is unlikely that this was a genuine class effect since Irish and Commonwealth immigrants in the West Midlands correlated strongly with the percent unskilled, but not with the skilled.

(4) Using partial correlations as a criterion, there was little evidence that any social variables were very powerful indicators of political deviance in some regions but not in others. Only two effects stand out: Agriculture was specially important in the East Midlands, East Anglia and the South West, while immigration had different effect in different regions. East Anglia and the South West were primarily agricultural areas although agriculture's importance in the East Midlands seems more related to the structure of party competition than a large amount of agricultural activity. Immigration effects in five regions and all elections are shown in Table 9. They have always been reputed to interact with region (i.e. to be specially strong in special regions) and the Table confirms this.[4]

Scotland and the North West, as the regions nearest to Ireland, have the reputation of containing large numbers of Irish and of displaying political deviance related to the presence of Irish immigrants. The West Midlands has a similar reputation regarding Commonwealth immigrants. In fact, all five regions had comparable levels of Northern Irish per capita; the greatest density of Southern Irish was in London, followed by the West Midlands and the South East. Prosperity was clearly more attractive than proximity to their homeland.

Table 9 shows the proportions of political deviance from the basic class alignment attributable to the presence of immigrants. In Scotland the net effects were small; in the North West there was a larger (over 10%) net effect in 1955 which declined thereafter. What effect there was, both in Scotland and the North West, showed anti-immigrant reaction as the larger force. In Inner London the net Irish effect was small and declining, but there was clearer evidence of a larger but declining anti-Commonwealth effect. However in Inner London the quantity of deviation from the class alignment was unusually small in total. In the South

Table 9
The Interaction between Region and Immigration

Region or Nation	Immi- gration type	Constituency Average of immigrants per 10,000 population	1955	1959	1964	1966	1970
			% of residual variation in LEAD explained				
Scotland	NI	56	4	2	0	0	1
	EIRE	83	3	2	1	3	1
	IRISH	139	4	3	1	2	1
	CIMM	51	5	5	7	5	5
	TIMM	190	6	4	3	4	3
North West	NI	47	10	6	9	6	3
	EIRE	161	9	2	2	1	1
	IRISH	208	11	3	3	2	1
	CIMM	88	7	3	4	4	4
	TIMM	296	9	3	4	3	3
West Midlands	NI	54	30	28	15	7	2
	EIRE	202	32	32	18	9	3
	IRISH	255	32	32	18	9	3
	CIMM	251	32	40	40	33	14
	TIMM	506	38	45	35	25	10
Inner London	NI	59	7	6	6	6	4
	EIRE	436	7	7	6	3	3
	IRISH	495	6	6	5	4	4
	CIMM	700	17	17	15	12	12
	TIMM	1195	15	15	13	10	10
South East	NI	39	6	7	5	2	1
	EIRE	184	−1	−1	−2	−6	−12
	IRISH	223	0	0	−2	−5	−10
	CIMM	227	0	0	−1	−4	−8
	TIMM	450	0	−1	−2	−5	−11

East the net immigrant effect benefited Labour especially towards the end of the sixties, although it never explained more than 12% of deviance.

The West Midlands was unique. Although the levels of both Irish and Commonwealth immigration were very close to those in the South East the results showed strong pro-Conservative deviations correlated with both Irish and Commonwealth immigrants. In 1955 the two effects were about equal, but the Irish effect stayed steady in 1959 and declined quickly thereafter. The Commonwealth effect peaked in 1964 and in 1966 when it explained 40% of pro-Conservative deviations; after 1964 it declined sharply. The deviations from the class alignment in the West Midlands were not specially small, as in London.

If patterns in the West Midlands had been more stable over time we could view the difference between the West Midlands and the South East immigrant effects as the result of interactions with different social environments, but the speed of change suggests more political explanations. In the early sixties local Conservative leaders in the West Midlands made an issue of the problems caused by immigration in specific localities. Although the issue received much greater nationwide publicity later in the decade and its effect may or may not have been large across the whole electorate, it was no longer so localised in impact and thus no longer so important for local deviations from general alignments. [5]

These conclusions are based on deviations from within-region class alignments using EMPL as the class indicator. They are not much altered if we use the best predictor at each election in each region, except in the West Midlands. In this area skilled workers were the single best predictor of LEAD in 1955, 1959 and 1964 and the deviations from an alignment based on skilled workers hardly correlated with immigration. We think the correct interpretation is to view this result in reverse: to see West Midlands percent skilled workers as a hybrid indicator that coincidentally selected working class areas without specially high immigrant levels. Immigration did not explain political deviations from this alignment since high levels of immigrants went with high levels of unskilled workers and the pro- and anti-Conservative effects cancelled.

(5) There was more variability between regions on other political responses than Conservative versus Labour choice. Liberal votes from 1955 to 1970 correlated particularly well with agriculture within Scotland, Wales, the South West and the West Midlands. Elsewhere there was no single dominant factor explaining Liberal votes.

Explanations of turnout varied spatially as they did temporarily, but within the same set of affluence and related variables. In 1955 unemployment was the best indicator in over half the regions but in every other year no single factor predominated. Car ownership was a recurrent predictor in the South West, housing in the West Midlands (GPHS), and unemployment in the North West. Elsewhere there was a great deal of year to year variation.

6   A Three-Way Battle

So far we have discussed partisanship in terms of choice between the two major parties, votes for the Liberals and turnout. At least this admits that there was more to voting than choosing between Labour and Conservative, but it is unrealistic in that it presents these three choices as separate and independent of each other. Few social characteristics actually helped the Conservatives and damaged Labour without affecting Liberal performance and conversely. The last section of Table 7 showed that in three-way contests the equations for Conservative voting were not the inverse of equations for Labour voting. The variables were different and when one variable appeared in both equations its coefficients differed in size as well as sign.

A more rigid analytical framework makes this point even more clearly. Table 10 shows equations predicting Conservative, Labour and Liberal vote shares in three-way contests using the same two predictors, EMPL and AGRI, for each party. A necessary consequence of the arithmetic of regression is that the unstandardised slopes linking all three parties to a particular social predictor must sum to zero. In 1955, for example, each 1 % of EMPL put the Conservative vote up by 1.76 %, the Labour vote down by 2.13 % and the Liberal vote up by 0.37 % providing agriculture was controlled. The standardised slopes do not have this simple property.

In all years the political polarisation corresponding to class was somewhere between Conservative versus Labour and Labour versus the rest since the Labour slope on EMPL was steeper than the Conservative; the Liberals shared the middle class advantage. By 1970 the political alignment with AGRI was almost purely a Liberal versus Labour alignment, a type of political polarisation that has yet to be measured. However before 1970 the AGRI alignment was somewhere between Liberal versus Labour and Liberal versus the rest.

The coefficients for three party contests can be compared with those for two party contests. Since EMPL was a good predictor of Liberal candidature the two party contests occurred, on average, in more working class seats where we might expect somewhat steeper slopes on class. However, while Labour slopes on class were 0.33 less steep in three party seats, the Conservative slopes were 0.72 less. Where Liberal candidates were present the Conservatives clearly lost some of their middle class advantage. Similarly the Conservative's positive slope of 0.05 on AGRI was turned into a negative slope of 0.09, a change of 0.14; Labour's slope steepened by 0.37 showing its extra disadvantage in rural areas where it was not the sole anti-Conservative candidate. So the Liberal vote was aligned with class, mainly at the expense of the Conservatives, and aligned with agriculture or rurality mainly at the expense of Labour.

Table 10

Class, Agriculture and Three Parties

	1955		1959		1964		1966		1970	
	EMPL	AGRI	EMPL	AGRI	EMPL	AGRI	EMPL	AGRI	EMPL	AGRI
In two party contests TWOCON = VCON = (100 % − VLAB)										
slopes	2.22	0.15	2.38	0.02	2.50	−0.10	2.49	0.05	2.44	0.14
standardised slopes	(78)	(8)	(79)	(1)	(75)	(−5)	(78)	(3)	(77)	(7)
In three party contests										
slopes VCON	1.76	−0.19	1.77	−0.12	1.61	−0.06	1.56	−0.05	1.71	−0.01
VLAB	−2.13	−0.39	−1.94	−0.39	−2.08	−0.42	−2.11	−0.49	−2.09	−0.43
VLIB	0.37	0.57	0.17	0.51	0.47	0.48	0.55	0.54	0.39	0.44
standardised slopes VCON	(63)	(−15)	(73)	(−10)	(69)	(−5)	(69)	(−5)	(71)	(−1)
VLAB	(−67)	(−27)	(−73)	(−28)	(−72)	(−29)	(−73)	(−34)	(−72)	(−28)
VLIB	(17)	(58)	(10)	(59)	(25)	(50)	(27)	(53)	(21)	(41)

7 Summary

1 From 1955 to 1970 the Britain-wide levels of partisanship and the spatial patterns of party support were stable within narrow limits.

2 However, although the pattern of party support changed little from one election to the next, the similarity of partisanship declined over time about as fast as would be predicted by a simple causal chain.

3 The Z model of individual and environmental class both affecting partisanship implied that environmental processes greatly magnified the individual level class effect, at least doubling it in 1966. The environmental process would be acting as an amplifier of class polarisation if the individual effect varied over time and the environmental effect varied with it. However, if the environmental effect varied in the opposite direction to changes in the individual effect, then the environmental process would be acting as a dampener. Alternatively the environmental process might have a neutral effect on trends.

4 Over the 1955–70 period the environmental process did not amplify trends in class polarisation.

5 There is some evidence that the environmental process dampened trends in class polarisation. The individual level class depolarisation found by sample surveys simply did not happen at the constituency level. If anything, constituency class polarisation increased.

6 A wide ranging check for secondary social patterns in partisanship was made using forty three census indicators to predict nine different measures of partisanship in each of the five election years, within eleven regions as well as within Britain as a whole and within its constituent nations. Results were as follows.

7 Basic equations were defined as those multiple regressions such that none of the forty three possible predictors not already included within the basic equation could improve the proportion of partisan variation explained by as much as 5%. Despite this seemingly lax criterion, basic equations for Conservative versus Labour used only one predictor, EMPL, at four elections and only added a Welsh control at the fifth.

8 Basic equations for Liberal voting never included more than two predictors. In all but one equation these predictors were agriculture and a class measure.

9 Basic equations for turnout included as many as three non-class measures plus class and class marginality.

10 By definition none of the remaining variables could be a powerful explanation of partisan deviations from the basic alignments. However the text assesses the size and direction of correlations between partisan deviance and: (a) a complex class breakdown; (b) the property owning democracy; (c) the urban/rural dimension; (d) immigration; (e) unemployment; (f) sex; (g) age; and (h) three special industries—agriculture, mining and defence.

11 Region-wide deviance was not of major importance except for the Welsh bias

to Labour rather than Conservative, although lesser effects and trends were noted.

12　The predictive power of EMPL in all regions and at all elections was impressive.

13　However immigration explained a substantial part of the deviations from the class alignment in some regions until the late sixties. Irish immigration had little net impact in Scotland or North West England where an effect might have been expected. Commonwealth immigration had a large net pro-Conservative effect in the West Midlands, a smaller one in London and none, or even a small pro-Labour effect, in the South East despite the similar levels of immigration in those regions.

14　Analyses restricted to seats with three-way contests exposed the inadequacies of bipolar analysis in a particularly elegant way. In these seats the class alignment was largely Conservative versus Labour, the urban-rural alignment was even closer to Liberal versus Labour.

CHAPTER 4

Units, Measures and Methods for Longer Term Analysis

1 Introduction: Essential Features of Longer Term Analysis

The problems of analysing voting outside the narrow time span between 1955 and 1970 are the same as before but worse. Even within 1955–70 it was impossible to ignore the Liberals and unsatisfactory to compartmentalise the analysis into Conservative versus Labour and Liberal versus the rest. Yet the Liberals never gained as much as 12% of votes cast. In 1929 they took twice that percentage and in 1974 well over one and a half times. At a certain level, a quantity of votes brings a qualitative change. Between 1955 and 1970 the Liberals could be described as a minor party but in 1923 they beat the Conservatives in Wales and Labour in England and, although third throughout the UK, they were within 1% of Labour. At least as a constant label for particular parties the major/minor distinction is not relevant for the long term. So one priority must be to develop some method of analysis which can cope with three parties without introducing arbitrary distinctions between them.

In most respects the data for the period before 1955 is much less rich than later. There was no major academic survey of the full British electorate before 1966 and no Gallup poll for any election before 1945. Gallup started in 1937 but both pollsters and public were far more concerned about the prospects for war than about the last British election.[1] We know from studies of more recent Gallup polls that political responses in the middle of a parliament give a very poor guide to electoral behaviour even when the mid-term is not dominated by a European War.[2] Census data is available from the Censuses of 1921, 1931 and 1951–there was none during the war–but, although they may have been excellent for the Registrar General's purposes, their measures of class are thin compared to those in the 1966 Census. Until 1951 good class measures were calculated for the country as a whole but not for small areas. As compensation, the earlier censuses which were poor on class were good on religion. So at a time when we should guess that religious patterns were stronger the census conveniently provided religious measures.

There also are boundary problems: parliamentary boundaries were changed in 1945, 1950, 1955 and 1974. So constituency election results can be related to themselves only within the periods 1918–35, 1950–51, 1955–70 and February–October 1974. Census boundaries never matched parliamentary boundaries, although constituency volumes were published for the Censuses of 1966 and 1971 using aggregations of small census tracts which approximated the 1955–70 and 1974 parliamentary boundaries. Before that the basic unit for most published census data was the county or county borough although some information was published for smaller units.

This chapter describes some solutions to the problems of incompatible boundaries, definitions of social measures and analysis of three party or even multi party voting systems.

2   Units

2.1 Matching Census and Parliamentary Boundaries

Votes for Parliament were counted and declared at the constituency level. There was no possibility, legal or illegal, of recovering parliamentary voting data at lower precinct levels as is the case in Europe or the United States. Consequently the only units that could provide voting data for every election between 1918 and 1974 were constituencies whose boundaries survived all four redistributions intact or groups of adjacent constituencies whose common external boundaries remained unaltered.

At all times constituency boundaries were defined in terms of some level of local government boundaries in existence at that time. Boundary commissions were instructed to 'respect local boundaries' and it was unusual for a parliamentary constituency to lie across the boundary of one of the primary local government units—a county or county borough. County boroughs were towns within a county; over time they increased in number and individually extended their boundaries, but for most of our period they were fairly static. Between the 1926 Local Government Act and 1958 it has been calculated that county borough extensions transferred only 300,000 people and 223,000 acres from the landward areas of counties to the boroughs. So as a general rule we may think of county and county borough boundaries as fixed; parliamentary constituencies as subdivisions of a county borough or of the landward area of a county; and parliamentary redistributions occurring within a county borough or within the landward area of a county.

For long term analyses spanning 1918–74 we defined a set of 161 so-called 'constant units'. Boundary changes involving 2% or less of population were accepted as leaving a boundary unchanged. These constant units were essentially boroughs and landward areas of counties. Every part of Britain was allocated to one or other of these constant units so that they covered rural as well as urban Britain. The 1966 boundaries were used as a starting point. Outside London constituencies were grouped into the county boroughs in which they were located. All constituencies within a county, but outside the county boroughs, were grouped to form a county remainder. In London constituencies were allocated to their old LCC (London County Council = Inner London) borough and the new GLC (Greater London Council) ignored. There were few troublesome exceptions and this procedure gave 184 units. This number was increased by defining more 'boroughs' which were groups of constituencies corresponding to areas defined by a group of larger local government units, municipal boroughs or large urban districts, for which a full range of census data was available. The number of units was then reduced by eliminating those whose boundaries cross-out earlier constituency or local government boundaries. Finally, after census data had been compiled for the 173 units remaining, computer checks were run using the census tables of population and acreage for current boundaries at the times of preceding censuses. 161 units were left after eliminating those which failed this test. At all stages eliminated units were combined with others, usually the county remainder.

The 161 constant units were defined before the elections of 1974. They corresponded very closely to groups of constituencies at each election between 1918 and 1970 and also to groups of census areas used in the 1921, 1931, 1951 and 1966 Censuses. To extend the file, voting data for 1974 was compiled by taking the group of 1974 constituencies which corresponded most closely to each of the 161 constant units. Despite the fact that local government boundaries also suffered a major revision between 1970 and 1974, the correspondence between the 1974 constituencies and the constant units remained close in most cases but the match was not quite so good as in earlier years. So for 1974 boundary mismatches may slightly depress correlations compared to other years.

2.2 Effect on Regressions of Aggregation Beyond the Constituency

Constant units produced by grouping constituencies are somewhat artificial although they did correspond to towns, counties and local governments. Still, we were driven by necessity, not choice; it would be foolish to pretend otherwise. There is some interest in how boroughs voted, just as in how individuals voted, but the only votes that elected M.Ps and so helped to determine governments, were the votes of constituencies. We have seen in Chapters Two and Three that the patterns and trends in constituency voting were not the same as in individual voting. If borough votes followed some third pattern they would be less interesting for they would not then explain how M.Ps were elected.

2.2.1 Effects on Slopes and Correlations
There is no logical necessity for regression slopes and correlations to be the same when using data at different levels of aggregation and we know they differ sharply between individual and constituency levels. The regression model for constituency data has the form

$$y_i = \alpha + \beta x_i + \varepsilon_i$$

where α, β are regression coefficients to be estimated; x_i and y_i are the values of social and political variables for the i th constituency; ε_i measures the i th constituency's deviance from the underlying socio-political pattern. For ordinary least squares regression estimates of α and β to be valid the ε_i should be random disturbance terms, independent of each other and of the values of x_i; they should have equal variances and zero expectations, that is each constituency should be as likely to deviate to the Conservatives as to Labour and each constituency should be as likely as any other to deviate by any specific amount.

If the i th and j th constituency are of similar size and we group them together, the values of the social and political measures and the error deviance for the combined unit, $\bar{x}$, $\bar{y}$, $\bar{\varepsilon}$ are

$$\bar{x} = (x_i + x_j)/2 \quad \bar{y} = (y_i + y_j)/2 \quad \bar{\varepsilon} = (\varepsilon_i + \varepsilon_j)/2$$

Now, since $y_i = \alpha + \beta x_i + \varepsilon_i$ and $y_j = \alpha + \beta x_j + \varepsilon_j$ we can add these two equations and divide by two to show

$$\bar{y} = \alpha + \beta \bar{x} + \bar{\varepsilon}$$

The form of the relationship and the parameters α and β are unchanged by aggregation. However we do not know: (1) whether ordinary least squares is an appropriate estimation procedure for estimating α and β; (2) how the correlation associated with this grouped data equation compares with that for the ungrouped data.

Ordinary least squares regression must be appropriate if, and only if, the $\bar{\varepsilon}$ satisfy the same criteria as the original error terms ε_i and ε_j of which the most critical were that they were independent of the x values. To calculate the effect of aggregation on the correlation coefficient we note that

$$r^2 = 1 - \frac{\text{unexplained sum of squares}}{\text{total sum of squares}}$$

$$= 1 - \frac{\text{variance of } \varepsilon}{\text{variance of } y}$$

at least when there are a large number of data points.

A random grouping of constituencies into pairs would halve the variance of ε, of x and of y, in accordance with the law of large numbers. Thus it would leave the correlation unchanged. It would also leave the regression slope estimates unchanged because $\bar{\varepsilon}$ would remain independent of $\bar{x}$. If the grouping put together constituencies with similar x values it would again leave $\bar{\varepsilon}$ independent of $\bar{x}$ and so leave slopes unchanged, but the correlation would be inflated because the variance of ε would be halved while the variance of y would be less reduced, in as much as y depended upon x. Finally if the grouping was by the dependent variable y it would inflate both slope and correlation. The correlation would rise because the variance of y would be preserved better than the variance in ε, again in as much as y depended upon x as well as ε. The slope would be inflated because the highest and lowest y values would occur where both x and ε were either high or low together which would destroy the independence between $\bar{x}$ and $\bar{\varepsilon}$. They would become positively correlated and part of the apparent slope of $\bar{y}$ on $\bar{x}$ would be due to the concurrent effect of ε.

Blalock has used some American county data to illustrate and confirm these consequences of three idealised aggregation schemes.[3] He also showed that for his data, grouping by geographic proximity was close to grouping by x. Slopes inflated very little but correlations much more.

As a methodological test, the 1966 Census data and the 1955–70 election results for constituencies were grouped into boroughs and county remainders ('borough' units), then further grouped into complete counties, and finally grouped into eleven regional data-points. These four different data sets were then analysed by stepwise regression. Table 1 shows some selected results using a variety of political measures and eighteen census variables. Stepwise regressions tended to select the same social measures at different levels of aggregation, although results for the regional data set differed most from constituency results and borough data produced the most similar results. Correlations did not rise uniformly with the level of aggregation. In general they fell until the regional level where there were so few data points that correlations were likely to be spuriously high. Table 2 shows the results for a number of pre-specified regressions applied to the different data sets. There was no consistent tendency for slopes to rise or fall with the level of aggregation. Once again borough analyses were closest to constituency results and regional data gave the least similar results.[4] For a prediction of the Conservative share of the two party vote from EMPL, the slope was 2.6 using constituency data, 2.7 using borough data. Similarly for a prediction from the non-manuals, MID, the slope was 0.93 using constituency data and 0.84 using borough data. For a prediction of the Liberal vote as a share of the electorate from AGRI, the slope was 0.51 using constituency data, 0.50 using borough data.

Although it was inescapable necessity that forced us to use borough level units for long term analysis, it would appear that regression slopes are not much altered, but correlations are reduced by using these units instead of constituencies. It would also appear that these borough level units are much more useful than county or regional data sets because slopes calculated from such data are considerably less accurate substitutes for constituency slopes.

These conclusions were reinforced by calculating multiple regressions using constituency, borough, county and regional measures of the same variable as simultaneous predictors (Table 3). The higher level terms did not improve the fit except in the case of MID where the betterment was slight but the coefficient of the higher level term which improved the fit had the opposite sign to the coefficient for the constituency term. If we took these equations seriously we should have to postulate an 'embattled citadel effect' whereby middle class constituencies became more Conservative when surrounded by working class constituencies. The idea is attractive but the evidence for it is weak.

Table 1
Stepwise Regressions at Four Levels of Aggregation

Political Partisanship	Aggregation Level	First Social Predictor (R%)		Second Social Predictor (R%)		R^2% using all 18 predictors
TWOCON	C	EMPL	67	AGRI	69	81
	B	EMPL	61	UNEMS	64	76
	T	EMPL	49	UNEMS	61	77
	R	EMPL	64	UNEMS	69	NA
VCON	C	EMPL	49	NI	56	65
	B	EMPL	35	UNEMS	46	59
	T	UNEMS	34	SKIL	51	67
	R	UNEMS	53	AMEN	69	NA
VLAB	C	EMPL	69	AGRI	74	84
	B	EMPL	66	AGRI	71	83
	T	EMPL	57	AGRI	59	76
	R	EMPL	74	AMEN	81	NA
VLIB where stood	C	AGRI	19	SEMI	24	31
	B	AGRI	44	OLD	58	65
	T	AGRI	54	EMPL	64	80
	R	EMPL	64	OLD	77	NA
ELIB where stood	C	AGRI	29	SEMI	33	44
	B	AGRI	43	OLD	57	63
	T	AGRI	51	SEMI	67	76
	R	EMPL	61	OLD	77	NA
TURN	C	AMEN	36	OWN	49	61
	B	OWN	35	AMEN	50	64
	T	PROF	8	CIMM	21	59
	R	TIMM	76	CARS	98	NA

Note: (1) Political variables defined as in Chapter Two except for the addition of ELIB, the Liberal vote as a percent of the electorate.
(2) Social predictors were PROF, EMPL, CLERK, MID, SKIL, SEMI, UNSK, COUN, OWN, AMEN, CARS, AGRI, NI, EIRE, CIMM, TIMM, OLD, UNEMS all defined in closely similar ways to those given in Chapter Two. Since these were exploratory analyses some slight variations in definition occurred, but none of any great importance.
(3) Aggregation Levels: C = constituency units; B = borough level units; T = county level units; R = a set of eleven regions as units.
(4) NA = not applicable since more predictors (eighteen) than data points (eleven).

Table 2
Pre-Specified Regressions at Four Levels of Aggregation

Aggregation Levels	Prediction Equation and coefficients			R^2
	TWOCON =	a	b MID	
C		0.16	0.93	47
B		0.19	0.84	31
T		0.23	0.83	16
R		0.22	0.73	23
	TWOCON =	a	b MID	c MID^2	
C		−0.08	2.4	−2.0	52
B		−0.12	2.6	−2.4	37
T		−0.38	4.6	−5.6	21
R		−1.01	8.4	−11.5	32
	TWOCON =	a	b EMPL	
C		0.18	2.6	67
B		0.17	2.7	61
T		0.13	3.1	49
R		0.05	3.9	64
	TWOCON =	a	b EMPL	c $EMPL^2$	
C		0.06	5.0	−9.7	70
B		0.06	4.9	−9.1	63
T		−0.06	6.5	−14.2	50
R		−1.18	26.7	−103.4	76
	TWOCON =	a	b MID	c OWN	
C		0.11	0.78	0.21	52
B		0.11	0.77	0.24	39
T		0.23	0.82	0.01	16
R		0.10	0.75	0.26	39

Aggregation Levels	TWOCON = a	b EMPL	c UNEMS	d AGRI	R^2
C	0.22	2.3	−2.0	0.32	71
B	0.24	2.4	−4.2	0.17	65
T	0.24	2.7	−6.1	0.09	61
R	0.25	2.6	−6.8	0.10	76

Aggregation Levels	ELIB where stood =	a	b AGRI	R^2
C		0.10	0.44	29
B		0.06	0.56	43
T		0.04	0.69	51
R		0.06	−0.00	0

ELECTORAL DYNAMICS

Table 2 [continued]

Aggregation Level	Prediction Equations and coefficients				R^2
	ELIB where stood =	a	+ b AGRI	+ c SEMI	
C		0.13	0.44	−0.07	33
B		0.10	0.56	−0.10	44
T		−0.09	0.69	−0.13	67
R		0.18	0.10	−0.66	20
	ELIB all seats =	a	+ b AGRI		
C		0.04	0.51		21
B		0.04	0.50		31
T		0.04	0.48		25
R		0.06	−0.00		00

Note: ELIB where stood involves different areas at different levels of aggregation.

Table 3
Multi Level Regressions

Using full non-manual middle class to predict TWOCON:–

TWOCON =	a	+ $b_1 MID_c$	+ $b_2 MID_b$	+ $b_3 MID_t$	+ $b_4 MID_r$	+ (R^2%)
	0.16	0.93				(47)
	0.18	1.02	−0.16			(48)
	0.22	1.02	0.11	−0.39		(49)
	0.20	1.02	0.11	−0.51	0.18	(49)

Using employers and managers to predict TWOCON:–

TWOCON =	a	+ $b_1 EMPL_c$	+ $b_2 EMPL_b$	+ $b_3 EMPL_t$	+ $b_4 EMPL_r$	(R^2%)
	0.18	2.6				(67)
	0.17	2.5	0.20			(67)
	0.15	2.5	−0.00	0.32		(67)
	0.13	2.5	0.00	0.10	0.45	(67)

The similarity of slopes at different levels of aggregation and, in particular, the lack of a consistent trend upwards or downwards with more aggregation can be explained by the contact-makes-consensus model. Contacts are much more frequent between individuals who live relatively close together. The environmental effects of the local mix of social characteristics would appear to operate powerfully but over a narrow area. Thus slopes in survey data differ sharply from those in constituency data, but thereafter further aggregation is unaffected by any environmental effects of concentrations of social characteristics.

2.2.2 Weighting So far results indicate that individuals were influenced by their own social characteristics and by those of their immediate neighbourhood, but not by those of the wider environment in which they lived. Wider environments had a strong influence but not via the social characteristics we have measured. Local news media, personalities, history and temper could all affect partisanship over a broad local area, but their contribution would be to the error term unless they happened to correlate strongly with the explicit social predictors used in our regressions. Calculating the variance of residuals from several constituency regressions firstly over all constituencies and then within boroughs and counties showed that about half the deviance from constituency regressions could be attributed to borough-wide, but unspecified influences, unrelated to the social composition of the borough. Such local influences destroy the statistical independence of errors from each other without changing their independence from the explicit social predictors. They increase the variance of ordinary least squares estimates of regression coefficients and would invalidate statistical significance tests on those coefficients (one reason why we have been reluctant to apply such tests) without biasing the slope estimates.

Borough-wide errors explain why correlation coefficients went down as the level of aggregation was increased beyond the constituency. Further aggregation suppressed the truly random part of constituency deviance according to the law of large numbers, but not the borough-wide part of the deviance. Aggregation had no effect on the borough-wide component until the degree of aggregation far exceeded the span of these powerful area-wide deviances. In Tables 1, 2 and 3 correlations eventually did begin to rise as expected but only on aggregation from the county to the regional level.

The constituency error term ε can be written $\varepsilon = \varepsilon_c + \varepsilon_b$ where ε_c stands for influences at or below the constituency level and ε_b for the area-wide errors common to all constituencies in the borough. Since the variances of ε_c and ε_b were roughly equal, we let variance $\varepsilon_c = \sigma^2 =$ variance ε_b. Then when N_b constituencies were grouped into borough b, the variance of the grouped error term became

$$\frac{\text{variance } \varepsilon_c}{N_b} + \text{variance } \varepsilon_b = \left(\frac{N_b + 1}{N_b} \right) \sigma^2$$

and the appropriate weighting factor to obtain the most efficient estimate of the regression coefficients was $\dfrac{N_b}{N_b + 1}$ which ranged from 0.5 for a single constituency to a maximum of 0.94 for a fifteen constituency borough or a logical maximum of 1.00 for an infinitely large borough. So despite considerable differences between the sizes of different borough units we should not weight by the number of constituencies within the unit, nor by population; the weighing requirement was so low that it could safely be omitted. To confirm this the analyses in Table 3 were repeated using $N_b/(N_b + 1)$ weighting. The results differed very slightly from those obtained without weighting and they were not always improved by weighting.

2.2.3 *Split Level Regressions*   As an alternative to regressions using social and political data at the borough level it is possible to predict constituency voting from borough level census information. This form of analysis appears similar to the classical errors-in-predictor variables situation. As is well known, the consequences of errors in the predictors are that both correlations and slopes are underestimated. In reality a split level regression is fundamentally different from the errors-in-predictors model. The constituency value of the social predictor can be written as $x_c = \bar{x}_b + \Delta_c$ where $\bar{x}_b$ is the borough level value. Then the constituency regression has the form

$$y_c = \alpha + \beta x_c + \varepsilon_c$$
$$= \alpha + \beta \bar{x}_b + \beta \Delta_c + \varepsilon_c$$

A multiple regression using $\bar{x}_b$ and Δ_c would be equivalent to a simple regression using x_c. A simple regression using just $\bar{x}_b$ would inevitably show a lower correlation, but it would give the same slope estimate if, and only if, the omitted predictor Δ_c was uncorrelated with $\bar{x}_b$. It is easy to show by writing down a few terms from the formula that Δ_c must be exactly uncorrelated with $\bar{x}_b$ if all the constituencies in the borough are of equal size because deviations from the borough average must sum to zero within each borough. If constituency sizes vary this result is approximate. By contrast, the more usual errors-in-variables model postulates a visible variable x equal to a true causative variable χ plus a random error ξ uncorrelated with χ. Then the model is

$$y = \alpha + \beta \chi + \varepsilon$$
$$= \alpha + \beta(x - \xi) + \varepsilon$$
$$= \alpha + \beta x - \beta \xi + \varepsilon$$

and unfortunately x and ξ are correlated, it is χ and ξ that are not.

Once again the theoretical conclusions were tested on the 1966 data and confirmed. Using MID as a predictor of Conservatism, the constituency slope of 0.93, which became 0.84 using borough data, dropped only to 0.81 using a split level regression. Using EMPL as a predictor, the slope of 2.6 went up to 2.7 using either all borough data or borough social with constituency voting. However correlations dropped sharply. For EMPL, R^2 equalled 67% for constituencies, 61% for boroughs but only 39% in the split level regression despite the almost identical slope. These few examples were typical of the full test

All the analyses reported for 1966 were repeated, with similar results, for each election between 1955 and 1970.

2.2.4 *Time as the Ultimate Spatial Aggregate*   We have identified two types of environmental effects: those related to the social composition of a narrow area and others unrelated to social characteristics and operating over areas as broad as a borough or county. The ultimate environmental effects are those like the pull of party leaders or the events and issues of the day which have an effect across the whole country. By definition such Britain-wide influences cannot explain any of the within-Britain variation in partisanship, but their power can be compared with that spatial variation. One method would be to treat the votes in each constituency at each election as separate units and predict partisanship throughout the 1955–70 period, for example, using the same regression methods as before but with five new dummy variables as additional predictors, one for each election year. Mathematically there would be no distinction between these five time-regions and the spatial-regions used already. Standard data analysis programmes require some time consuming data reorganisation before they can treat different elections within a single constituency as separate units and a computationally simpler procedure will do much the same job.

To predict constituency partisanship at any election we could use the British overall partisanship at the preceding election. Such a prediction would entail two sorts of errors. First, there would be a swing between one election and the next. So the predictions (all equal to each other) would be biased. Second, the actual constituency results would all vary from the British figure. Hence the repeated use even of the correct British figure for the second election would imply errors due to the variance of constituency results around the British figure.

Using the standard formula for the mean square error of a prediction scheme we have—

$$\text{mean square error} = \text{bias squared} + \text{variance}$$
$$= \text{British swing squared}$$
$$+ \text{variance of constituency results}$$

By this formula the mean British swing in the Conservative share of the two party vote accounted for 1 % of mean square error between 1955 and 1959, 6 % between 1959 and 1964, 6 % again between 1964 and 1966, and 10 % between 1966 and 1970. Spatial variation in Conservatism accounted for the remainder.

If there were no year to year swings, no environmental effects of either the borough-wide or neighbourhood social mix types and none of the inexplicable constituency deviance, but only the variation in constituency partisanship that would follow from the individual-level class differences shown in surveys, the mean square error would be approximately one-fourteenth the size that actually occurred. Figure 1 displays, very approximately, how various influences combined to produce the total mean square error.

3   Variables

3.1 Political

There was no election at which all British seats were contested by all three major parties. Except for 1929 the most frequent type of constituency contest at every interwar election was a two party fight.[5] Even in 1923 when there were 536

Figure 1. Decomposition of partisan variance.

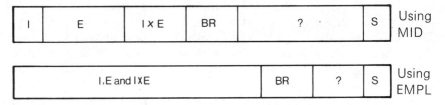

  I   individual class effect
  E   environmental class effect
I × E   interaction of individual and environmental class effects
 BR   borough-wide residuals
  ?   otherwise unexplained
  S   Britain-wide swing

Conservative candidates, 427 Labour and 457 Liberal for 615 seats there were more straight fights than any other type of contest. The difference between elections such as 1923 and those between 1955 and 1970 was that many of these straight fights were not between Labour and Conservative candidates.

1950 was the first election without any unopposed returns for mainland Britain: in 1918 as many as eighty two candidates (outside Ireland) were returned to Parliament without opposition and consequently without a vote being cast. The number gradually declined to three in 1929, went up to fiftyone in 1931 and declined again to only two in 1945.

To construct party voting percentages and turnout rates for the constant units, the actual votes in constituencies where voting occurred were summed over all seats within the unit. Where candidates were returned unopposed they were given a notional vote equal to the average turnout rate in opposed seats multiplied by the electorate in the unopposed seat. The remainder of the electorate were allocated to abstention. It is probably true that if the unopposed candidate had been opposed his opponent would have gained some of the votes allocated to him, but it is equally true that if the two candidates in a straight fight had been opposed by a third candidate they would both have taken less votes than they actually received. In that sense the notional vote allocated to an unopposed candidate is consistent with our acceptance of votes recorded elsewhere. The measures of party support that result are equivalent to the survey question 'how did you vote in the recent election?' They measure votes not sympathies. Obviously votes were even more conditioned by the choices offered to the electorate in the interwar years than in 1955–70. In 1918 and 1922, for example, there were four main party groups – Conservative, Labour, Asquith Liberals and Lloyd George Liberals – but less than fifty four-way contests in either year.

Two member or undivided boroughs, abolished before the 1950 election require further arbitrary decisions. For all but five of the contests in two member seats it was possible to obtain details of the numbers voting for every combination of candidates.[6] All voters who cast two votes for the same party or used only one of their votes were allocated to the appropriate party. Voters who cast one vote for party A and another for party B were divided equally between the two parties since the voting arrangements did not allow any statement of preference.

Candidates stood under many labels in the interwar period and some, indeed, obtained the endorsement of various public bodies including one or more political parties rather than standing as the candidate of a party. To simplify the analysis candidates were divided into four party groups plus a composite 'others' category. The purpose was to classify votes, not the candidates themselves, into groups supporting the Conservatives and allies, independent Liberals, Labour and similar parties, a Centre group consisting of those who wanted a permanent Liberal/Conservative coalition with or without Lloyd George and finally, those who could not be fitted into any of these four groups. Where any candidate saved his deposit by obtaining over one-eighth of votes cast, but was initially categorised as an 'other', an effort was made to discover whether he had the informal endorsement of one of the main parties. If so his vote was reallocated to that party. There were also cases where a candidate for a major party was not readopted at a subsequent election and chose to stand as an independent. When this happened and the defecting candidate did not go on to join another major party group at some future election his votes were reallocated to his original party.

3.2 Social

Since elections occurred more frequently than the census it was only possible to analyse all elections by comparing an election in one year with a census in another. For that reason it is important to know how persistent were the social patterns. By chance there was an election within a year of every census except for 1961 when the nearest election was 1959. So it would seem possible to restrict attention to the elections nearest to census years, but in the event the different censuses either provided measures of different concepts or different measures of the same concept. And as was noted in Chapter Three, there are dangers in changing the census used to measure social characteristics when areas have large and persisting political deviances.

3.2.1 Definitions

Earlier censuses gave information on all the concepts measured by our 1966 Census variables. Detailed lists and definitions of variables will be given as they are used. Here we consider three concepts that were only measured in the earlier censuses and one which was measured very differently.

From the 1951 Census we took measures of education, not of the education currently going on in the localities, but the educational attainments of the full adult population measured by terminal education age. Second, the 1931 Census coincided with the great depression. Unemployment was almost at its peak. So the measure of unemployment in the 1931 Census differed from that in 1966 not because it was defined differently but because it was a different sort of experience on a completely different scale. Third, there were measures of religion in the earlier censuses. Finally occupational class was measured in a different way in each census.

No British census (outside Ireland) has asked the population to state their religion but in 1921 and 1931, under the heading of occupations, the census listed the numbers of Anglican, Catholic and 'other' clergy. In 1951 Anglican clergy were still listed separately but not the others. From these figures we can define several measures of religion. Clergy of one denomination expressed as a percentage of all clergy give a measure of the local strength of that denomination especially if it is remembered that the units of analysis were areas as large as boroughs or county remainders. The total clergy per capita of population gives a measure of religiosity in the area. Three measures, Anglican, Catholic and non-conformist clergy per capita, can be used together to detect both sectarian and religiosity effects. For example, if all three were used in a multiple regression predicting partisanship, positive coefficients on all three would suggest a religiosity effect. Positive on one but negative on another would indicate a sectarian effect and positive on one but zero on the other would suggest a combination of sectarian and religiosity effects.

The number of clergy per capita was never large in any area. Using them to measure religion is somewhat like using the locations of active naval commanders to measure the strengths and balances of rival navies in the world's oceans. Some commanders captain aircraft carriers, others patrol boats. The measure is far from perfect. However some alternative measures of religion are analogous to accepting the published naval strengths as accurate or asking civilians which navy they feel more sympathetic towards.

The occupational classification used in 1966 was not available for the constant units at any earlier census. The 1951 census used five 'social classes' instead of the 'socio-economic groups'. These were: (1) professional; (2) intermediate; (3) skilled; (4) semi-skilled; (5) unskilled. The second of these social classes the so-called 'intermediate' class included many of those included in the 1966 employers and managers category but with some differences. The 1966 measure included many self-employed persons with employees who were excluded from the 1951 measure. Many managers in gardening, fishing, coal mining and other rough and dirty occupations were also excluded from social class two in 1951. Conversely social class two included some very respectable but not very managerial occupations like nurses, teachers, social workers, authors and actors.

A second occupational classification available for some units in 1951 divided occupied males into: (1) general managers; (2) branch managers; (3) office managers; (4) operatives; (5) out of work; (6) own-account. The operatives and out of work were available in 1931. This provides a simple measure of class in 1931 either by taking the operatives as a percentage of all those in work or by taking the sum of the operatives and the out of work. These operatives measures, the 1951 class two and the 1966 employers and managers, all measure the distinction between controllers and controlled in the workplace. No measure of class was available in the 1921 census.

3.2.2 Persistence   Over-time correlations between similarly defined measures were generally high, in some cases extremely so. The two versions of the operatives measure for 1931 correlated at 0.99 with each other and showed almost identical pairs of correlations with other class measures. Table 4 shows the correlations taken over all constant units in England between operatives (plus unemployed) in 1931 and 1951, class two in 1951 and employers and managers in 1966. It also shows similar over-time correlations for measures of religion and agriculture.

Despite the dislocation of a major war and the elapse of twenty years, the correlation between operatives in 1931 and 1951 was 0.92, much the same as the correlation between both 1931 operatives and 1951 operatives and 1951 social class two. The 1966 employers and managers correlated at 0.89 with 1951 class two but a little less with the 1931 measure.

Though religion was only measured twice and with a gap of only ten years, the numbers of Anglican and non-conformist clergy per capita correlated over time at 0.98 or 0.91. Catholic clergy per capita varied considerably more.

The levels employed in agriculture dropped by a third between 1921 and 1951 but the correlations over time remained above 0.98, although there was some more variability during the further decline between 1951 and 1966.

Table 4
Persistence of Social Patterns in England

Correlations between:—

(A) Class measures

	1931 NOPR31	1951 NOPR51	1951 CL251	1966 EMPL66
Non-operatives (1931)	100	92	89	77
Non-operatives (1951)		100	89	84
Social Class 2 (1951)			100	89
Employers and Managers (1966)				100

(B) Religious measures in 1921 and 1931

Anglican clergy per capita		98
Catholic clergy per capita		71
Non-conformist clergy per capita		91
Ratio of Anglican to Anglican plus non-conformist clergy		88

(C) Agriculture measures

	1921	1931	1951	1966
1921	100	99	98	93
1931		100	99	96
1951			100	98
1966				100

For England and Wales these patterns of over-time correlations were similar although the non-conformist correlation was higher.

3.2.3 Comparisons with Measures used in Other Studies   In previous studies class and religion have been measured in different ways from those proposed here and the census data is sufficiently rich to permit some comparisons.

It can be argued, and indeed has been, that the basis of social 'class' is not related to the control of industry, that class is not based on occupation but on religion (the established church), region (close to the centre), race, consumption or education. On a less metaphysical plane, non-occupational measures are sometimes used for class simply because they are available measures while occupation is not. Among others, class has been measured by the density of housing (overcrowding), by industrial sector (business and commercial, etc.) and even by the presence of servants. Kinnear was quite explicit that because 'the 1921 Census did not break down census groups according to income, nor did it usually state what proportion of a given census group was managerial' he would 'arbitrarily define' four census sectors 'as constituting the middle class'. They were: (1) commerce and finance; (2) public administration; (3) professional; (4) clerks.[7] Similarly Blewett followed Pelling in using the percent female indoor domestic servants as a measure of the middle class before 1918.[8] Since housing data were among the little information tabulated for wards within cities Kinnear used persons per room as a measure of class within selected cities.[9]

Table 5 shows the correlations between the direct class measures used in this study and various measures of sector, servants and housing density. The correlations were generally lower than the correlations between different direct measures of class taken at widely separated time points. Irrespective of when the direct class measure was applied the surrogate measures became less accurate guides to occupational class as the century wore on. All these substitutes for class, except housing, were better indicators of the presence of professionals than managers. They also correlated much less with Labour voting than the direct, managerially orientated, class measures. (1931 voting is given purely as an example, other years showed the same pattern)

As an alternative to our census measures of religion Kinnear used church year books to calculate non-conformist church membership in boroughs and counties throughout England. Unfortunately non-conformist membership could be high either because the area was non-conformist or because of a high level of general religiosity. Kinnear himself noted that in Sheffield where only 7% were members of non-conformist churches, an apparently low figure, only 4% attended Anglican Easter Communion.[10]

Kinnear's religious data was not available for all the constant units, but over those for which it was available it correlated far better with our non-conformist ministers per capita than with the non-conformist share of the local clergy. This confirms that it depended upon both non-conformity and religiosity (see Table 6). Our Table also shows that Anglican and non-conformist clergy per capita were positively correlated, further evidence of a religiosity dimension.

Table 5
Comparison of Direct Class Measures with the Surrogates used in Previous Studies

All entries are correlations over English constant units.

			Direct Class Measures					1931 Labour Vote
Surrogates		Professional Classes		Managerial Classes				
		CL151	PROF66	NOPR31	NOPR51	CL251	EMPL66	VLAB31
Sector:	finance 1921	58	50	37	37	48	41	−35
	finance 1931	58	52	33	33	47	42	−32
	public admin 1921	42	34	7	9	24	27	−19
	public admin 1931	35	27	2	3	10	26	−20
	professional 1921	87	86	51	52	64	65	−55
	professional 1931	92	90	53	57	68	71	−55
	fin. + pub. ad. + prof. 1921	68	62	36	37	50	47	−40
	fin. + pub. ad. + prof. 1931	76	69	34	37	51	53	−42
Servants	female 1921	89	79	64	66	65	79	−65
	female 1931	91	80	57	62	59	75	−60
	female 1951	77	68	38	47	39	66	−45
	male 1921	62	57	26	30	24	52	−40
	male 1931	63	57	25	29	21	51	−36
	all 1921	89	79	61	64	62	78	−64
	all 1931	90	79	54	59	56	74	−59
Persons per room	1921	−52	−46	−71	−66	−76	−63	69
	1931	−49	−45	−67	−64	−74	−63	66
	1951	−24	−23	−39	−41	−48	−39	41
1931 Labour vote		−64	−56	−80	−76	−79	−76	100

Table 6
Correlations between Various Religious Measures

	1931 Census Measures			Kinnear's Non-conformist membership figures (1922)
	ANG	MIN	RANG	
Anglican clergy per capita	100	55	66	10
Non-conformist ministers per capita		100	−13	49
Ratio of Anglican to Anglican plus non-conformist clergy			100	−15

Note: The Table gives correlations with 1931 Census data which is used in Chapters Five and Six. The 1921 Census data gave closely similar correlations.

4   Methods

4.1 Symmetric Representation for Three Party Systems

To describe the outcome of an electoral contest between three parties it is only necessary to specify the vote shares gained by two of them since the third must have recieved 100% minus the sum of these two vote shares. In general the outcome of a contest between N parties can be completely specified by N − 1 numbers. Although the vote shares for each of N − 1 parties is sufficient to describe the result, other sets of N − 1 numbers will do equally well. For example, in a Conservative versus Labour versus Liberal contest it is sufficient to specify the Conservative lead over Labour and, secondly, the Liberal percentage. Diagrammatically the outcome of a three party fight can be represented by plotting the Conservative lead over Labour horizontally and the Liberal percentage vertically. It is easy to show that any possible outcome can be represented by some point within the triangle whose vertices correspond to Conservative leads of 100% and minus 100%, at which points the Liberal vote must be zero, and thirdly the point representing a Liberal vote of 100%, where the Conservative lead over Labour must be zero. Such a triangle is not symmetric. It is twice as wide as it is high. Symmetry can be achieved by stretching the vertical axis in ratio of $\sqrt{3}$ to 1. The symmetric triangular diagram that results is shown in Figure 2.

Figure 2. Symmetric triangular diagram to display three party election outcome.

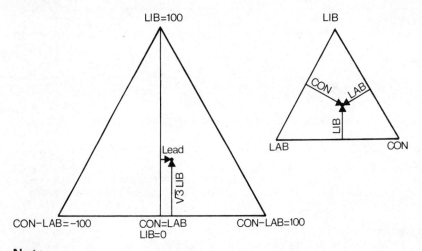

Note:
Both representations illustrate the result CON=40%, LAB=30%, LIB=30%. Thus LEAD=10% and $\sqrt{3}$ LIB=52%. Both diagrams are drawn to the same scale. The rectangular co-ordinate diagram has side lengths =200% and the homogeneous co-ordinate diagram has side length 115%.

The same symmetric diagram and the same point representing an election outcome could be drawn by plotting the Conservative lead over the Liberals against $\sqrt{3}$ times the Labour percentage or the Labour lead over the Liberals against $\sqrt{3}$ times the Conservative percentage. Apart from a size reduction in the ratio of 1 to $\sqrt{3}$ of the same diagram can be derived using what are called 'homogeneous' co-ordinates. The Conservative, Labour and Liberal percentages are each plotted inside an equilateral triangle, perpendicular to the sides, as shown in the second part of Figure 2. It obviously makes no important difference whether we enlarge or shrink the scale of this diagram, but it is convenient for discussion to standardise the scale so that each side of the triangle has a length of 100 %. This can be done, for example, by plotting half the Conservative lead over Labour against $\sqrt{3}/2$ times the Liberal percentage. With this standard form we can state some of the useful properties of the diagram[11]:–

(1) It is symmetric whatever co-ordinates are used to construct it. It does not distinguish in any way between the three parties.

(2) No information is lost. The individual party percentages can be calculated from the position of the point.

(3) Each vertex corresponds to one party taking 100 %.

(4) The full triangle can be divided into four half-size triangles.

Points within the central subtriangle correspond to no party winning over 50 % of the vote. Points in each of the peripheral triangles correspond to an absolute majority for one party (Figure 3). It can also be divided into three diamond shaped

Figure 3. Areas representing absolute majorities.

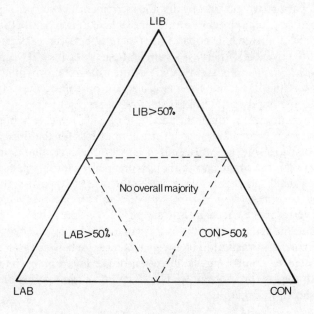

areas corresponding to which party came first, and into six according to which pair of parties held the top two places (Figure 4).

Figure 4. Areas representing party victories.

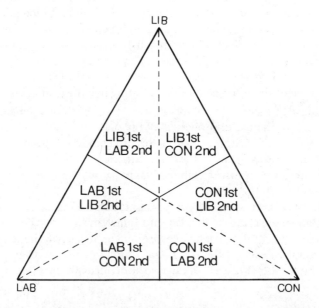

(5) Comparing two election results the movement between two points in the diagram can be decomposed into three movements, each parallel to a side. The lengths of these movements equal 'Butler swings' between each pair of parties, defined as the average of party A's gain and party B's loss. 'Two party swings' defined as the change in party A's share of the total vote for A plus B equal the projections of the line joining the two election outcomes, projected from one vertex onto the opposite side like a shadow.[12] (see Figure 5)

(6) Movements in the diagram parallel to a side indicate a pure change in support between two parties with no net gain or loss for the third. Movements perpendicular to a side indicate a gain or loss for one party that does not change the gap between the other two. Although one party can only gain 100% of the vote by eventually closing the gap between the other two parties, this funnelling effect only becomes a logical necessity in the extreme. Movements directly towards a vertex represent changes in support for one party which leave the other two dividing the remaining votes in the same proportions as before.

(7) The partisan orientation of any general change between two elections can be interpreted by comparing the direction of the line joining the two election points with the six (or twelve if we take account of sign) points of the political compass shown in Figure 6.

Figure 5. Butler and two-party swings.

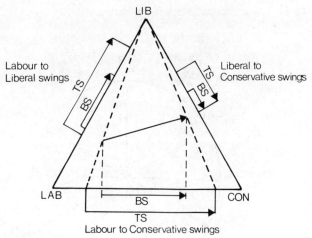

TS   two-party swing
BS   Butler swing

(8) It can be shown that the length of the line joining the two election outcomes, which measures the size of generalised swing, equals half the square root of

$$(\Delta CON^2 + \Delta LAB^2 + \Delta LIB^2 - 2\Delta CON\Delta LAB - 2\Delta LAB\Delta LIB$$

$$- 2\Delta CON\Delta LIE)$$

where ΔCON, ΔLAB and ΔLIB are the changes in each party's share of the vote. This formula is perfectly symmetric. It reduces to the Butler swing when any one party experiences no change. Where one party gains and both the others decline by the same amount, equal to half this gain, this generalised swing reduces to $\sqrt{3}/2$ times the gain. This is rather less than a conventional swing formula would give for a swing between the gaining party and the rest, but more than conventional definitions would give for swings between any pair of the parties.

Where there are more than three parties or where we wish to distinguish three parties and abstention as four separate fractions of the electorate, the method can easily be extended: it requires a regular tetrahedron for a four-option system and a symmetric N–1 dimensional hypersolid for an N–option system. So a direct mathematical generalisation is more possible in theory than practice. As an approximation which retains the easily drawn two dimensional triangular diagram, votes for parties beyond the third can be reallocated to the top three parties either on grounds of second preferences, political similarity or arbitrarily, by dividing them equally between the top three parties or by calculating vote shares for the top three as percentages of the total votes given to them. It will be

Figure 6. The political compass for Butler swings.

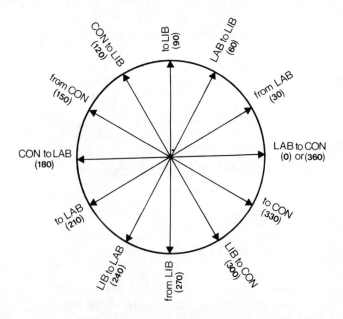

Notes:
(1) The numbers in brackets are the number of degrees of orientation taking due east as zero and rotating anticlockwise.
(2) In tables presenting political alignments in chapters five and six the orientations of alignments are indicated by their directions, in degrees, on this compass. For convenience, the tables also show the nearest of the 12 compass points. The conversion table is as follows:

Degrees	Nearest point
345–15	L→C
15–45	L→*
45–75	L→I
75–105	*→I
105–135	C→I
135–165	C→*
165–195	C→L
195–225	*→L
225–255	I→L
255–285	I→*
285–315	I→C
315–345	*→C

Where C, I, L, * represent Conservative, Liberal, Labour and "both". The meaning of "both" varies.

convenient to group centre votes either with the Conservatives or the Liberals on grounds of political similarity and to divide others equally between the top three.

4.2 Factor Analysis of Three Party Outcomes

One use for symmetric triangular diagrams is for displaying the distribution of party support in a three option system by producing a scatterplot containing one point for each constant unit. Figure 7 shows what the distribution looked like for England (alone) in October 1974 when there were Conservative and Labour candidates in every seat and Liberals in all but one seat.

The shape of this two dimensional scatter can be summarised by calculating the two principal components of the variation. Some factor analysis routines are unsuitable for this purpose since they automatically standardise the input variables to have equal variances. They always produce the same answer: the first principal component is the sum or difference of the standardised input variables. When principal components derived in this way are plotted back onto the triangular diagram the lines drawn depend entirely upon which pair of input variables were used. For example, the points in the scatterplot are completely defined by any of these pairs of values: CON and LAB; CON and LIB; LIB and LAB; CON lead over LAB and LIB percent. However each pair would produce different principal components if put into a standard factor analysis programme.[13]

What is required is to find the principal components of the variation in the actual scatterplot without any adjustments for the standard deviations of input variables. Since there are only two dimensions it is as easy to derive and use a special purpose formula as to use a rather special factor analysis programme.

Let y be the vertical co-ordinate and x the horizontal for the scatterplot. We seek the line $y = ax + c$ such that the sum of squared perpendicular deviations of points from this line is at a minimum. This line is the first principal component. The second is perpendicular to it.

The sum of squares of perpendicular deviations is

$$\sum_i \frac{(y_i - ax_i - c)^2}{1 + a^2}$$

Minimising this function by differentiating with respect to a and c gives

$$c = \bar{y} - a\bar{x}, \quad \text{i.e.} \quad c \text{ is chosen so as to run the line through}$$

the centre of gravity $\bar{x}, \bar{y}$ of the scatterplot

and $a = -Q \pm \sqrt{Q^2 + 1}$

where $Q = \left(\frac{\sigma y}{\sigma x} - \frac{\sigma x}{\sigma y} \right) / 2r$

where σx, σy and r are the standard deviations of x and y and r is the correlation between x and y. Note that if x and y had been standardised to equal variance Q $= 0$ and $a = \pm 1$.

This formula produces the same principal component lines irrespective of which direction is taken as horizontal. It may be any side of the triangle or even a direction that is not parallel to a side. If we take the horizontal as the line between the Conservative and Labour vertices then $x = (\text{CON} - \text{LAB})/2$ and y $= \sqrt{3}\ \text{LIB}/2$ where CON, LAB, and LIB are the party percentages of the vote.

$$\text{then } Q = \left(\frac{\sqrt{3}\,\sigma_{\text{LIB}}}{\sigma_{\text{LEAD}}} - \frac{\sigma_{\text{LOAD}}}{\sqrt{3}\sigma_{\text{LIB}}} \right)/2r_{\text{LIB LEAD}}$$

where LEAD = CON − LAB. In October 1974, for constant units in England, $\sigma_{\text{LIB}} = 7.2$, $\sigma_{\text{LEAD}} = 23.1$ and $r = 0.62$ whence $Q = -1.06$ and $a = 2.5$ or $a = 0.40$. The lines with these two perpendicular slopes have been drawn through the scatterplot in Figure 7. They can also be drawn on the political compass diagram which shows that the principal variation in the scatterplot at an angle of 22° was much nearer to a Labour versus the rest orientation ($= 30°$) than a Conservative versus Labour orientation ($= 0°$).

While principal component directions calculated as described are a useful summary of the distribution of partisanship, they can be over simple, as in October 1974. At this election the distribution was very clearly curvilinear. In

Figure 7. Distribution of election result and principal components of distribution.

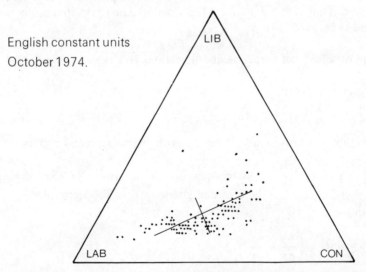

English constant units
October 1974.

Note: Axis lengths equal 3 standard deviations.

areas where Labour was ahead of the Conservatives, Liberal votes did not vary much and the essential variation was Labour versus Conservative. However where the Conservatives beat Labour the Conservative vote varied little: the scatter was directed at about 60° to the horizontal, parallel to the Labour versus Liberal side of the triangle. In these areas it was Labour and Liberal votes that were inversely related. At other elections the principal components were less misleading.

The formula for the standard deviations in the two principal component directions is

$$\sqrt{\frac{\sigma^2 x + 2 a r \sigma_x \sigma_y + a^2 \sigma^2 y}{1 + a^2}}$$

and with $x = \text{LEAD}/2$ and $y = \sqrt{3}\ \text{LIB}/2$ this becomes

$$\sqrt{\frac{\sigma^2_{\text{LEAD}} + 2\sqrt{3} a r \sigma_{\text{LEAD}} \sigma_{\text{LIB}} + 3 a^2 \sigma^2_{\text{LIB}}}{4(1 + a^2)}}$$

Applied to the October 1974 results this gives a standard deviation of 12.3 % in the principal direction and 4.6 % in the secondary direction. The orientations of the principal and secondary axes only become significant when their sizes are considerably different. The dimensionality of the partisan distribution can be measured by the ratio of these sizes. A large value indicates an approximately unidimensional distribution.

4.3 Regression Methods for Three Party Systems

When the notion of political orientation is added regression analyses can be generalised in two different ways. First, we can calculate for each predictor variable not only the size of its effect on partisanship but the political orientation of its effect. Second, we can calculate one principal direction for the whole complex of social alignments.

4.3.1 Political Orientations of Several Social Alignments

If we use a fixed set of social predictors in separate multiple regressions, each predicting a single party's share of the vote, then the coefficients relating one social variable to each of the political variables must sum to zero. Collectively the separate regressions indicate that, for example, a 1 % increase in EMPL goes with higher votes for one or more parties and lower votes for the others; the sum of these voting advantages and disadvantages must come to zero. The voting changes associated with a 1 % change in EMPL (unstandardised effects) or the percentage voting changes associated with a single standard deviation of change in EMPL (semi-standardised effects) can be plotted on the political compass diagram just as if they were swings over time instead of differences across space.

As an example, Table 10 of Chapter Three showed that in three way contests in

1966 the unstandardised slopes when predicting Conservative, Labour and Liberal votes from EMPL and AGRI were

$$
\begin{array}{lll}
\text{CON} & 1.56 \text{ EMPL} - 0.05 \text{ AGRI} \\
\text{LAB} & -2.11 \text{ EMPL} - 0.49 \text{ AGRI} \\
\text{LIB} & 0.55 \text{ EMPL} - 0.54 \text{ AGRI}
\end{array}
$$

Since unstandardised or semi-standardised (but not standardised) slopes can be manipulated arithmetically, the slopes for predictions of $(\text{CON} - \text{LAB})/2$ and $\sqrt{3}\ \text{LIB}/2$ are just half the difference between CON and LAB slopes, and $\sqrt{3}/2$ times the LIB slope. So in the example they were

$$
\begin{array}{lll}
\text{LEAD}/2 & 1.84 \text{ EMPL} + 0.22 \text{ AGRI} \\
\sqrt{3}\ \text{LIB}/2 & 0.48 \text{ EMPL} + 0.47 \text{ AGRI}
\end{array}
$$

A 1 % increase in EMPL would correspond to a horizontal movement of 1.84 and a vertical movement of 0.48, i.e. to a political orientation of arctan $48/184 = 15°$ halfway between Conservative versus Labour $(0°)$ and Labour versus the rest $(30°)$. Similarly the political orientation of AGRI was arctan $47/22 = 65°$, very close to Labour versus Liberal $(60°)$ but slightly on the Liberal versus the rest side (Figure 8).

Figure 8.   Class and rurality in three-way contests 1966.

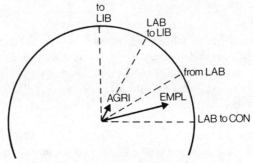

Note: Lengths proportional to unstandardised regression coefficients.

4.3.2 Principal Political Orientation of a Complex of Social Alignments   The method of the last section produces, quite correctly, a different political orientation of each social predictor. So it is not possible to say which is the principal orientation of social alignments.

The logic of stepwise regression is that we select as predictors those social variables which best predict partisanship. This logic can be extended to the three party or multi party situation by selecting as the principal political orientation of social alignments that political orientation whose partisanship can best be predicted from a multiple regression on the social variables. In general this direction will not be the same as the principal direction of partisanship defined by a factor analysis of the partisan scatterplot, since the criterion of optimality is different. It could be that the principal direction of partisan variation was between Conservative and Liberal, but none of the available social predictors explained that variation, while the social measures were good predictors of the limited amount of variation in a Labour versus the rest direction. Then the principal direction of partisanship defined by the partisan scatter would be the minor orientation of the social variables and conversely. In the event such gross discrepancies did not occur in our results for Britain.

Figure 9. R² values for different partisan orientations.

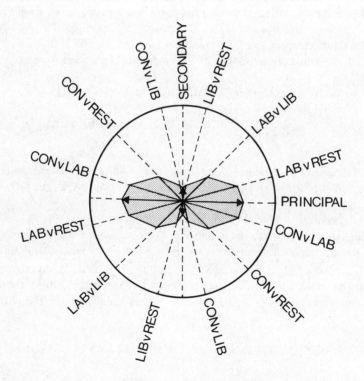

Notes:
(1) Lengths of lines in this diagram are proportional to R² values obtained when predicting partisan variation in the direction of the line.
(2) Class, Religion and Agriculture used as predictors.
(3) 1924 election result.

As an example, Figure 9 shows the R^2 values obtained when using 1931 operatives, Anglican, Catholic and non-conformist clergy per capita and percent in agriculture, to predict partisan variation in six different basic political directions: each party versus the rest, and each party versus one other. In this example 1924 election results were used. The Figure shows that the degree of fit depended very much on the partisan direction chosen. The Figure also shows the principal direction of social alignments and the R^2 value for that political orientation.

The procedure for determining the principal orientation is known as canonical correlation or canonical regression. Computer programmes accept two sets of variables as input and calculate the linear functions of each set which correlate most highly with each other.[14] In the example, this means the linear function of a set of partisan measures which correlated most highly with a linear function of the class, religious and rural measures. As before, the choice of partisan measures is not critical provided they define and do not overdefine positions within the triangular diagram. Suitable choices would be any pair of party percentages or LEAD and LIB. Once the canonical regression results have been converted into (1) a partisan orientation, (2) a social prediction function exactly equivalent to a multiple regression formula, and (3) an R^2 measure of the degree of fit, the results will be the same irrespective of the choice of partisan inputs.

Using LEAD and LIB as inputs the two canonical functions were

$$\text{partisan function} = 0.97\ \text{LEAD} + 0.27\ \text{LIB}$$
$$\text{social function} = 0.82\ \text{CLASS} + 0.36\ \text{ANG}$$
$$- 0.01\ \text{MIN} + 0.15\ \text{PRS} - 0.19\ \text{AGRI}$$
$$R^2 = 65\%$$

Where CLASS was the percent non operatives, ANG, MIN and PRS the Anglican, non-conformist and Catholic clergy per capita and AGRI the percent in agriculture.

These coefficients apply to the standardised versions of input variables and are automatically scaled to make the variance of both partisan and census functions unity. If the census coefficients are multiplied by the canonical correlation, R $= 0.81\ (= \sqrt{0.65})$, they become exactly equal to the standardised regression coefficients calculated by an ordinary regression programme, using the census variables to predict a political index whose values equal those of the partisan function

$$0.66\ \text{CLASS} + 0.29\ \text{ANG} - 0.01\ \text{MIN} + 0.12\ \text{PRS} - 0.16\ \text{AGRI}$$

The partisan function can be transformed into a function of $x = \text{LEAD}/2$ and $y = \sqrt{3}\ \text{LIB}/2$ as follows:–

$$\text{partisan function} = 0.97\frac{\text{LEAD}}{\sigma_{\text{LEAD}}} + 0.27\frac{\text{LIB}}{\sigma_{\text{LIB}}}$$

$$= \frac{0.97}{\sigma_{\text{LEAD}}}\frac{\text{LEAD}}{2}2 + \frac{0.27}{\sigma_{\text{LIB}}}\frac{\sqrt{3}}{2}\frac{\text{LIB}}{2}\frac{2}{\sqrt{3}}$$

$$= 2\frac{0.97}{\sigma_{\text{LEAD}}} \times + \frac{0.27y}{\sqrt{3}\sigma_{\text{LIB}}}$$

orientation of this function is given by the ratio of the coefficients of y and x:

$$\text{i.e. orientation} = \arctan\left(\frac{1}{\sqrt{3}}\quad\frac{\text{canonical coeff. of LIB}}{\text{canonical doeff of LEAD}}\quad\frac{\sigma_{\text{LEAD}}}{\sigma_{\text{LIB}}}\right)$$

$$= \arctan\left(\frac{1}{\sqrt{3}}\quad\frac{0.27}{0.97}\quad\frac{0.2627}{0.1556}\right)$$

$$= \arctan 0.27$$

$$= 15°$$

$$= \text{halfway between LAB versus rest and LAB versus CON}$$

The standard deviation of partisanship in this direction may be calculated from the formula

$$\sqrt{\frac{1}{1+a^2}(\sigma^2 x + a^2\sigma^2 y + 2ar\sigma_x\sigma_y)}$$

$$= \sqrt{\frac{\sigma^2_{\text{LEAD}} + 2\sqrt{3}ar\sigma_{\text{LEAD}}\sigma_{\text{LIB}} + 3a^2\sigma^2_{\text{LIB}}}{4(1+a^2)}}$$

as with the factor analysis of partisanship, but now a represents the orientation of the canonical function of partisanship, i.e. $a = 0.27$ in the example, and the standard deviation of partisanship in the direction determined by the complex of social alignments is 13 %.

The coefficients in the social prediction function may now be changed into semi-standardised coefficients by multiplying by 13 % and into unstandardised coefficients by dividing each semi-standardised coefficient by the standard deviation of the appropriate social predictor.

Once canonical correlation has determined a principal partisan direction for social alignments it goes on to calculate a second direction which is determined by two conditions: (1) partisan variation in the second direction should be uncorrelated with that in the first and (2) subject to this orthogonality condition the direction chosen should be the one which correlates most highly with the social predictors. For a three party system it can be shown that this second condition is redundant, the direction is completely determined by the first condition. A paradoxical feature of the orthogonality condition is that though the variation in the second direction must be uncorrelated with that in the principal direction, the two directions need not be perpendicular to each other. This may be shown algebraically but it can be proved very simply using the October 1974 partisan distribution in Figure 7. If the principal direction of social alignments for that election turned out to be in a Conservative versus Labour direction, that is horizontal, then partisan variation in the perpendicular direction, the vertical or Liberal versus the rest direction, would necessarily be correlated with that in the principal direction, since higher values of Liberal voting went with larger Conservative leads over Labour. In the example of canonical correlations for 1924 the secondary orientation of social alignments was, in the event, 104°, which was almost perpendicular to the principal direction, but that was accidental and less exactly true in other election years.

The canonical method is a powerful automatic technique with obvious virtues. Its vices are much the same as those of stepwise regression applied to a two party system. Just as stepwise regressions may select one of two almost equally good, but correlated, predictors and then ignore the other, so the canonical method may give a false sense of uniqueness by selecting one orientation rather than other almost equally good directions. In 1924, for example, the R^2 value for the principal orientation was 65%, only a little better than the 62% achieved when predicting either Labour versus the rest or Labour versus Conservative. The principal orientation indicated by the canonical analysis was exactly half way between these two directions. It seems likely that small changes in the election results could shift the principal orientation quite a long way on either side of the direction actually selected. Nonetheless, if the principal orientation at successive elections repeatedly falls within a narrow segment of the political compass, it would be perverse to attribute all the results to chance.

5 Summary

Units of analysis
1 Outside the 1955–70 period constituency boundaries changed; before 1955 they never coincided with census tabulation boundaries.
2 We defined 161 so-called 'Constant-Units' which were both constant and compatible, i.e. they did not change over time; both census and electoral data was available for them at all times.
3 These constant units were boroughs or complete counties minus some of the

boroughs within them; together they covered the whole of Britain.

4 Within 1955–70 the effects on regressions of using constant units instead of constituencies could be tested empirically. We also tested the effects of using counties or regions as units of analysis. At constant unit or county level, results were fairly similar to constituency analyses.

5 In general, slopes went neither up nor down as higher level units were used, although they were far steeper at all aggregate levels than at the individual level. This showed that the environmental effects of a concentration of individual characteristics operated over a very narrow area.

6 In general, correlations went down as constant unit and then county data was used in place of constituency data, but they rose again at the regional level. This was brought about by strong patterns of borough-wide or even county-wide political deviance unrelated to social characteristics.

7 Further implications of county-wide deviance were that constant units should not be weighted by population and standard tests of statistical significance were not valid.

8 A simple method of comparing the explanatory power of random, environmental, individual and temporal effects on partisanship showed individual and temporal effects to be the smallest.

Variables

9 When constructing measures of voting for constant units, actual votes were added up. However where candidates were returned unopposed it was necessary to assign them a notional vote.

10 Because of Liberal splits a Centre voting category was defined to include mainly votes for Coalition Liberals (1918), National Liberals (1922), and Liberal Nationals (1931–45). After 1950 votes for National Liberals were always treated as Conservative votes. Before 1945 there were sometimes advantages in treating Centre votes separately from those given to other parties.

11 Among other social variables from the Censuses of 1921, 1931, 1951 and 1966 it was possible to construct direct measures of religion (1921, 1931) and occupational class (1931, 1951, 1966).

12 Over time correlations between similarly defined measures were high.

13 Correlations between direct class measures and the class surrogates used in previous studies were surprisingly low. These surrogates tended to correlate rather better with professionals than with employers and managers; they were relatively poor predictors of Labour voting.

14 Correlations between the census measures of religion showed that church membership data used in previous studies was a joint product of sect and religiosity. These concepts could be distinguished using census data.

Three Party analysis

15 The outcome of a three party election can be completely described by a single point within a symmetric triangle.

16 This triangular representation can be used to define political orientation which is measured on a 360 degree political compass.

17 A generalised size of political change of polarisation can be defined corresponding to a particular orientation.

18 Using a variant of simple factor analysis we can describe the distribution of constituency results in a three party election by a major and minor axis within the triangular diagram. If the proportion of the variation associated with the major axis is large, the orientation of the axes is an important descriptor of the distribution.

19 Multiple regression results in a three party system can be simply described by quoting a separate size and orientation for the political response to each social predictor.

20 Using canonical regression we can define a single political orientation that correlates most highly with a whole complex of social predictors.

CHAPTER 5

Basic Social Alignments 1918–74

1 The Limits of Temporal Change

1.1 Trends in the Levels of Party Votes

Over the full 1918–74 period changes in the levels of party votes were much larger than in the narrow 1955–70 period; 1918 itself was different in kind from any pre-war election. Because of the impact of religion and nationalism it is necessary to restrict this chapter to England. England included about 85% of the British Electorate and 83% of parliamentary seats. Table 1 shows the English trends in seats contested, party votes and turnout from 1910 onwards. At its most aggressive before the war Labour only contested 14% of seats and won only 7% of votes in 1910 while in 1918 it contested 61% rising steadily to 96% in 1929. There was a slight fall following the collapse of the Labour government in 1931 but from 1945 onwards Labour contested nearly all seats. Meanwhile its vote rose from 21% in 1918 to 37% in 1929, dropped 10% in the 1931 disaster, but recovered completely at the next election and reached a new high of 49% in 1945. It stayed high until between 1966 and 1974 when it again dropped by 10%.[1]

The Conservatives always contested most seats except when they were in coalition or, in 1922, had only just left one. Their Centre party allies maintained an independent existence until 1968, but their degree of independence declined and from 1950 onwards we shall treat their votes and candidates as Conservatives. If the Centre had to be included with another party it would be reasonable to put them with the Conservatives from 1931 to 1945, with the Liberals in 1922 and, with less assurance, in 1918 also. Whether split or united the Liberals contested a majority of the seats achieving substantial proportions of the vote right through the twenties. In 1923 they contested more seats and got more votes than Labour and although they were disheartened by their 1929 performance they took a quarter of the vote and contested 87% of seats. Their vote collapsed in 1931 when they contested less than a fifth of the seats. In 1950, when they again fought on a wide front their vote did not rise to its old levels: next year they fought less than a fifth of the seats and their vote hit a new low of just 2%. They enjoyed a minor revival centred on 1964 but it was not until 1974

Table 1
Trends in Votes and Candidates 1918–74

(England)	Adjusted % of Vote				% of Seats Contested				Turnout	
	CON	CEN	LIB	LAB	CON	CEN	LIB	LAB	Raw	Adjusted
1910 JAN	50		43	7	99		89	14	87	95
1910 DEC	53		40	5	96		79	10	68	96
1918	46	15	13	21	73	24	48	61	50	61
1922	45	7	19	27	84	19	56	70	68	78
1923	42	–	29	28	92	–	75	72	68	77
1924	49	1	18	32	91	2	58	85	77	82
1929	39	–	24	37	97	–	87	96	79	83
1931	61	4	6	28	88	10	18	88	72	82
1935	51	4	6	38	87	11	27	93	70	77
1945	37	3	9	49	92	9	53	99	75	78
1950	41	3	9	46	92	8	82	99	84	88
1951	46	3	2	49	92	8	18	100	83	94
1955	48	3	3	47	94	6	19	100	77	82
1959	48	2	6	44	95	5	37	100	79	90
1964	43	1	12	44	98	2	63	100	77	88
1966	42	1	9	48	98	2	53	100	76	82
1970	48	–	8	43	100	–	55	100	72	79
1974 FEB	40	–	21	38	100	–	88	100	79	84
1974 OCT	39	–	20	40	100	–	100	100	73	82

Note: (1) Turnout adjusted for unopposed returns, two member seats and age of register.
(2) In most analyses the Centre has been combined with the Conservatives from 1950 onwards, even though separate manifestos were issued.
(3) Votes adjusted for unopposed returns and two member seats.

that they once more contested most seats and pushed their vote up above the 1924 level. Figure 1 shows the changing levels of party support diagrammatically.

Turnout, after adjustment for technical factors, averaged 82%. It was particularly low in 1918 and particularly high during the fifties. If the newly enfranchised needed time to get involved in the electoral process they needed either a very short time or a very long time. Turnout was up to 78% at the first election after 1918 and up to the long run average by 1924. In October 1974 it was again on the long run average of 82%.

1.2 Trends in the Distribution of Party Votes

The distribution of party support can be measured using the triangular factor analysis technique described in Chapter Four. All the way through the interwar years the distribution was markedly two dimensional, but from 1950 onwards the pattern came much closer to a unidimensional scatter which was not reduced by the Liberal revival in 1974. (see Table 2). During the heyday of the two party

Figure 1. English voting trends 1910–74.

Notes:
(1) Centre included with Liberals in 1918–22 and with Conservatives 1931–66.
(2) 18*, 31* are points representing 1918 and 1931 elections grouping Centre with Conservative in 1918 and with Liberal in 1931.

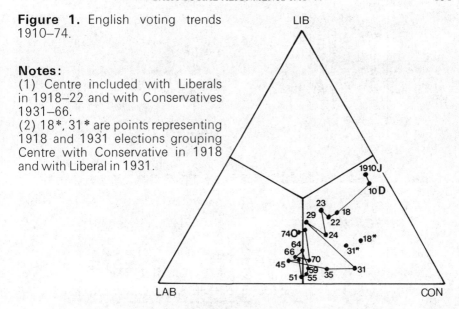

system, from 1950 to 1955, the principal axis of partisan variation was close to Labour versus Conservative, the minor axis close to Liberal versus the rest and the amount of variation in the principal direction was between six and nine times that in the secondary direction. However from 1959 onwards while uni-dimensionality remained strong the orientation changed. The principal axis moved nearer to the Labour versus the rest direction and the secondary axis lay between Conservative and Liberal. Labour variation was, on average, six times the size of the Conservative versus Liberal variation.

Interwar orientations were less clearly defined, although they are recorded in the Table, because variation in the principal direction was only a little greater than in the secondary direction.

From the changing distribution of party support it seems likely that the social structure of partisanship did change. From 1959 to 1974 the orientation and unidimensionality suggest that whatever characteristics went with Conservative support went also with Liberal support; whereas at interwar elections the lack of unidimensionality suggests that a variety of social characteristics were associated in different ways with the different parties, that cross-cutting alignments cross-cut in political orientation as well as social origin.

Figure 2 shows the actual distributions for 1923, 1950 and February 1974 which illustrate the three types of distribution. In all three years the Liberals were united and contested over three-quarters of the seats.

1.3 Continuities in Party Votes

Correlations between Labour shares of the vote at different elections were

Table 2
Distribution of Partisanship 1918–74

(English Constant Units)

	Principal Partisan Axis			Secondary Partisan Axis			Unidimensionality (= ratio of variation along principal axis to variation along secondary axis)
	Degrees	Orientation Nearest Compass-point	St. Dev. (%)	Degrees	Orientation Nearest Compass-point	St. Dev. (%)	
1918	149	CON	15	59	LAB v LIB	12	2
1922	176	LAB v CON	14	86	LIB	11	1
1923	21	LAB	14	111	LIB v CON	12	1
1924	0	LAB v CON	14	90	LIB	12	1
1929	28	LAB	13	118	LIB v CON	8	2
1931	146	CON	14	56	LAB v LIB	10	2
1935	4	LAB v CON	12	94	LIB	9	2
1945	23	LAB	12	113	LIB v CON	6	3
1950	10	LAB v CON	10	100	LIB v CON	4	6
1951	4	LAB v CON	11	94	LIB	4	8
1955	5	LAB v CON	11	95	LIB	4	9
1959	21	LAB	11	111	LIB v CON	6	4
1964	29	LAB	12	119	LIB v CON	5	5
1966	24	LAB	11	114	LIB v CON	4	7
1970	20	LAB	11	110	LIB v CON	4	6
1974 FEB	31	LAB	12	121	LIB v CON	6	5
1974 OCT	22	LAB	12	112	LIB v CON	5	7

Note: (1) LAB means LAB versus REST; Similarly for LIB, CON.
(2) Unidimensionality is measured to nearest integer.

Figure 2(a). Distribution of partisanship 1923.

English constant units.

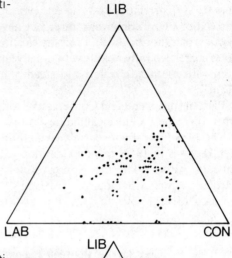

Figure 2(b). Distribution of partisanship 1950.

English constant units.

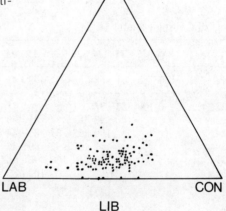

Figure 2(c). Distribution of partisanship 1974 February.

English constant units.

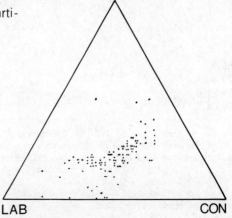

high. Using English constant units, the correlation between consecutive elections never fell below 0.96 in the 1950–74 period and for any pair of elections in that period the correlation was never less than 0.89. Between 1922 and 1945 correlations were somewhat lower but never fell below 0.87 for a consecutive election pair, nor below 0.71 for any election pair. By contrast the 1918 Labour votes correlated rather badly with other years. The correlation was as low as 0.68 even with the next election and steadily fell away for more distant elections (Table 3).

Patterns of Liberal and Conservative voting were far less consistent especially when there were Centre candidates to take votes from either or both.

The 1918 Liberal vote correlated so little with any other year that it suggests Centre votes in 1918, mainly Coalition Liberal votes, should be put with the Liberals rather than the Conservatives. Liberal votes in 1929 correlated particularly well with other years, except 1918–22, and especially so with 1974. If we used Liberal votes in 1929 and 1970 to predict the October 1974 vote, a

Table 3
Correlations Between Labour Vote Shares 1918–74

(English Constant Units)

	18	22	23	24	29	31	35	45	50	51	55	59	64	66	70	74F	74O
1918	100	68	61	58	56	55	49	48	48	42	42	45	44	41	40	37	35
1922		100	87	85	81	82	76	71	75	74	75	76	72	71	67	62	61
1923			100	93	87	84	81	79	79	77	78	78	78	77	74	71	72
1924				100	93	87	85	84	83	80	81	83	82	80	79	76	78
1929					100	92	89	88	90	88	89	89	89	88	87	84	84
1931						100	90	86	90	88	89	89	86	86	85	82	81
1935							100	87	88	86	88	86	85	85	83	82	82
1945								100	91	90	90	89	90	88	88	85	87
1950									100	97	96	95	94	93	93	90	90
1951										100	98	96	95	94	93	89	89
1955											100	97	95	95	93	89	89
1959												100	97	95	94	90	89
1964													100	98	97	92	93
1966														100	98	94	94
1970															100	96	96
1974 FEB																100	98
1974 OCT																	100

Note: (1) Between 1950 and 1974 the correlations between votes at adjacent elections ranged between 0.96 and 0.98. Most seats were contested.
   (2) Between 1922 and 1945 the correlations between votes at adjacent elections ranged between 0.87 and 0.93. The percent of seats contested rose from 70% in 1922 to 97% in 1945.
   (3) In 1918 only 61% of seats were contested. Votes in that year never correlate with those in other years at over 0.68.

Table 4
Correlations Between Conservative Vote Shares 1918–74

(English Constant Units)

	18	22	23	24	29	31	35	45	50	51	55	59	64	66	70	74F	74O
1918	100	78	63	63	62	55	55	50	54	51	49	44	39	38	32	37	40
1922		100	82	79	74	56	65	59	67	63	62	60	56	55	50	50	55
1923			100	87	84	59	66	66	73	69	69	65	67	67	61	66	68
1924				100	85	61	67	66	71	67	68	66	63	65	58	64	67
1929					100	62	70	71	76	70	71	67	66	65	60	64	69
1931						100	86	79	55	49	51	50	40	46	40	46	49
1935							100	90	63	60	62	59	54	58	54	54	59
1945								100	69	69	70	65	62	65	61	62	65
1950									100	94	94	88	86	87	85	82	87
1951										100	97	89	85	89	85	81	86
1955											100	91	87	90	85	83	87
1959												100	91	90	87	85	85
1964													100	93	93	88	89
1966														100	95	92	94
1970															100	91	93
1974 FEB																100	96
1974 OCT																	100

Note: There was a separate Centre vote category in 1918–22 and 1931–45.

multiple regression would weight 1970 only twice as heavily as 1929; if we used 1929 and 1964 they would get equal weight.

Single party correlations in a multi party system are biased downwards. What may persist from election to election may be the support pattern for one party but it might equally be the polarisation of support between some pair of parties. This can be checked by obtaining the canonical correlations between votes at different elections (Table 6). The canonical correlations are the highest correlations between any pair of partisan orientations, one chosen for each election. With English data the highest correlations were usually obtained by correlating approximately similar partisan orientations but if, for example, one party replaced another, or two parties interchanged their bases of support, the canonical correlations would have detected the continuity underlying the change of party names.

After the Second War the principal orientation of partisan continuity was the bipolar Conservative versus Labour axis, at least from one election to the next. However in the twenties, and in the three long term correlations shown, 1929–50,

Table 5
Correlations Between Liberal Vote Shares 1918–74

(English Constant Units)

	18	22	23	24	29	31	35	45	50	51	55	59	64	66	70	74F	74O
1918	100	39	18	28	13	4	4	14	−4	−1	14	11	9	12	14	19	17
1922		100	62	63	42	24	28	20	14	19	23	33	29	27	29	21	32
1923			100	73	67	36	43	34	36	19	19	19	28	29	24	25	35
1924				100	60	49	48	32	27	14	19	26	19	21	25	31	40
1929					100	44	56	60	59	28	43	40	45	51	44	44	57
1931						100	76	45	44	22	30	26	23	30	26	32	48
1935							100	52	58	20	47	30	32	42	29	33	52
1945								100	71	35	43	50	63	60	57	43	53
1950									100	53	53	52	57	55	46	38	45
1951										100	46	36	43	38	31	18	23
1955											100	56	51	59	44	32	37
1959												100	74	69	73	56	56
1964													100	80	78	55	57
1966														100	80	70	72
1970															100	74	77
1974 FEB																100	85
1974 OCT																	100

Note: (1) There was a separate Centre vote category in 1818–22 and 1931–45.
        (2) During the fifties Liberal voting almost died out.
        (3) A renewed effort with many more candidates was made between 1959 and 1970.
        (4) In 1974 candidatures became almost complete.

1950–74 and 1929–74, there was a stronger bias towards a unipolar Labour versus the rest orientation.

When Centre candidates were numerous we used all four party groups and the principal direction of partisan continuity was a line through the body of a solid tetrahedron which is difficult to display. One method is to calculate the projections of this line onto the four surfaces of the tetrahedron and then look at its direction in terms of CON versus LAB versus LIB, CON versus CEN versus LIB, CON versus CEN versus LAB and CON versus LIB versus CEN. Of these the most interesting is probably CON versus CEN versus LIB. Between 1918 and 1922 the canonical analysis showed polarisations between Conservative and Centre and again between Centre and Liberal which did no more than reflect the electoral pacts whereby both Conservatives and Liberals avoided opposing Centre candidates. However between 1922 and 1923 the direction of 1922 partisanship which most closely matched the more normal 1923 patterns was halfway between Conservative versus (free) Liberals and Conservative versus the total of free and 'National' Liberals (who were the Centre candidates in 1922).

Table 6
Canonical Correlations Between Votes 1918–74

(English Constant Units)

Years	Correlation	Orientation in first year (degrees)		Orientation in second year (degrees)	
1918–22	85		*		*
1922–23	90		*	3	C v L
1923–24	94	17	C v L/L v rest	15	C v L/L v rest
1924–29	95	13	C v L/L v rest	15	C v L/L v rest
1929–31	92	23	L v rest		*
1931–35	92		*		*
1935–45	94		*		*
1945–50	94		*	17	C v L/L v rest
1950–51	99	8	C v L	12	C v L/L v rest
1951–55	99	2	C v L	3	C v L
1955–59	99	10	C v L	10	C v L
1959–64	98	7	C v L	3	C v L
1964–66	99	1	C v L	3	C v L
1966–70	99	3	C v L	5	C v L
1970–74 F	98	8	C v L	5	C v L
1974F–74 O	99	2	C v L	1	C v L
1929–1950	91	19	C v L/L v rest	20	C v L/L v rest
1950–1974 Oct	93	14	C v L/L v rest	0	C v L
1929–1974 Oct	86	25	L v rest	18	C v L/L v rest

Note: (1) Asterisks indicate four party groups existed and the orientation cannot be so simply
    described. See text.
 (2) C v L = CON v LAB is nearest compass point (0)
    L v rest = LAB v rest is nearest compass point (30)
    C v L/L v rest = midway between these two orientations.

2 Four Basic Social Divisions

Analysis of the 1955–70 constituency results using the 1966 Census showed
that the two social divisions most important for partisanship were class,
specifically the concentration of employers and managers, and rurality which
was especially important for Liberal support. To these we should add religion,
partly because it was only omitted from the constituency analyses for lack of
data, and partly because we should expect it to be more important in the earlier

part of the 1918–74 period. Distinguishing the two facets of religion, sect and religiosity, produces a total of four basic social divisions.

This choice has two methodological implications. First, the patterns of sectarian choice were so different in Scotland and possibly in Wales that the analysis must be restricted to England, at least in its basic form. Second, it is easier to analyse the political effects of these four divisions in a combined analysis than to treat each separately, since they were spatially correlated and correlated among individuals as well. Middle class areas scored higher on religiosity and rural areas had more managers, more clergy and more Anglicans than the cities.

3　Cohort Analyses of Survey Data

3.1　Two Interpretations of Cohort Analysis

Butler and Stokes divided respondents in their Election Study survey by date of birth, dividing them into four 'cohorts' according to whether they came of voting age: (1) before 1918; (2) between 1918–35; (3) in 1945–50; or (4) between 1951–66. These were called the 'pre-1918', 'interwar', '1945' and 'post-1951' cohorts. By asking for respondent's memories of their father's class, religion and vote when they themselves were growing up it was possible to construct two earlier cohorts consisting of the memories of cohort 1's fathers and of cohort 2's fathers. These collections of memories were christened the 'pre-1885' and 'pre-1900' cohorts respectively. Butler and Stokes standard method of analysis was to tabulate the current party identification (1963) of the four living cohorts and the remembered partisanship of the two extra cohorts as measures of party support. Using these measures they compared the social structure of party support in the different cohorts.[2]

Such cohort analyses can be very informative if the old socio-political patterns are taken as given or can be calculated from election results. Then cohort analysis uses known history to explain the patterns of party support within the present day electorate. We can see to what extent old alignments persist. However it would be a bad example of circular reasoning if we used such cohort analyses as evidence both for the existence and the persistence of past alignments. Indeed cohorts give very little information at all about the social alignments of former years. If religious divisions have a much greater political impact on 1963 party identification in the oldest cohort than in the youngest, it is reasonable to suppose that religion was especially relevant to politics at some time during the oldest cohorts' life. Assuming that their politically 'formative' years were during their youth, we could even place the time of that high political relevance. However since their lives after those early years have some effect on their partisanship, and the current year especially influences their party identification, we cannot take the 1963 value of the religious effect on 1963 party identification as a measure of the religious effect at pre-1918 elections. Whatever the influences of their early years the pre-1918 cohort had over half a century of post-1918 political experience and they had to make their 1963 choice from a totally different configuration of parties. Furthermore, even if we could determine how the pre-1918 cohort voted before 1918, it would not tell us how the full pre-1918 electorate behaved then.

3.2 Cohort Analysis of the Class and Sectarian Alignments

Since the published tabulations are not sufficient to calculate sectarian effects within each class of each cohort and vice versa, we have reanalysed the Election

Table 7
Cohort Analysis of Sectarian Effects within Classes and Class Effects within Sects using 1963 Party Identification

Cohort		*Anglican Effect*				*Middle Class Effect*		
	Within Class	*CON*	*On LAB*	*LIB*	*Within Sect*	*CON*	*On LAB*	*LIB*
fathers of pre –1918	W	27	– 5	– 22	A	35	– 19	– 15
	M	45	7	– 51	N	17	– 31	14
	Av	36	1	– 37	Av	26	– 25	– 1
fathers of interwar	W	25	7	– 31	A	33	– 36	3
	M	47	– 7	– 40	N	11	– 22	12
	Av	36	0	– 36	Av	22	– 29	8
pre-1918	W	18	– 20	2	A	29	– 29	0
	M	30	– 2	28	N	17	– 47	30
	Av	24	– 11	– 13	Av	23	– 38	15
interwar	W	22	– 15	– 7	A	48	– 46	– 2
	M	29	– 9	– 20	N	41	– 52	11
	Av	26	– 12	– 14	Av	45	– 49	5
1945	W	3	– 5	2	A	42	– 51	9
	M	29	– 14	– 14	N	16	– 42	25
	Av	16	– 10	– 6	Av	29	– 47	17
1951–66	W	1	– 2	1	A	41	– 48	7
	M	11	– 7	– 4	N	31	– 43	12
	Av	6	– 5	– 2	Av	36	– 46	10

Note: (1) Anglican effect = party percent among Anglicans minus party per cent among non-conformists. Class effect defined similarly.
(2) W = working, M = middle, A = Anglican, N = Non-conformist, Av = average.
(3) Middle class = Butler/Stokes grades one to four (non-manual).

Study survey. We took the opportunity to adopt the revised (manual versus non-manual) class division used by Butler and Stokes in their second edition but otherwise replicated their methodology. Table 7 shows the class and sectarian effects on partisanship, each controlled for the other.

In the first two cohorts, consisting of the memories of respondents' fathers, the Anglican effect was symmetric between Conservative and Liberal; it had no impact on Labour support. The class effect, especially in the very first cohort, was symmetric between Conservative and Labour, having little effect on Liberal support. The sectarian effect was one and a half times as large as the class effect.

The next cohort consisted of old people reporting their 1963 party identification. In this and the succeeding cohorts, simple symmetric effects on pairs of parties were no longer evident. The strongest sectarian effect was associated with the Conservatives and the strongest class effect with Labour. The non-conformist advantage was shared between Liberal and Labour, the middle class advantage between Liberal and Conservative. The class effect on Labour was always larger than the sectarian effect on the Conservatives. Sectarian effects were clearly in decline both absolutely and in comparison with class effects, but it was a long drawn out decline. For the Conservatives the sectarian effect exceeded the class effect in the first three cohorts, remained over half the size in the next two cohorts and only became insignificant in the last. In all cohorts the sectarian effect was much stronger in the middle class and in the last two cohorts it survived only in the middle class.

A cohort analysis of 1963 party identification is most useful as evidence of the consequences, during the sixties, of old voting alignments. As an alternative we used respondents' memories of their own earliest votes. This would still not tell us about bygone electorates, but it might show how each cohort had behaved at the time indicated by the cohort name. The results of this cohort analysis of earliest votes are shown in Table 8. The sectarian effects were smaller and so, generally, were the class effects. Between their earliest votes and their 1963 party identification, six groups of respondents changed their 1963 party support by more than 15% and each one moved its partisanship in a direction consistent with an intensification of the religious alignment. In particular partisan movements in the 1951–66 cohort suggest a resurgence of the sectarian alignment, at least if we compare the open choice of 1963 party identification with the very much more restricted set of options open to new voters in the fifties. Middle class non-conformists voting for the first time in the fifties were faced with a temporarily unattractive Labour party and usually no Liberal candidate. At their first vote they all opted for the Conservatives, but only 54% had Conservative identifications in 1963. Such changes serve to emphasise that cohort analysis based on 1963 partisanship is time-specific to 1963 and also to remind us of the difference, often forced, between party identification and voting. The time-specific nature of the 1963 cohort analysis was also shown by the general tendency for pre-1918 and interwar cohorts to shift towards Labour between first vote and 1963, while the 1945 cohort had shifted away and the post-1951 cohort towards Labour. The persisting patterns in 1963 represented levels

Table 8
Cohort Analysis using Memory of First Vote

Cohort	Anglican Effect				Middle Class Effect			
	Within Class	On CON	LAB	LIB	Within Sect	On CON	LAB	LIB
pre-1918	W	−6	6	− 1	A	32	−27	−5
	M	30	6	− 37	N	−4	−27	31
	Av	12	6	− 19	Av	14	− 27	13
interwar	W	25	−8	− 17	A	27	− 31	4
	M	18	1	− 19	N	34	− 40	6
	Av	22	−4	− 18	Av	31	− 36	5
1945	W	17	− 15	−2	A	21	− 23	2
	M	23	− 13	− 11	N	15	− 25	11
	Av	20	− 14	−7	Av	18	− 24	7
1951–66	W	− 11	13	−2	A	34	− 46	12
	M	− 34	17	17	N	57	− 50	−7
	Av	− 23	15	8	Av	46	− 48	3

Note: (1) This table repeats Table 7 except that:
    (a) Partisanship is measured by memory of first vote.
    (b) Class is measured by memory of father's class.
    (c) Religion is measured by memory of father's and mother's religion. Those whose
        parents disagreed on religion, very few, are excluded.
(2) Note that the sectarian effect in the youngest cohort is large but has the 'wrong' sign.
    Comparison with Table 7 shows how much this cohort moved into line with general
    patterns after their first vote. This must qualify any simple interpretation of Table 7.

of support as less extreme, patterns as more extreme, than indicated by the
memories of first votes.

3.3 Cohorts and the Social Structure of Issues

Given the decline in sectarian effects on 1963 party identification across
cohorts and the rise of class effects, at least between the pre-1918 cohort and the
later ones, we might guess that the same trends would appear in a cohort analysis
of issues: the pre-1918 cohort would show a recognisably pre-1918 pattern of
attitudes to issues and so on. In Table 9 we have repeated the social analysis of
issue positions which was first introduced in Chapter Two, but this time there are
separate breakdowns within each cohort.

It was certainly not the case that sectarian effects were always strongest in the
old cohorts and weakest in the youngest. On immigration the sectarian effect was
only a little less in the younger cohorts, on the Empire the smoothed slope

Table 9
Cohort Analysis of Social Structure of Issues
Cohort

Attitude	Class or Sectarian Effect	pre-1918	interwar	1945	1951–66	Smoothed estimate of trend
% more nationalisation	C	−14	−12	−16	−4	8
	S	−3	−2	−4	−1	1
% too much TU power	C	23	27	27	11	−11
	S	21	14	11	−5	−24
% unilateralist	C	−3	3	−15	3	0
	S	3	−16	−12	−20	−20
% very strongly against immigration	C	−2	0	−12	−12	−13
	S	23	3	8	18	−3
% gave up Empire too fast	C	8	20	13	4	−6
	S	−7	17	9	5	8
% accept UDI or negotiate	C	16	33	12	23	0
	S	5	5	10	3	0
% feel Queen and Royal Family very important	C	−15	2	−7	−9	3
	S	20	10	14	10	−8
% no increase in social services	C	20	22	22	11	−8
	S	−1	−12	−1	−4	1
% prefer tax-cut to more social services	C	26	7	5	−2	−26
	S	21	7	12	5	−13

Note: (1) Class effects are the average of the middle classes effects among Anglicans and non-conformists.
(2) Sectarian effects are the average Anglican effects in the two classes.

indicates an increased sectarian effect and on unilateralism there is clear evidence of a very much larger sectarian effect in the younger cohorts. Where the sectarian effect did decline was on the issues of the Queen, taxes, and above all, on trade union power. The Queen was perhaps a reminder of pre-1918 constitutional issues, but taxes and trade unions were not old, dead issues. However they do recall the social gospel of the pre-1918 cohort: both class and sectarian effects on these issues were strong and about equal in size. Middle class Anglicans were 43% more anti-trade unions and 47% more anti-taxation than working class non-conformists. In the youngest cohort the sectarian effect on these issues was small and ambiguous in contrast to the large sectarian effects on internationalist issues.

4 The Sectarian Environment

Just as we split up respondents to the 1966 Election Survey by the social class mix in their area to see the effects of environmental class so we can divide them by the religious mix in their localities. Using RANG31, the ratio of Anglican to Anglican plus non-conformist clergy in the 1931 Census, respondents were divided into four groups. If RANG31 was not a good measure of the sectarian division within the population at large, or if religious patterns changed greatly between 1931 and 1966, the breakdown of respondents' religion within each group of areas would not match the values of RANG31. However Table 10 shows that the ratio of active Anglicans, who attended church more than once a year, to the total of active Anglicans plus non-conformists among survey respondents in 1966, replicated the 1931 clergy-based census measure quite well.

Although RANG31 seemed a good measure of the religious environment the effects of that environment on attitudes and votes were somewhat surprising. The general tendency of the class environment was to bias attitudes and votes towards middle class norms in middle class areas, but on trade union power there was evidence of middle class reaction against the environment rather than consensus. With the sectarian environment there was a general tendency among Anglicans of both classes and working class non-conformists to incline towards the attitudes of the locally dominant sect. However there was evidence across a wide range of issues for a strong reactive tendency among middle class non-conformists and this pattern extended to voting as well as attitudes. Because the number of non-conformists, especially in Anglican areas, was small, the figures in Table 11 for them are particularly subject to sampling errors. Equally important for aggregate level patterns, sheer weight of numbers made the consensual

Table 10
The Sectarian Environment; Check on Measures

	Value of RANG31, the ratio of Anglican to Anglican plus non-conformist clergy in the 1931 Census.			
	< 57%	57%—69%	69%—76%	> 76%
Ratio of Active Anglican to Active Anglican plus non-conformist respondents in 1966 survey:–	63	64	73	82
middle class respondents only	46	65	72	84
working class respondents only	73	64	74	80

Note: (1) Active Anglicans attended church more than once a year.
       (2) Middle class = non-manual.
       (3) England only.

response of Anglicans and of those who were neither active Anglicans nor non-conformists outweigh the reactive responses of the non-conformists. Thus, as Table 11 shows, RANG31 was positively linked to the attitudes and voting of the complete samples in both middle and working classes.

In Anglican areas the political party and all the political attitudes favoured by the Anglicans were more popular except on immigration, where there was an effect in the opposite direction among working class respondents only. The size of the effects may be related to the amount of sectarian variation. The most Anglican quartile of areas were 19% more Anglican than the least Anglican. So on trade union power, the Empire, Rhodesia, the Queen and voting, each 1% more Anglican biased political attitudes within classes by about half a percent towards the Anglican norm. On unilateralism, nationalisation and the social services the effect was smaller, but each 1% more Anglican still biased the political response by about a quarter percent. These sectarian effects were the sum of effects due to sectarian substitution plus consensual biases among most respondents, offset by reactive biases particularly among middle class non-conformists.

5   Contemporary Voting Patterns Analysed by Census Data

5.1   Social Predictors and Spatial Controls

Four measures of class will be used in the basic area analyses, the proportions non-operatives in 1931 and 1951, the proportion in social class two in 1951, and the proportion employers and managers in 1966: NOPR31, NOPR51, CL251, EMPL66. Operatives were adjusted for unemployment. All were measures of the controllers versus controlled division. Since CL251 correlated very highly with the operatives measures, the more complex analyses were only computed twice, once using CL251 and once using EMPL66. Most attention will be given to those using CL251 as the class measure: in time it was the closest to the mid-point of our period and it was a particularly good substitute for all the other measures.

Religion will be measured by the Anglican, non-conformist and Catholic clergy per capita in 1931 (ANG31, MIN31, PRS31) and by the ration of Anglican to Anglican plus non-conformist clergy (RANG31). These were measured at the latest time for which data was available and they correlated highly with the 1921 measures.

Rurality will be measured by the percent in agriculture in 1931. This correlated very highly with agriculture in later years.

This choice of a consistent set of basic social predictors is equivalent to dividing areas into fixed, unchanging groups and then plotting the political trends in the different groups. From 1918 until the fifties these fixed measures were highly accurate indicators of social patterns, although by the sixties they were becoming less accurate. A class polarisation analysis will show how very little our conclusions would change if we gradually switched from 1931 to 1951 to 1966 class measures. Conclusions about religious polarisation would change

Table 11
Political Responses to the Sectarian Environment

(England only)

| Attitude or Vote | Class | RANG 31 | | | | | | | | | | | | Smoothed slope estimates of environment's effect | | |
| | | < 57% | | | 57–69% | | | 69–76% | | | > 76% | | | | | |
		A	N	All	A	N	All	A	N	All	A	N	All	A	N	All
% more nationalisation	M	14	14	23	17	34	21	16	18	17	15	21	16	1	2	−8
	W	37	39	32	10	26	25	26	17	26	33	30	28	1	−11	−3
% too much TU power	M	72	70	70	93	72	77	79	76	76	82	64	83	5	−4	11
	W	64	31	49	70	54	58	69	56	63	60	55	62	−4	22	13
% unilateralist	M	24	29	15	8	19	13	13	29	13	6	23	8	−15	−2	−6
	W	14	31	19	13	21	15	10	30	16	11	22	17	−4	−5	−2
% very strongly against immigration	M	42	35	36	42	26	41	41	25	46	35	21	38	−7	−13	3
	W	55	29	49	49	46	54	52	29	47	36	47	44	−16	11	−7
% gave up Empire too fast	M	34	42	41	53	59	49	60	45	53	55	35	54	21	−11	13
	W	44	32	35	38	40	40	51	31	45	37	43	43	−2	7	9
% accept UDI or negotiate	M	49	73	52	56	54	56	62	52	57	73	44	62	23	−27	9
	W	31	37	32	30	25	31	53	42	43	45	48	43	20	15	14
% feel Queen and Royal Family very important	M	49	44	49	59	49	52	69	37	59	80	64	63	31	14	15
	W	53	50	53	62	61	60	72	71	60	75	54	62	23	7	8
% no increase in social services	M	53	62	54	64	48	50	56	60	53	64	55	65	8	−3	11
	W	40	46	34	27	50	37	39	37	40	40	39	37	4	−10	4
% prefer tax cut to more social services	M	62	58	56	57	40	59	62	54	56	62	38	66	2	−14	8
	W	60	59	47	64	42	54	51	51	54	54	48	55	−9	−7	7
% Conservative of two party vote 1966	M	77	85	70	73	43	63	79	80	73	86	43	76	10	−27	8
	W	15	24	17	35	19	28	43	28	33	44	17	34	29	−4	17

Note: (1) This Table is restricted to those living in England (even Wales has been excluded).
(2) N=non-conformist, A=active Anglicans, All=all respondents including inactive Anglicans, Catholics, etc.
(3) Positive environmental effects are consensual, negative are reactive, except on nationalisation and unilateralism where the signs reverse.

rather more because the different class measures correlated differently with the religious measures. This would seem to be a spatial or definitional effect, not a true time trend.

Table 12 shows the correlations, over English constant units, of all six basic predictors used in the multiple regressions that follow. The variables clearly tap both a sectarian and a religious dimension for Anglican and non-conformist clergy correlated positively at 0.55. The middle class, by both measures, correlated with clergy of all sorts, with agriculture and rather more weakly with Anglicanism (RANG31). Agriculture also correlated with religiosity, with Anglicanism and especially with that combination of sect and religion, the Anglican clergy. These intercorrelations make a multiple regression approach essential if the effects of class, religion and rurality are to be disentangled.

Table 12
Correlations between Basic Social Predictions used in Multiple Regressions

	CL251	EMPL66	ANG31	MIN31	PRS31	RANG31	AGRI31
CL251	100	89	52	56	14	21	46
EMPL66		100	49	35	26	36	37
ANG31			100	55	25	66	80
MIN31				100	−5	−13	59
PRS31					100	28	−1
RANG31						100	44
AGRI31							100

Although Scotland and Wales were excluded, even within England non-conformity was stronger on the periphery and some control for English peripherality seems worthwhile. In this chapter England will be treated as a whole, but in the next we consider the differences between central England, the whole of England, England and Wales taken together, and Scotland.

5.2 Class Polarisation 1918–74

To start with we ignore all the social correlates of class and simply relate class to voting. At least this makes for easy comparisons with other studies. Both Butler and Stokes[3] and Rose[4] have calculated class polarisations in 1970 within five cohorts of a sample survey. Rose used a cumulated Gallup survey containing 9634 respondents. So each cohort contained large numbers of respondents and cohort partisanship estimates should have been particularly free from sampling errors. While Butler/Stokes cohorts were defined by the time when respondents came of age, Rose's were defined by when they were adolescents. Both cohort studies show that the oldest and youngest cohorts were the least class polarised in 1970; the highest class polarisation occurred among forty one to fifty six year olds ('1945') in the Butler/Stokes survey and among fifty to sixty four year olds ('interwar') in Rose's survey. Yet both agree that class polarisations peaked in some intermediate cohort and the peak was especially sharp in the Butler/Stokes study (Table 13).

By contrast, although the area data showed a particularly good fit between class and voting in intermediate years it also showed remarkable stability of

Table 13
Cohort Analyses of Class Polarisation 1970

	Butler/Stokes			Rose/Gallup		
Cohort	Cohort Ages in 1970	Class Polarisation 1970	Cohort	Cohort Ages in 1970	Class Polarisation 1970
pre –1918	over 73	28	pre-Great War	over 65	24
interwar	56–73	33	depression	50–64	33
1945	41–56	46	wartime	35–49	27
1951–66	25–41	29	prosperity	25–34	22

Note: (1) Class polarisation = Conservative share of 1970 two party support in middle class minus share in working class.
(2) Calculated from Butler/Stokes p. 205 and Rose p. 251. Butler/Stokes figures are for party identification, Rose for party vote.
(3) Names of cohorts and age bands are those used by source cited.

slopes from 1922 onwards. (Tables 14 and 15). By all class measures Liberal votes were correlated most highly with class in 1929 and in the period 1959–74; Conservative correlations were highest in 1950 and 1951; Labour correlations were also highest in the early fifties although they were comparably high in 1929, 1931 and in the whole period from 1950 to 1974.

The slopes shown in Table 15 are semi-standardised. They show the effect on the percent voting for each party of a single standard deviation shift in the class predictor. So they are standardised across class measures but do not enforce any standardisation of political responses.

Although there were variations around the trend, the class effect on Conservative voting gradually declined while the Labour slope after 1922 remained steady. If anything, Labour's class polarisation was low, not high in the early fifties, despite the specially good fit in those years. In 1918 the Liberals and Centre, taken together, did better in working class areas; in 1922 they had no class advantage and thereafter the Liberal vote became polarised towards middle class areas. This middle class bias reached a peak by 1929, fell away over the next two decades, then reappeared in 1959; from 1959 to 1974 it remained steady apart from a slightly higher value in February 1974.

Figure 3 shows the trends in class slopes using the four class measures. These trends, particularly for Labour, would not be greatly changed if we took the 1931 class measure for early votes, 1951 for the intermediate years and 1966 for the most recent. Indeed the differences between the values and trends for the two 1951 measures are as large as any differences between pairs of measures. Definition, not timing, seems critical.

Table 14
Class Correlations with Partisanship in England 1918–74

Party Class Measure	Conservative				Liberal				Labour			
	Non-operatives		CL251	EMPL66	Non-operatives		CL251	EMPL66	Non-operatives		CL251	EMPL66
	1931	1951			1931	1951			1931	1951		
1918	38	39	47	50	−13	−16	−25	−27	−40	−38	−35	−37
1922	46	49	56	56	11	4	0	−7	−72	−69	−71	−67
1923	57	54	63	66	24	12	12	2	−72	−60	−67	−60
1924	55	51	61	65	26	17	13	3	−77	−67	−73	−69
1929	56	56	63	69	59	46	49	36	−84	−75	−82	−77
1931	44	39	49	54	27	27	20	11	−81	−75	−80	−76
1935	58	56	67	71	38	32	26	18	−76	−70	−75	−73
1945	71	68	76	75	48	40	45	35	−79	−74	−79	−74
1950	70	69	82	80	47	42	42	35	−83	−79	−86	−82
1951	71	69	81	79	32	31	30	21	−81	−78	−88	−82
1955	68	67	80	80	47	40	40	24	−81	−78	−88	−83
1959	62	61	71	72	56	50	57	49	−81	−77	−88	−84
1964	69	65	74	74	51	45	57	52	−79	−72	−84	−81
1966	68	64	77	77	67	61	65	59	−82	−76	−85	−83
1970	69	63	75	75	61	57	62	58	−80	−73	−84	−82
1974 FEB	67	68	75	77	61	58	56	47	−80	−78	−82	−77
1974 OCT	73	74	80	79	61	55	55	47	−80	−77	−82	−76

Note: (1) Alternative class measures defined and discussed in Chapter Four.
(2) Centre grouped with Liberals in 1918–22, with Conservatives thereafter.
(3) All correlations x100.

Table 15
Semi-Standardised Class Slopes 1918–74 [England]

Party	Conservative				Liberal				Labour			
Class	Non-operatives				Non-operatives				Non-operatives			
Measure	1931	1951	CL251	EMPL66	1931	1951	CL251	EMPL66	1931	1951	CL251	EMPL66
1918	9.3	9.6	11.7	12.2	− 3.2	− 3.9	− 6.0	− 6.4	− 5.8	− 5.5	− 5.1	− 5.3
1922	8.5	9.0	10.3	10.2	1.8	0.7	0	− 1.2	− 10.6	− 10.3	− 10.6	− 10.0
1923	8.5	8.1	9.4	9.8	3.3	1.7	1.7	0.3	− 11.9	− 9.9	− 11.1	− 10.0
1924	8.4	7.9	9.4	10.1	3.5	2.3	1.7	0.5	− 11.5	− 9.9	− 10.8	− 10.3
1929	6.1	6.1	6.9	7.5	6.3	4.9	5.2	3.8	− 12.3	− 11.0	− 11.9	− 11.2
1931	7.2	6.4	7.9	8.7	3.2	3.2	2.4	1.3	− 10.5	− 9.8	− 10.4	− 9.9
1935	6.8	6.6	7.8	8.3	3.6	3.0	2.4	1.7	− 10.4	− 9.6	− 10.2	− 10.0
1945	6.6	6.4	7.1	7.0	4.1	3.4	3.8	2.9	− 11.1	− 10.4	− 11.1	− 10.5
1950	7.1	7.0	8.3	8.0	2.5	2.2	2.2	1.9	− 9.5	− 9.0	− 9.9	− 9.4
1951	7.8	7.6	9.0	8.7	1.5	1.4	1.4	1.0	− 9.3	− 9.0	− 9.9	− 9.4
1955	7.7	7.5	8.9	9.0	2.0	1.7	1.7	1.0	− 9.5	− 9.1	− 10.3	− 9.6
1959	6.0	5.9	6.9	7.0	4.3	3.8	4.3	3.7	− 10.1	− 9.5	− 10.9	− 10.5
1964	6.0	5.7	6.4	6.4	4.1	3.6	4.6	4.2	− 9.9	− 9.1	− 10.7	− 10.3
1966	6.1	5.7	6.9	6.9	4.2	3.9	4.5	4.0	− 10.5	− 9.7	− 11.0	− 10.6
1970	6.3	5.8	6.8	6.9	4.2	3.9	4.3	4.0	− 10.3	− 9.4	− 10.8	− 10.5
1974 FEB	6.0	6.1	7.0	7.2	5.7	5.4	5.4	4.5	− 11.0	− 10.8	− 11.8	− 11.0
1974 OCT	7.2	7.3	8.2	8.1	4.5	4.1	4.3	3.7	− 10.9	− 10.6	− 11.7	− 10.9

Figure 3. Trends in class polarisation using four alternative census measures of class.

Note: Data from table 15.

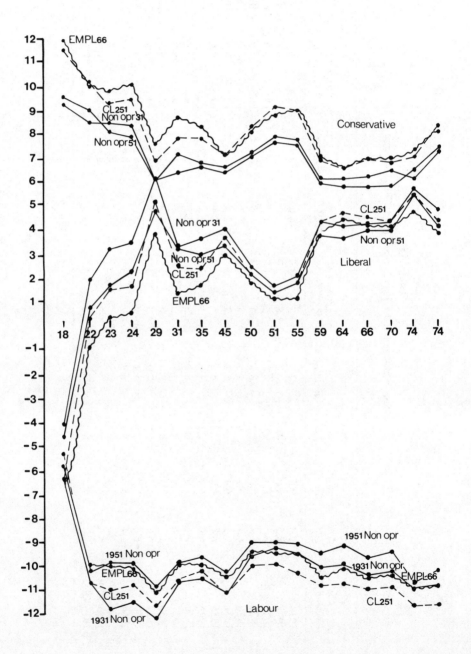

5.3 Class, Sectarian, Religious and Rural Alignments 1918–74

As a standard method of multivariate analysis party shares of the vote and the turnout rate were predicted using four multiple regression equations. The social predictors were

(1) CL251, RANG31, AGRI31
(2) CL251, ANG31, PRS31, MIN31, AGRI31
(3) as (1) plus CL251 × RANG31
(4) as (2) plus CL251 × ANG31, CL251 × PRS31, CL251 × MIN31.

Results for the first and second equations are shown in Tables 16 and 19. Four more multiple regressions using EMPL66 in place of CL251 were also used. Results differed in detail but the trends were broadly similar to those found when using CL251.[5]

Each equation corresponds to a model relating voting and society. In the first equation votes are predicted from class, sect and rurality with no explicit allowance for religiosity. The second equation allows for religiosity as well as sect. An Anglican sectarian effect would give a positive slope on ANG31 and a negative slope on MIN31; a pure religiosity effect would give positive slopes on both; a combination of an Anglican effect and a religiosity effect would give a high positive slope on ANG31 but an approximately zero slope on MIN31. The third and fourth equations allow the religious variables to display larger or smaller effects in middle class areas compared with working class areas.

The results showed that the interactive models seldom explained much more of the partisan variation than did the linear models. Only in 1923 was there strong evidence of an interactive effect when the third equation explained 5% more of Conservative variation and 12% more of Liberal variation than did the first equation. Averaging over all elections the addition of interactive terms to the first equation increased the predictability of Conservative voting by only 1%, Liberal by 2% and Labour by less than 1% Adding interactive terms to the second equation, complicating an already complex model, increased Conservative predictability by 3%, Liberal 5%, and Labour 1%. Partly because they improved the fit so little, but more because they complicate the explanation so much, we shall report few of the findings using interactive models.

5.3.1 Class Controlling for sect and rurality:

(1) The class effect was at its strongest in 1918 when the Conservatives did badly in working class areas and all other party groups did badly in middle class areas. The political orientation of the class effect in 1918 was close to being Conservatives versus the rest. This was true whether Centre votes were put with the Conservatives or the Liberals.

(2) From 1922 to 1955 the class effect was orientated close to the Conservative versus Labour direction, although in 1929 and 1945 it was halfway between this and Labour versus the rest.

Table 16
Class, Sectarian and Rural Polarisations for Each Party 1918–74

Year	Semi-standardised slopes on CL251					Semi-standardised slopes on RANG31					Semi-standardised slopes on AGRI31				
	CON	CEN	LIB	LAB	TURN	CON	CEN	LIB	LAB	TURN	CON	CEN	LIB	LAB	TURN
1918	15.5	−7.4	−3.1	−5.1	1.5	8.4	−7.5	1.1	−2.0	−0.8	−12.2	8.3	3.3	0.5	0.7
1922	11.3	−2.5	2.2	−11.1	−0.2	6.7	−2.0	−2.1	−2.6	−2.6	−5.1	1.2	1.4	2.4	2.2
1923	9.5		0.6	−10.0	−1.0	4.7		−3.3	−1.4	−2.2	−2.0		3.6	−1.6	2.6
1924	9.6		−0.3	−9.2	−0.6	4.8		−3.5	−1.3	−1.8	−2.9		5.8	−2.8	0.8
1929	7.5		2.5	−9.9	−1.0	4.1		−2.5	−1.6	−2.5	−3.2		6.6	−3.4	2.9
1931	11.5	−2.9	0.9	−9.4	−0.1	4.5	0.4	−2.6	−2.4	−1.5	−10.0	6.5	4.2	−0.7	0.7
1935	11.1	−3.1	0.5	−8.5	−1.1	3.8	0	−1.8	−1.9	−2.1	−7.3	5.0	4.7	−2.5	1.8
1945	8.3	−1.6	2.6	−9.5	0.6	3.9	−1.5	−1.0	−1.4	−1.7	−4.3	3.9	2.9	−2.7	0.2
1950	7.9		1.3	−9.2	0.2	2.2		−0.7	−1.5	−1.2	−0.8		1.8	−1.1	0.6
1951	7.8		0.9	−10.1	0	1.5		−0.1	−1.4	−1.3	0.3		0	−0.3	0.5
1955	8.7		1.2	−9.8	0.6	1.7		−0.4	−1.3	−1.2	−0.6		1.0	−0.4	1.6
1959	6.2		4.3	−10.4	0.6	1.9		−0.1	−1.7	−1.3	0.3		−0.1	−0.2	1.8
1964	5.3		4.4	−9.7	1.6	1.8		−0.1	−1.7	−1.0	1.3		0.1	−1.3	2.6
1966	5.8		3.9	−9.7	2.4	1.6		0.6	−2.1	−0.6	1.0		0.7	−1.8	2.3
1970	5.5		4.0	−9.5	2.3	2.0		0.2	−2.1	−0.8	1.7		0.3	−1.8	3.4
1974 F	6.0		3.8	−9.8	2.1	2.1		0.4	−2.5	−1.4	0.6		2.7	−3.4	3.2
1974 O	7.1		2.5	−9.6	2.0	2.4		−0.2	−2.1	−1.1	0.7		3.3	−4.0	3.3

(3) From 1959 to 1974 class was orientated close to Labour versus the rest although in October 1974 it was again halfway between this and Labour versus Conservative.

(4) In size, class polarisation declined from 1918 to 1929, sharply at first but more slowly later. Thereafter it varied up and down by small amounts always remaining within the range 8.3 % to 9.3 % partisan shift per standard deviation of class. It was weakest in 1935 and 1970, strongest in 1955. (Tables 16 and 17)

Controlling for sect, religiosity and rurality showed the same sharp decline in the size of class polarisation between 1918 and 1929, and the same steadiness thereafter, with the stongest polarisation after 1929 being 8.9 % and the weakest 7.5 %.

Table 17
Generalised Partisan Polarisations by Class, Sect and Rurality 1918–74

Year	Class Polarisation		Sectarian Polarisation		Rural Polarisation	
	Orientation (degrees)	Size (%)	Orientation	Size	Orientation	Size
1918	319 * →C	13.8	313 I →C	7.6	122 C→I	11.9
1922	0 L→C	11.2	323 * →C	5.9	149 C→ *	4.4
1923	3 L→C	9.8	317 * →C	4.2	94 * →I	3.1
1924	2 L→C	9.4	315 * →C	4.3	91 * →I	5.0
1929	14 L→C	9.0	323 * →C	3.6	89 * →I	5.7
1931	5 L→C	9.1	328 * →C	4.3	111 C→I	3.9
1935	3 L→C	8.3	332 * →C	3.3	89 * →I	4.1
1945	16 L→ *	8.4	336 * →C	2.1	65 L→I	2.8
1950	8 L→C	8.7	342 * →C	2.0	84 * →I	1.6
1951	5 L→C	9.0	356 L→C	1.5	— –	0
1955	6 L→C	9.3	347 L→C	1.6	97 * →I	0.9
1959	24 L→ *	9.1	357 L→C	1.8	338 * →C	0.3
1964	27 L→ *	8.4	357 L→C	1.8	4 L→C	1.3
1966	24 L→ *	8.5	15 L→C	1.9	23 L→ *	1.5
1970	25 L→ *	8.3	4 L→C	2.1	8 L→C	1.8
1974 F	23 L→ *	8.6	9 L→C	2.3	48 L→I	3.1
1974 O	14 L→C	8.7	356 L→C	2.3	51 L→I	3.7

Note: (1) Orientation and sizes calculated from Table 16 using the methods of Chapter Four.
(2) C = CON, L = LAB, I = LIB, * = gains from or losses to both other parties, → indicates the party gaining from the polarisation as measured i.e. from middle class, Anglican, or rural.

Again, 1955 and 1970 were the years of high and low post-1929 polarisation. Controls for religiosity altered the orientation of the class effect a little. In 1918 it was halfway between Conservative versus the rest and Conservative versus Liberal. Then throughout the early twenties it lay between Conservative versus Labour and Conservative versus the rest, but closer to the latter. From 1929 to 1955 it lay close to Labour versus Conservative and from 1959 to 1974 closer to Labour versus the rest as we found before. (Table 18)

5.3.2 *Sect* Controlling for class and rurality:

(1) In 1918 the orientation of the Anglican effect was marginally closer to Conservative versus Liberal than Conservative versus the rest, but from 1922 to 1950 the nearest political compass point was always Conservative versus the rest.

Table 18
Class Polarisation, Controlling for Sect, Religiosity and Rurality 1918–74

Year	Party Polarisations (semi-standardised slopes)					Generalised Polarisations Orientation	Size
	CON	CEN	LIB	LAB	TURN		
1918	15.4	−8.5	−4.0	−5.0	0.2	313 I → C	14.9
1922	13.0	−2.8	−0.5	−9.7	−1.9	346 L → C	11.7
1923	9.9		−3.0	−6.9	−3.4	343 * → C	8.8
1924	10.2		−3.4	−6.8	−1.8	341 * → C	9.0
1929	7.4		1.0	−8.3	−2.4	6 L → C	7.9
1931	9.8	−1.5	0.3	−8.5	−1.4	2 L → C	8.4
1935	10.0	−1.8	−0.4	−7.9	−2.5	358 L → C	8.1
1945	7.0	−0.7	1.2	−7.6	0.2	9 L → C	7.1
1950	7.9		0.6	−8.5	0.1	3 L → C	8.2
1951	8.2		0.8	−9.0	−0.6	0 L → C	8.7
1955	8.4		0.9	−9.3	0	1 L → C	8.9
1959	6.4		3.4	−9.9	−0.1	20 L → *	8.7
1964	5.6		3.0	−8.6	0.7	20 L → *	7.6
1966	5.8		2.8	−8.6	1.5	18 L → *	7.6
1970	5.7		2.8	−8.4	1.2	19 L → *	7.5
1974 F	5.9		3.0	−9.0	1.2	19 L → *	7.9
1974 O	6.9		1.4	−8.1	0.8	9 L → C	7.6

Note: (1) Slopes, etc. in this Table are taken from multiple regressions using CL251, ANG31, MIN31, PRS31, AGRI31 as predictors.
(2) See Tables 16 and 17 for class effects controlled for Sect and Rurality only.
(3) When comparing generalised polarisations with party polarisations note that a polarisation between one party versus the rest would produce a single party polarisation figure equal to $2/\sqrt{3} = 1.15$ times the generalised polarisation figure. This scale factor means that the generalised figures are frequently lower than some single party figures. It is best to compare single party effects with each other, and generalised effects with other generalised effects.

Then from 1951 to 1974 the sectarian orientation was always closest to Conservative–Labour.

(2) In size, sectarian polarisation declined from 1918 to 1951. The decline was sharp in 1918–22 and temporarily interrupted in 1931, but the general tendency was one of continuous decline.

(3) From 1951 to 1974 sectarian polarisation increased again until it reached half the size it had been during the twenties.

(4) During the twenties, the sectarian effect was about half the size of the class effect. By 1951 it had dropped to one-sixth but by 1974 it was up again to a quarter the size of the class effect.

5.3.3 Religiosity   The presence of clergy seldom indicated a good Labour vote. At every election the Anglican clergy effect on Labour voting was negative and its size ran from minus 2.5 % in 1918 to minus 6.2 % in 1922. In October 1974 it was minus 5.3 %. However this effect was not balanced by an equally large non-conformist clergy effect in the opposite direction. At six elections Labour did worse where the density of non-conformist clergy was high; even when the effect was positive it never exceeded 1 % and was usually much smaller. Catholic clergy, like Anglicans, depressed Labour votes. The religious effect on Labour votes seems to have been a combination of a positive sectarian effect associated with non-conformity and a negative religiosity effect associated with clergy in general. From 1922 to 1929, and again in 1945, the sectarian effect was sufficiently weak to make Labour support lower where non-conformist clergy were numerous, but in 1918, 1931–35 and 1950–74 the sectarian effect outweighed religiosity and Labour did better where non-conformist clergy were numerous.

Conservative votes were always higher where Anglican clergy were numerous and always lower where non-conformist clergy were numerous, indicating that for the Conservatives the sectarian effect outweighted any religiosity effect which may have existed. The unstandardised slopes showed that Conservative votes were more sensitive to variations in the numbers of non-conformist clergy per capita; the spatial variation in non-conformist clergy was very much less than the variation in the density of Anglican clergy, so the actual variation in Anglican clergy made a somewhat greater political impact. If individual clergymen of whatever denomination could be regarded as equal units of religiosity then we should interpret the regression results as indicating an anti-Conservative religiosity effect additional to the sectarian effect, because the positive political response to Anglican clergy was so weak. However, if we took one standard deviation of Anglican and non-conformist clergy as equal units of religiosity, the results would indicate a pure sectarian effect on Conservative voting. Since it was a state church and well endowed, the density of Anglican clergy was twice as large and four times as variable as the density of non-conformists. Taking the unstandardised and semi-standardised slopes as corresponding to extreme ways of measuring religiosity we should interpret the results as evidence for a minor anti-Conservative religiosity effect outweighed by a sectarian effect.

Patterns of Liberal voting were necessarily the inverse of Labour and

Conservative patterns, taken together. Thus the Liberals tended to do well where either Anglican or non-conformist clergy, or both, were numerous, but their votes were especially sensitive to the presence of non-conformists. Whether unstandardised or semi-standardised slopes are used, the evidence is of both a sectarian and a pro-Liberal religiosity effect. Between the wars the sectarian effect was clearly stronger and the slope on Anglican clergy occasionally negative, but after the Second War religiosity dominated and the semi-standardised slopes from 1950 to 1966 showed a larger positive effect from Anglican clergy than from non-conformist. (Table 19)

5.3.4 Rurality   Controlling for class and sect:

(1) The orientation of the rural effect was to Liberal from Conservative in 1918 and 1931, and to Liberal from the rest in 1923–29, 1935, and 1950–55. In 1922 it was from Conservative to the rest.

(2) In 1945 and 1974 the orientation was from Labour to Liberal, in 1959 and 1964, from Labour to Conservative and in 1966 from Labour to the rest.

(3) The size of the rural effect was large in 1918, if the Centre were grouped with Liberals, dropped sharply in 1922 and stayed between 3.1% and 5.0% throughout the twenties. It died out completely in 1951 and then increased again, reaching 3.7% in October 1974.

Controlling for religiosity as well as class and sect produced similar trends in the size of rural polarisation although the minimum was 0.6% in 1950, not 1951, and the subsequent increase smaller, so that it reached only 2.0% in October 1974. However, as with class effects, the introduction of a religiosity control changed the orientation of the rural effect. In 1918 it was from Conservative to Liberal as before, but then from Labour to the rest in 1922–23, and from Conservative to the rest in 1924. From 1929 to 1945 it was again from Conservative to Liberal. Rural polarisation was minimal in 1950 to 1955, but in 1951 and again from 1959 to 1966, the rural effect was between Liberals and the rest, but always to the disadvantage of Liberals in rural areas. In 1970 the Liberals were still doing badly in rural areas but the orientation was from Liberal to Conservative. Then in 1974 polarisation switched back to Liberals versus the rest but now, as between the wars, the Liberals did better in rural areas.

Thus, taking account of the Liberals advantage in areas of high religiosity, which tended to be rural, the most striking feature of the trends in rural polarisation were the Liberals advantages in rural areas between the wars and in 1974, and their disadvantage in these same areas during the fifties and sixties. (Table 20) This is perhaps the clearest of many indications that Liberal voting strength between 1959 and 1970 had a different basis from other years.

5.3.5 The Centre   For simplicity we have usually grouped the Centre either with the Conservatives or with the Liberals in 1918–22 and 1931–45 and always with the Conservatives after 1950. On a balance of arguments it is best to group the Centre with the Liberals in 1918–22 and the Conservatives in 1931–45. They reunited with the Liberals in 1923 but steadily merged with the Conservatives

Table 19

Religious Polarisation, Controlling for Class and Rurality 1918–74

Party Polarisations

Year	Slopes on Anglican Clergy					Slopes on Non-conformist Clergy					Slopes on Catholic Clergy				
	CON	CEN	LIB	LAB	TURN	CON	CEN	LIB	LAB	TURN	CON	CEN	LIB	LAB	TURN
1918	11.4	−10.3	1.5	−2.5	1.9	−7.1	6.1	0	1.0	2.4	0.7	1.0	0.4	−2.1	−0.3
1922	5.9	−3.1	2.6	−5.3	0.8	−7.8	2.7	5.2	−0.2	3.9	1.3	−0.8	0.6	−1.1	−0.3
1923	5.9		0.3	−6.2	2.0	−4.8		8.3	−3.6	4.7	1.1		1.0	−2.1	0.5
1924	4.8		0	−4.7	0.4	−4.8		7.2	−2.4	2.8	1.2		0.6	−1.8	−0.3
1929	5.5		−1.3	−4.2	0.3	−3.0		4.3	−1.3	3.6	1.1		0.2	−1.3	−0.9
1931	11.6	−4.4	−2.5	−4.7	2.4	−2.9	−0.7	2.9	0.6	2.2	2.3	−1.0	−0.2	−1.1	−0.7
1935	8.3	−4.4	−1.2	−2.7	1.4	−2.6	−0.5	2.6	0.5	3.2	2.1	−1.0	0.3	−1.4	−0.8
1945	7.1	−4.4	1.2	−4.0	−0.7	−1.2	0.3	2.6	−1.7	1.6	1.9	−0.6	0.3	−1.7	−0.3
1950	2.3		0.9	−3.2	0.5	−1.7		1.4	0.3	1.2	1.2		−0.6	−0.6	−1.0
1951	1.5		2.0	−3.5	0.6	−1.3		0.9	0.4	1.5	1.6		−1.0	−0.6	−1.2
1955	2.1		0.7	−2.8	1.6	−1.1		0.5	0.6	1.5	1.3		−0.5	−0.9	−1.3
1959	1.7		1.8	−3.6	1.1	−1.8		1.0	0.8	1.7	0.7		0	−0.7	−1.0
1964	1.2		3.7	−4.8	2.1	−1.8		1.8	0	1.7	0.7		−0.3	−0.3	−1.1
1966	2.5		2.0	−4.5	2.6	−1.4		1.3	0	1.5	0.2		0.7	−0.8	−1.3
1970	2.7		1.6	−4.3	2.5	−1.9		1.9	0.1	2.1	0		0.8	−0.8	−1.0
1974 F	4.0		0.4	−4.4	1.1	−1.6		1.2	0.4	2.1	−0.4		1.1	−0.7	−1.0
1974 O	4.3		0.6	−5.3	1.7	−1.4		1.9	−0.4	2.5	−0.4		1.1	−0.7	−0.8

Table 19: [continued]

	Generalised Polarisations					
	Anglican		Non-conformist		Catholic	
	Orientation	Size	Orientation	Size	Orientation	Size
1918	312 I → C	10.3	127 C → I	6.7	41 L → *	1.9
1922	355 L → C	5.7	119 C → I	7.9	7 L → C	1.2
1923	2 L → C	6.1	95 * → I	7.3	28 L → *	1.8
1924	0 L → C	4.8	101 * → I	6.4	18 L → *	1.6
1929	347 L → C	5.0	103 * → I	3.8	7 L → C	1.2
1931	340 * → C	6.4	130 C → I	3.3	7 L → C	1.2
1935	342 * → C	3.5	129 C → I	2.9	11 L → C	1.3
1945	17 L → *	3.5	80 * → I	2.3	9 L → C	1.5
1950	16 L → *	2.9	130 C → I	1.6	331 * → C	1.2
1951	35 L → *	3.1	137 C → *	1.2	322 * → C	1.4
1955	14 L → C	2.6	152 C → *	1.0	338 * → C	1.2
1959	32 L → *	3.1	147 C → *	1.6	0 L → C	0.7
1964	47 L → I	4.4	120 C → I	1.9	333 * → C	0.6
1966	27 L → *	3.9	121 C → I	1.4	50 L → I	0.8
1970	22 L → C	3.8	121 C → I	2.0	60 L → I	0.8
1974 F	5 L → C	4.2	134 C → I	1.5	81 * → I	1.0
1974 O	6 L → C	4.8	107 C → I	1.7	81 * → I	1.0

after 1931. However the Tables allow us to discuss the Centre, the Liberals and the Conservatives as three separate groups of votes.

In 1918–22 the pattern of Centre voting was an exaggerated charicature of the pattern of support we should expect for pre-1918 Liberals, so much so that the actual Liberal pattern in 1918 was not as expected. The Centre did very badly in places where the Conservatives did particularly well: in middle class, Anglican and urban areas. The differences between Conservative and Centre support followed the pattern we should have expected from pre-war Unionist versus Liberal electoral battles.

From 1931 to 1945 the pattern of Centre support again matched our expectations of a Liberal pattern, but very much less so than in 1918 or even 1922. Again they did badly in middle class, Anglican and urban areas but, except for the rural effect, the pattern in 1931–45 was weak. We return to the pattern of Centre voting in the next section.

5.3.6 Interaction Our whole presentation of the regression results in terms of additive class and religious effects is an admitted over simplification. The distortion was greatest in 1923 when the interaction between class and religion most improved the data fit. As a guide to the power of interaction in 1923, Table

Table 20
Rural Polarisation, Controlling for Class, Sect and Religiosity 1918–74

Year		Party Polarisations				Generalised Polarisation	
	CON	CEN	LIB	LAB	TURN	Orientation	Size
1918	−13.7	10.1	2.7	0.9	−2.0	123 C →I	13.3
1922	−3.1	1.5	−3.3	5.0	−1.1	201 * →L	4.4
1923	−2.1		−1.2	3.3	−1.6	201 * →L	2.9
1924	−2.2		1.5	0.7	−1.4	138 C →*	2.0
1929	−3.8		4.6	−0.7	0.1	111 C →I	4.3
1931	−14.8	10.0	3.6	1.2	−2.5	134 C →I	4.3
1935	−10.2	8.2	3.8	−1.8	−1.4	92 * →I	3.3
1945	−6.9	6.2	0.6	0.2	−0.7	132 C →I	0.7
1950	−0.6		0.3	0.4	−0.8	153 C →*	0.6
1951	0.6		−1.9	1.3	−1.2	258 I →*	1.7
1955	−0.7		0.1	0.6	−0.8	171 C →L	0.7
1959	0.6		−1.8	1.2	−0.3	259 I →*	1.6
1964	2.0		−3.3	1.3	0.1	263 I →*	2.9
1966	0.5		−0.9	0.4	−0.6	274 I →*	0.8
1970	1.4		−1.5	0.1	0.4	297 I →C	1.5
1974 F	−0.7		2.2	−1.4	0.9	80 * →I	2.0
1974 O	−0.8		2.3	−1.3	0.6	83 * →I	2.0

Note: (1) Slopes, etc. in this Table are taken from multiple regressions using CL251, ANG31, MIN31, PRS31, AGRI31 as predictors.
(2) See Tables 16 and 17 for rural effects controlled for Sect and Class but not for Religiosity.

21 shows the estimated sectarian effect in areas which were half a standard deviation more or less middle class than average. Since the Table shows semi-standardised slopes, reflecting the effect on partisanship of one standard deviation of shift in RANG31, the difference between slopes at the two levels of class may be compared with the sizes of the slopes themselves, since this difference also represents the effect of a one standard deviation shift.

The sectarian effect was twice as powerful in the middle class areas and it was orientated between Conservative and Liberal rather than between Conservatives and the rest.

5.3.7 Turnout   From our post-war constituency analyses it would seem unlikely that the basic variables used to predict partisanship would also be good predictors of turnout. However, for completeness, the Tables also show the effect of class, religion and rurality on turnout.

Using class, sect and rurality (Table 16) class had a small positive effect in 1918, small negative effects from 1922 to 1935, then small positive effects thereafter, very small until 1959 but somewhat larger from 1964 to 1974. Turnout was always lower in Anglican areas but the effect was small between the wars and

Table 21
Interactive Effects in 1923

| Partisanship | Semi-standardised slope on sect (RANG31) | |
	in areas half a standard deviation more working class than average	in areas half a standard deviation more middle class than average
CON	3.4	6.7
LIB	−1.8	−5.8
LAB	−1.6	−0.9
(CON−LAB)/2	2.5	3.8
$\sqrt{3}$ LIB/2	−1.6	−5.0
size of effect	3.0	6.3
orientation	328°	308°

Note: (1) These slopes in a multiple regression using CL251, RANG31, AGRI31 and CL251 × RANG31.
(2) Overall size and orientation calculated by the formulae of Chapter Four. For example, in working class areas size = $\sqrt{2.5^2 + 1.6^2}$, orientation = arctan $(-1.6/2.5)$.

very small after 1950. Turnout was always higher in rural areas, particularly in 1922–23, 1929 and from 1964 onwards. The effect was at its highest in 1970 and 1974. The combination of sizeable class and rural effects from 1964 onwards meant that the multiple regression explained a fifth of turnout variation in 1964, a quarter in 1966 and almost a third in 1970–74. Before 1959 it had explained very little, usually less than a tenth.

When religiosity was included as a predictor this picture changed. The class effect followed the same trends, but was more negative between the wars, less positive afterwards and never more than small and positive. Turnout was generally lower in rural areas and although the pattern changed to a positive effect in 1970 and 1974 it was very small. There was consistent evidence that turnout was high, nearly every time, where both Anglican and non-conformist clergy were numerous. Turnout was especially sensitive to non-conformist clergy. It was lower in Catholic areas but the effect was very small. This combination suggests a positive link between religiosity and turnout super-imposed on sectarian effects, increasing turnout in non-conformist areas, reducing it in Catholic areas and having an intermediate effect on Anglican areas.

5.4 Principal Social Alignments 1918–74

The different social alignments were orientated in different partisan directions at any one time as well as varying their orientations over time. Principal social alignments were the single partisan orientations that were, at any one time, the most predictable from the whole complex of social predictors. Table 22 gives the principal social alignments for the years 1923–29 and 1950–74, when there were only three partisan groups.

Using class, sect and rurality as social predictors, the principal alignment was close to being Conservative versus Labour in 1923–24 and 1964, close to Labour versus the rest in 1929, 1951–59 and 1966 and intermediate in other years. Using religiosity and sect made the orientation intermediate in 1924 and 1964 as well, and generally orientated the alignment a little closer to Labour versus the rest.

The fit between partisan variation in the principal direction and the complex of social alignments rose by 17% between 1923 and 1929. After 1950 it was only a

Table 22
Principal Social Alignments

Using Class, Sect and Rurality

Year	R^2	Orientation	Semi-standardised Slopes		
			CL251	RANG31	AGRI31
1923	58	2 L→C	9.7	3.2	0.4
1924	63	8 L→C	9.5	2.7	0.7
1929	75	28 L→*	8.6	1.4	2.9
1950	80	14 L→C	8.7	1.6	0.5
1951	80	24 L→*	8.8	1.3	0.3
1955	80	37 L→*	7.9	1.0	0.6
1959	79	23 L→*	9.2	1.6	0.3
1964	77	8 L→C	7.9	1.7	1.4
1966	79	20 L→*	8.5	1.9	1.6
1970	78	13 L→C	8.0	2.0	1.9
1974 F	80	11 L→C	8.3	2.4	2.4
1974 O	80	11 L→C	8.6	2.1	2.9

Year	R^2	Orientation	Semi-standardised Slopes				
			CL251	ANG31	MIN31	PRS31	AGRI31
1923	63	3 L→C	8.3	6.1	−0.3	1.6	−2.8
1924	68	13 L→C	7.8	4.8	0.3	1.7	−1.1
1929	79	28 L→*	7.2	3.7	0.9	1.4	0.6
1950	82	14 L→C	8.2	2.9	−0.7	0.7	−0.4
1951	82	25 L→*	8.1	3.0	−0.4	0.6	−0.9
1955	82	36 L→*	7.5	2.3	−0.5	0.7	−0.4
1959	82	24 L→*	8.8	3.1	−0.8	0.7	−0.9
1964	80	14 L→C	7.6	3.7	−0.5	0.4	−0.3
1966	82	25 L→*	7.6	4.0	−0.1	0.7	−0.3
1970	80	19 L→*	7.4	3.7	−0.3	0.7	0.2
1974 F	81	11 L→C	7.7	4.1	−0.8	0.4	0.7
1974 O	82	16 L→*	7.7	4.7	0	0.4	0.8

little higher and almost invariant. Class, sect and rurality explained between 77 %
and 80 % of partisan variation at all nine elections and class, sect, religiosity and
rurality between 80 % and 82 %.

Class was always the major determinant of partisan variation although
Anglican clergy, sect and rurality were also influential. Trends in the size of social
effects in the principal partisan direction followed trends in the size of their
effects on partisanship in general. Class effects stayed relatively constant,
religious effects declined until 1955 but then increased again. There was an anti-
Labour rural bias in 1929 and a steadily increasing rural effect from 1964 to 1974,
but controls for religiosity decreased or even reversed this bias. One difference
between social effects on the principal partisan alignment and the freely
orientated effects was that religious effects on the principal alignment in 1974
were as large as in 1924 and larger than in 1929, because during the half century
that intervened the orientation of religious effects had swung more into line with
the orientation of the dominant class effects.

The secondary direction of the complex of social alignments was always closest
to Liberal versus the rest, except in 1929 when it was marginally closer to Liberal
versus Conservative. The fit was never very good, although in the twenties the
social variables explained between a fifth and just over a third of partisan
variation. Using class, sect and rurality, the dominant influences in the twenties
were sect and especially rurality, but after 1950 none had very much effect.

Introducing a religiosity control showed non-conformist clergy as the
dominant influence in the twenties; again all effects were smaller after 1950.

6   The Contribution from Patterns of Candidature

6.1 Social Structure of Candidature 1918–45

Rates of candidature can be analysed using the same prediction equations that
were used for party votes. For each party group the rate of candidature was
defined as 100 % where the party group had as many candidates in a constant unit
as there were parliamentary seats. If the party only contested four out of five seats
in a unit, the rate would be 80 % and so on. In a very few cases party splits
produced more candidates than seats and the group's candidature rate could
then rise above 100 %. However, as a general rule, the candidature rate equalled
the percent of seats contested.

Table 23 shows the results, in terms of semi-standardised slopes, of multiple
regressions predicting candidature rates. Each slope represents the increase or
decrease in the candidature rate associated with a single standard deviation of
shift on the predictor. There is one critical difference between these equations and
the equations for votes. Slopes predicting votes must be zero-sum, one party's
gain must be another's loss, but not so with candidature rates. It is quite possible
for all parties to have more candidates in rural areas or all to have less. For
example, Labour and Conservative candidates were so widespread after the
Second War that it was impossible for their candidature rates to have any social

Table 23
Social Structure of Interwar Candidature

Semi-standardised slopes on

Year	CL251				RANG31				AGRI31			
	CON	CEN	LIB	LAB	CON	CEN	LIB	LAB	CON	CEN	LIB	LAB
1918	8.0	−13.0	−10.7	−8.7	8.7	−11.0	1.4	−4.2	−9.8	8.9	5.8	−4.7
1922	7.8	−6.7	2.5	−21.7	2.8	−9.2	−12.5	−7.6	−0.4	5.7	1.7	9.2
1923	5.8		−4.1	−13.6	−1.2		−7.8	−4.5	1.1		5.0	−1.5
1924	4.6		−0.2	−4.9	1.3		−11.2	−2.1	0.6		10.6	−6.2
1929	0		3.9	−2.3	0.2		−5.5	−3.3	0.5		5.8	0.4
1931	6.9	−4.5	4.7	−7.9	2.1	1.9	−6.4	−5.9	−11.8	6.9	5.7	−3.0
1935	7.4	−6.7	4.2	−0.9	0.5	0.9	−6.8	−1.3	−7.4	6.5	9.0	−6.6
1945	5.0	−5.0	13.6	−1.0	2.1	−1.8	−4.3	−1.3	−7.4	6.7	8.2	−1.5

Semi-standardised slopes on

Year	CL251				ANG31				MIN31				PRS31				AGRI31			
	CON	CEN	LIB	LAB	CON	CEN	LIB	LAB	CON	CEN	LIB	LAB	CON	CEN	LIB	LAB	CON	CEN	LIB	LAB
1918	8.5	−13.8	−9.5	−7.0	12.0	−14.3	−2.2	−4.8	−7.6	9.1	−2.9	2.0	0.8	−0.2	2.0	−7.9	−11.4	10.6	9.3	−4.7
1922	7.8	−7.2	−3.3	−21.0	4.2	−11.9	−4.2	−11.2	−2.5	8.6	15.2	4.0	0.9	−2.8	2.0	−0.1	−1.1	6.4	−6.5	12.1
1923	5.0		−11.3	−10.2	1.3		0.7	−9.4	1.0		17.2	−2.6	0.4		0.7	−2.5	−0.6		−5.6	4.0
1924	4.2		−7.2	−2.1	1.3		0.7	−6.9	−0.4		17.9	−3.0	1.2		−2.2	−0.8	0.5		−2.0	−1.1
1929	0.1		2.2	−2.9	0		−3.0	−2.3	−0.4		6.5	3.9	0.1		−1.5	−2.0	0.8		2.8	−1.1
1931	4.1	−2.3	2.3	−5.5	14.0	−5.0	−0.4	−13.5	−0.1	−2.0	6.9	−1.9	0.2	−1.8	−1.5	−2.1	−20.8	11.9	0.4	3.0
1935	5.4	−4.0	0.6	−1.1	8.0	−6.7	−1.3	0.3	0.2	−2.2	10.5	1.2	1.5	−2.4	−1.8	−2.0	−12.8	12.2	2.6	−8.1
1945	2.8	−2.8	8.2	−0.9	8.8	−7.8	1.5	−2.4	0.5	−0.5	10.0	1.2	1.2	−2.1	5.0	−0.6	−12.7	11.4	1.8	−0.9

structure; yet we saw in Chapter Three that during the sixties Liberal candidatures were heavily biased towards middle class areas.

The social structure of interwar candidature was very sharply defined. A major feature was the sharp 'Unionist' profile of Conservative candidature and 'Liberal' profile of Centre candidature in the years 1918–22 and 1931–45. It was at its strongest in 1918 when a single standard deviation shift towards the middle class was accompanied by an 8% increase in Conservative candidature and a 13% drop in Centre candidature. One standard deviation shift in the Anglican sectarian direction put Conservative rates up by 9% and the Centre down by 11%, while a similar shift to rural areas put the Conservative rate down by 10% and the Centre up by 9%. Whatever criteria Lloyd George may have used to decide which non-Conservatives should get the coupon, the effect was to withhold Conservative candidates in rural, non-conformist and working class areas and to issue Coalition coupons to non-Conservatives in these places. Many of those who voted Centre in 1918 may well have chosen to vote Conservative if they had been given the option, for the campaign had been strongly xenophobic. This has been said so often that it is easy to forget that they did not have that option and could not vote Conservative. Lloyd George's coupon ensured that at a time when many Liberals might have been especially tempted to vote Conservative, the areas most associated with Liberal support had temptation removed from before them and they got past 1918, at least, without voting Conservative.

In 1923 when the Liberals reunited, the Conservatives contested 92% of seats, the sectarian and rural patterning of their candidates was all but ended and only the middle class bias remained substantial. By 1929 they were contesting 97% of seats and all evidence of pattern had disappeared. Following the 1931 crisis a Centre group reappeared and so did patterns in Conservative and Centre candidatures; but this time sect was relatively unimportant and the pattern was principally a strong rural bias towards the Centre and a moderate middle class bias towards the Conservatives.

Liberal and Labour candidatures were also structured from time to time. In 1918 there was a bias towards Labour candidatures in working class areas: one standard deviation on class had a 9% effect on Labour candidature rates. However this class bias increased to 22% in 1922 before dropping back in stages to 2% in 1929. In 1931 it rose to 8% but was very small from 1935 onwards. In other ways too, Labour candidatures were strongly patterned in 1922: there was an 8% non-conformist effect and, surprisingly perhaps, a 9% rural effect. The latter was reversed at the next election, but the former declined only as far as 3% in 1929 to be followed by a jump to 6% in 1931. After 1935 the sectarian bias was small.

Sectarian bias was larger and more persistent in the pattern of Liberal candidatures. There was virtually none in 1918, partly because they avoided fighting Centre candidates, but in 1922 the non-conformist effect was 13%. It remained at 11% in 1924 but dropped to 6% in 1929. Then it rose slightly in 1931 and 1935 before dropping back to 4% in 1945. In 1918 there had been strong rural and working class biases in Liberal candidatures; by 1929 Liberal candidates were more frequent in middle class areas although the rural bias remained and even strengthened as time passed. So comparing 1918 and 1945, an 11 % working class bias changed to a 14 % middle class bias, while a 6 % rural bias increased to 8 %.

6.2 Effect on Voting 1918–45

Some of the patterns and trends in candidature rates are so similar to patterns and trends in votes that it is almost inconceivable that candidature patterns did not influence voting patterns; but there is no necessity in this view. It is logically possible that the parties were so politically sensitive that they managed to place their candidates just where their support was strong and so flexible that they were able to shift their candidates around as the bases of their support changed. While they might not be perfectly sensitive and flexible it would be surprising if their placing of candidates was not to some extent related to the likely patterns of their support.

In Table 24 we have multiplied the slopes of Table 23 by the average share of the vote achieved by each party's candidates. These adjusted slopes show what the slopes would be in equations predicting voting if the candidates of a particular party at a particular election all received the same percentage vote. Multiplying by average votes reduces all the slopes, but particularly those for parties which did badly even where they stood. For example, the class bias in Labour candidatures in 1923 was the same as in Liberal candidatures in 1945, except for a change of sign, but the slope resulting from uniform party votes would be twice as large for 1923 Labour as 1945 Liberal, because Labour in 1923 was much more successful where it stood than were the Liberals in 1945.

These adjusted slopes, equivalent to uniform votes per candidate, may be compared with the actual slopes in equations predicting actual voting (compare Table 24 with Tables 16–20). Some patterns in achieved votes were stronger than would have resulted from uniform votes per candidate, but some were not. The class and sectarian bias in Centre votes was not much different from that predicted by uniform votes per candidate, although the rural effect could not be completely expalined by candidature. The unsual pro-rural bias in Labour votes in 1922 can be completely explained by candidature and, indeed reverts to an urban bias once candidature is taken into account. However, even allowing for candidature patterns, there were strong class biases in Labour and Conservative votes, and strong sectarian and rural biases in Conservative votes. Labour and the Liberals had so many more candidates in non-conformist areas that they might expect greater votes there; but even if we take account of candidates, there were still non-conformist biases in their votes from 1924 onwards, although the effects were small. The sectarian effects on Liberal votes in 1922 and Labour in 1922–23 were not as large as even uniform votes would have produced.

After the Second War the only pattern of candidatures in England was the pattern of Liberal candidatures, for Labour and Conservative contested nearly all seats. The political impact of Liberal candidatures was limited by the

Table 24

Effect of Candidature on Voting if Votes per Candidate had been Uniform within Each Party

Semi-standardised slopes on

Year	CL251				RANG 31				AGRI31			
	CON	CEN	LIB	LAB	CON	CEN	LIB	LAB	CON	CEN	LIB	LAB
1918	4.9	-7.4	-3.0	-2.9	5.3	-6.2	0.4	-1.4	-6.0	5.0	1.6	-1.5
1922	4.1	-2.1	0.8	-7.8	1.5	-2.9	-4.0	-2.7	-0.2	1.8	0.5	3.3
1923	2.7		-1.5	-5.0	-0.5		-2.9	-1.7	0.6		1.9	-0.6
1924	2.3		-0.1	-1.7	0.4		-3.3	-0.7	0.3		3.1	-2.2
1929	0		1.1	-0.8	0.1		-1.5	-1.2	0.2		1.6	0.1
1931	4.6	-2.6	1.5	-2.5	1.4	1.1	-2.0	-1.9	-7.9	4.0	1.8	-1.0
1935	4.2	-3.2	0.9	-0.4	0.3	0.4	-1.5	-0.5	-4.2	3.1	2.0	-2.7
1945	2.0	-1.8	2.4	-0.5	0.8	-0.7	-0.8	-0.7	-3.0	2.5	1.5	-0.8

Semi-standardised slopes on

Year	CL251				ANG31				MIN31				PRS31				AGRI31			
	CON	CEN	LIB	LAB	CON	CEN	LIB	LAB	CON	CEN	LIB	LAB	CON	CEN	LIB	LAB	CON	CEN	LIB	LAB
1918	5.2	-7.8	-2.7	-2.3	7.3	-8.1	-0.6	-1.6	-4.6	5.2	-0.8	0.7	0.5	-0.1	0.6	-2.6	-7.0	6.0	2.6	-1.5
1922	4.1	-2.3	-1.0	-7.5	2.2	-3.7	-1.3	-4.0	-1.3	2.7	4.8	1.4	0.5	-0.9	0.6	0	-0.6	2.0	-2.1	4.3
1923	2.3		-4.3	-3.8	0.6		0.3	-3.5	0.6		6.5	-1.0	0.1		0.3	-0.9	-0.3		-2.1	1.5
1924	2.3		-2.1	-0.7	0.4		0.2	-2.5	-0.3		5.3	-1.1	0.4		-0.6	-0.3	0.3		-0.6	-0.4
1929	0		0.6	-1.1	0		-0.8	-0.8	-0.2		1.8	1.4	0		-0.4	-0.7	0.3		0.8	-0.4
1931	2.7	-1.3	0.7	-1.8	9.4	-2.9	-0.1	-4.3	-0.1	-1.2	2.2	0.6	0.1	-1.0	-0.5	-0.7	-13.9	6.9	0.1	1.0
1935	3.1	-1.9	0.1	-0.4	4.6	-3.2	-0.3	0.1	0.1	-1.0	2.3	0.5	0.9	-1.1	-0.4	-0.8	-7.3	5.8	0.6	-3.3
1945	1.1	-1.0	1.5	-0.5	3.5	-2.9	0.3	-1.2	0.2	-0.2	1.8	0.6	0.5	-0.8	0.9	-0.3	-5.1	4.2	0.3	0.5

Note: Since the slopes for the different parties at any one election do not sum to zero, not even when 'other' candidates effects are included (these are not shown), the uniform votes hypothesis is not logically possible for all parties simultaneously. However it provides a useful benchmark against which reality can be measured.

weakness of the party and still more by the party's position in politics. Its candidatures obviously had at least some effect on its own votes. Where it did not stand it did not receive even the small votes it might otherwise have got. However its candidatures had a small effect on the Labour versus Conservative balance because some of those inclined to vote Liberal would vote Labour in the absence of a Liberal candidate while others would vote Conservative. There was a slight tendency for Liberal interventions to hurt the Conservatives more than Labour; similarly Liberal withdrawals were more beneficial to the Conservatives, but the advantages and disadvantages, though consistent, were small. Averaging over all elections between 1950 and 1970 and controlling for voting changes in seats with Liberal candidates at both of a pair of elections, Liberal withdrawals increased the Conservative lead over Labour by 1.5 % and Liberal interventions decreased it by 1.9%. So the important effect of Liberal candidature patterns was on Liberal votes.

Between the wars this was not so because Conservative and Labour candidatures were also patterned and the lack of, for example, a Conservative candidate not only depressed the Conservative vote but substantially altered the balance between the other two parties. Averaging over all the elections between 1918 and 1945 and controlling for voting changes in seats with Conservative, Liberal and Labour candidates at each of a pair of elections, we can assess the full effects of withdrawals and interventions. Liberal withdrawals and interventions between the wars produced results strikingly similar to those for 1950–70 both in their small size and in the tendency for withdrawals to help the Conservatives rather more than interventions hurt them. However Labour and Conservative candidature changes had large effects on Liberal votes, moderate effects on abstention and trivial effects on each others votes. (Table 25). Liberal votes were particularly sensitive to Conservative interventions and withdrawals. The pattern of cross-voting in two member seats between the wars also suggests that

Table 25:
Effects of Interventions and Withdrawals 1918–45

Candidature change	Change in % of electorate			
	voting CON	voting LIB	voting LAB	abstaining
Labour intervention	−0.1	−8.1	*	−1.9
Labour withdrawal	+0.6	+8.4	*	+3.3
Conservative intervention	*	−16.6	−1.4	−4.5
Conservative withdrawal	*	+12.8	−0.1	+3.4

Note: (1) These are the averages of figures for each consecutive election pair. Individual election pairs gave consistent results.
    (2) Liberal here excludes Centre.
    (3) These changes have been controlled for the changes in party votes in seats with Conservative and Liberal and Labour candidates at both elections (control by substraction).

Conservatives and Liberals might vote for each others' candidates, and so would Liberal and Labour, but not Conservative and Labour. Cross-voting also suggests that larger percentages of voters were willing to vote Conservative or Liberal than Labour or Liberal.[6]

So even if there had been no pattern to Liberal candidatures, the patterns in Labour, and especially in Conservative candidatures, could be expected to cause pattens in Liberal voting. In the event Conservative candidature patterns were weak, except for a class bias, in the years when the Liberals were united. Although Conservative candidatures had a large effect on votes in individual seats they had little effect on the social patterns of votes. Even the Conservatives tendency not to stand in working class seats, thus increasing Liberal votes there, was offset by the Labour tendency not to contest middle class seats, thus giving the Liberals a compensating advantage at the other end of the class spectrum.

A combination of forced choices helps to explain why the voting patterns for Centre candidates were no more extreme on class and sect, if not on rurality, than would have resulted from uniform votes in all the seats they contested. Centre candidates were usually opposed by Labour but not by either Conservative or Liberal candidates, although they had more opposition in 1922. It is reasonable to suppose they got the bulk of the votes that would have gone to a Conservative and well over half those that would have gone to a Liberal. So in middle class and Anglican areas they would get large votes from Conservative sympathisers, while in non-conformist and working class areas they would get large votes from Liberal sympathisers.

6.3 Three-Way Contests in 1929, 1950 and 1974

We noted at the start of the last section that even if votes were completely uniform over seats contested the social pattern in party votes need not be entirely determined by elite decisions about placing candidates. The causal flow might run in the opposite direction.

One way to estimate what the structure of party voting would have been in the absence of forced choices is to look at the patterns of support in three-way contests. Unfortunately three-way contests were never the norm in the interwar years, except for 1929. When constituencies were grouped to form constant units the lack of a three-way contest in any constituency within the unit means that we cannot treat the constant unit votes as coming from a three-way contest. However there were sixty nine English constant units in 1929 that had three-way contests in every constituency, seventy five such units in 1950, and since only one constituency in October 1974 lacked a three-way contest, there is hardly a need to recompute 1974 patterns. These three years represent the twenties with its three party system and relatively strong rural and religious patterns, the establishment of the two party, almost pure class system and finally the trend towards a new three party system, again with religious and rural patterns to voting but orientated differently from the twenties.

Restricting the analysis to three-way units in 1929 cut the class, sectarian and rural effects by as much as two-fifths, but certainly did not eliminate them or greatly change their orientation. In the equation using clergy per capita, coefficients also went down but never by more than a quarter and again orientations were not greatly changed. (Table 26). In1950 the restriction to three-way contests hardly altered coefficients or orientations; indeed most of the slopes steepened slightly.

Thus, if we compare the trends from 1929 through 1950 to 1974, restricting attention to fully contested seats, class polarisation went up from 7.8 % in 1929 to 8.9 % in 1950 and stayed up at 8.7 % in 1974. Sectarian polarisation remained almost unchanged at 2.1 % in 1929 and 1950 and 2.3 % in 1974. However while class was nearest to Conservative versus Labour every time, the sectarian orientation switched from Conservative versus the rest in 1929 to Conservative versus Labour in 1974. Rural polarisation was 4.7 % in 1929, down to 1.9 % in 1950 but up again to 3.7 % in 1974. Its orientation moved from closer to Liberal versus the rest to Liberal versus Labour.

If 1929 was representative of the twenties, then social patterns in the vote were partly caused by candidature patterns. Although it was clearly a minor cause in 1929, in the early twenties when candidature patterns were much sharper, it may well have contributed rather more to voting patterns. According to this view, the apparent stability in class polarisation and the apparently precipitous decline in sectarian polarisation during the twenties, while indisputably real, possibly masked some increase in class polarisation of party sympathies and a slower decline in sectarian polarization of party sympathies. However this is a very passive view of candidature. We could also see the strong candidature patterns of the early twenties as a cause, not only of contemporary voting, but as one of the forces moulding the long term party sympathies of a newly enfranchised and politically shocked electorate. While some voters in constituencies without a Liberal candidate, for example, probably would have voted Liberal if given the option, this does not imply that they retained their Liberal sympathies after the lack of a candidate had forced them to chose between and vote for other parties.

7 Contradictions and Reconciliations

On several points the results in this chapter appear to conflict with each other or with those of earlier chapters. Since we have tried to extract the maximum amount of information from the available data it is possible that some contradictions arise from the high sampling errors associated with fine break-downs of survey data. We are more inclined to believe that the conflicts are more apparent than real and are open to political rather than technical explanations. The puzzles that need to be solved are

(1) If contact makes for consensus why did middle class non-conformists appear to react against Anglican environments?

(2) If contact makes for consensus, a process requiring time to reach fulfilment, why did social alignments start at their most extreme i.e. why did alignment trends follow a 'big bang' rather than a 'growth' pattern?

Table 26

Three-Way Contests in 1929, 1950 and October 1974

Semi-standardised slopes on

Year	CL251			RANG31			AGRI31		
	CON	LIB	LAB	CON	LIB	LAB	CON	LIB	LAB
1929	6.8	1.6	−8.4	2.4	−1.4	−1.0	−1.5	5.2	−3.6
1950	8.5	1.3	−9.2	2.2	−0.7	−1.8	−0.6	2.0	−1.0
1974 O	7.1	2.5	−9.6	2.4	−0.2	−2.1	0.7	3.3	−4.0

Semi-standardised slopes on

Year	CL251			ANG31			MIN31			PRS31			AGRI31		
	CON	LIB	LAB	CON	LIB	LAB	CON	LIB	LAB	CON	LIB	LAB	CON	LIB	LAB
1929	6.3	0.2	−6.6	4.3	−0.9	−3.3	−1.2	3.3	−2.1	0.8	0.7	−1.4	−2.9	4.1	−1.2
1950	8.6	0.3	−8.3	2.4	1.5	−3.9	−2.0	1.9	−0.1	0.9	−0.2	−0.8	−0.6	−0.2	0.8
1974 O	6.9	1.4	−8.1	4.3	0.6	−5.3	−1.4	1.9	−0.4	−0.4	1.1	−0.7	−0.8	2.3	−1.3

Generalised Polarisations

Three-Way contests

Year	CL251		RANG31		AGRI31	
	Orient	Size	Orient	Size	Orient	Size
1929	10	7.8	325	2.1	77	4.7
1950	7	9.0	343	2.1	83	1.8
1974 O	14	8.7	356	2.3	51	3.7

All seats

Year	CL251		RANG		AGRI31	
	Orient	Size	Orient	Size	Orient	Size
1929	14	9.0	323	3.6	89	5.7
1950	8	8.7	342	2.0	84	1.6
1974 O	14	8.7	356	2.3	51	3.7

Note: (1) The units with three-way contests were a different set each time.
(2) In computing semi-standardised coefficients the standard deviations of predictors throughout England have been applied even to the restricted sets of units with three party contests. They are really scaled unstandardised slopes, fully comparable between data nets.

(3) In particular why did one cohort analysis put maximum class polarization in the '1945' cohort when the area studies did not show that period as a time of high class polarisation?

(4) Why did area studies show increasing sectarian polarisation after 1951 when cohort studies showed a declining trend in more recent cohorts?

The phrase used in the Chicago school's classic study of environmental influence was 'contact is a condition for consensus'. This should really be revised to read 'contact is a condition for interaction'. Whether the results of social interaction produce consensus or antagonistic reactions must depend upon circumstances. The empirical finding that local contacts in working class environments made the middle class identify more with the working class (consensual effect) but feel more strongly anti-trade union (reactive effect) seemed quite plausible. Middle class non-conformists' apparent reactions against Anglican environments were so pervasive across a whole range of attitudes that the evidence of reaction seems excessive. Alternative possibilities, apart from sampling error, are that middle class non-conformists in Anglican areas had particularly strong contacts with each other, or that only the most strongly non-conformist resisted the class and environmental influences towards becoming Anglicans.

There are three explanations, all with some element of truth, of the 'big bang' pattern of trends in social alignments. First, there was a long period of eight years between the 1910 and 1918 elections. In particular, battle lines for the 1918 election were drawn up in August 1917 when Lloyd George dismissed Henderson from the War Cabinet, yet the election did not take place until December 1918. If we seek evidence for a classic S-shaped growth curve it is easy to find, but it relates not to class polarisation after 1918 but the establishment of constituency Labour parties. Growth was slow from 1900 to 1917, the number went up from 239 in 1917 to 492 in 1920 and thereafter further growth was slow. Although that is organisational data, it perhaps indicates that discussion processes were operating strongly in the closing years of the war. A second explanation for the strong start of social alignments may be that 'a week is a long time in politics'. After the elections of 1974 we are especially aware of how quickly political choices can change and how intense political debate can be over short periods of time. While the discussion process needs time, the length of a three week election campaign is probably sufficient. Lastly we have already noted that the social pattern of candidature in 1918 almost guaranteed sharp social alignments in 1918 itself and the restricted voting choices offered to the electorate in that year helped to start them voting for the parties appropriate to their social groups.

Cohort analyses could not really contradict analyses of contemporary election results because they were time-specific to 1966 and 1970, not to the times mentioned in the cohort names. Contemporary Gallup survey data for 1945 agrees with the area studies that 1945 was not a time of high class polarisation. (see Table 5 of Chapter Three) It is easier to interpret the cohort results if we do not try to be too time-specific, that is if we admit that cohorts lived through periods of time rather than suddenly appearing and instantly forming a completely rigid party attachment. Taking the median age of each cohort, class polarisation in the Butler/Stokes and the Rose studies was highest in the cohorts who had lived through every election from 1922 to 1931 before coming of voting age. In Butler/Stokes they also lived through the 1935 campaign, and in Rose the 1918 campaign. Since class divisions were undoubtedly more significant in the elections of these years than in earlier or later elections, the cohort findings are reasonable. However it must be noted that the variation in class polarisation across cohorts was much less in the large Rose sample than in the much smaller Election Study sample. Finally, as we showed in Chapter Three, trends in constituency polarisation were small and did not reproduce even the trends in contemporary survey data.

There are several explanations for the conflicting evidence on sectarian trends. While the sectarian alignment was weaker in more recent cohorts, the same Election Study data indicated that it was less weak in the sixties than in the fifties. Indeed the sign had reversed for some cohorts during the fifties. Secondly, the issue analysis by cohorts showed that the sectarian polarisation decline was associated with class and trade union issues which recalled pre-1918 electoral disputes. On some internationalist issues it held up or even increased in the more recent cohorts. However, most important, it would be excessively narrow minded to identify the non-conformist tradition only with the non-conformist themselves. The evidence is that Anglicans and others were infected by the political traditions of non-conformity in those areas where the non-conformists were relatively strong.

8 Summary

1 This chapter is restricted to England because religious and national effects were significant in the analysis of trends from 1918–74. England included 85 % of British electors. The basic analysis is extended to Scotland and Wales in the next chapter.
2 Unlike 1955–70 there were large changes both in levels of party support and in patterns of support.
3 Between the wars the distribution of partisanship was two-dimensional (in the sense defined in Chapter Four). After the Second War it was much closer to a unidimensional distribution even when Liberal support revived. The reasons were: partly a decline in influences that cut across the class alignment; partly a convergence in the political orientation of different social alignments; and partly a decline in random deviance.
4 Basic analyses were multiple regressions using two concepts that had proved important in the constituency analyses, class and rurality, and two which had only been omitted for lack of data, sect and religiosity.
5 Cohort analyses of survey data cannot be used to prove both the existence and the persistence of social patterns. It is necessary to assume the one property to prove the other.

6 Cohort analyses are most useful for measuring the degree of persistence of known historical patterns, since cohorts never represent electorates and cohort partisanship is always much affected by present day politics.

7 Two recent studies using cohorts have found class polarisation greatest in cohorts described as 'interwar' or '1945'. One study has also found a declining sectarian effect on partisanship with very little effect in the youngest cohorts.

8 However a cohort analysis of political attitudes revealed that on some issues the sectarian effect did not decline and on one, unilateralism, it increased. Sectarian decline occurred on the issues of the 'social gospel' – trade unions, taxes and symbols of state.

9 Survey respondents were categorised by a census measure of their sectarian environment. This measure correlated well with respondents' sectarian choice.

10 There was evidence of a consensual influence from the sectarian environment on Anglicans but, middle class non-conformists reacted against the environment.

11 Analyses of voting in constant units showed similar class polarisation trends irrespective of the date of the class measure.

12 Controlling for sect and rurality, class polarisation declined from 1918 to 1929 but was stable thereafter. Its orientation was Conservative versus the rest in 1918, Conservative versus Labour generally from 1922 to 1955, then usually Labour versus the rest.

13 Controlling for class and rurality, sectarian polarisation declined until 1951 but increased thereafter. Its orientation moved from Conservative versus Liberal in 1918, through Conservative versus the rest until 1951, to Conservative versus Labour thereafter. In the twenties it was half the size of class polarisation, by 1974 it was again up to a quarter the size of class polarisation.

14 Religious effects on Conservative votes came nearest to a purely sectarian effect. There were also anti-Labour and pro-Liberal religiosity effects.

15 The rural effect, controlling for class and sect, operated primarily to the Liberals advantage until 1959 when it became more a Labour disadvantage. In size it was roughly half as powerful as class in the twenties, died out in 1951 but was back up to a third the size of the class effect by 1974.

16 Controlling for religiosity indicated the same rural trends, but a smaller rural effect. In orientation it was pro-Liberal and anti-Conservative until 1955 and in 1974, but from 1959 to 1970 actually anti-Liberal.

17 Cohort analyses indicated larger sectarian effects in the middle class. So did the constant unit studies, but only in 1923 did they improve the fit substantially. Then sectarian effects were not only more powerful but differently orientated in middle class areas.

18 The basic model was a poor predictor of turnout.

19 The social structure of interwar patterns of candidature was sharply defined, especially for Centre candidates.

20 If all candidates for a party got equal percentage votes, candidature patterns

alone would largely explain patterns of Centre voting, but could not completely explain the patterns of Conservative, Labour or Liberal votes.

21 Restricting analyses to constant units with Conservative, Labour and Liberal candidates in all their constituencies, comparison of 1929, 1950 and 1974 showed:

(i) a steady or slightly increasing Conservative versus Labour class effect.

(ii) a steady or slightly increasing sectarian effect veering from Conservative versus the rest to Conservative versus Labour.

(iii) a rural effect with a minimum in 1950 veering from pro-Liberal to pro-Liberal anti-Labour.

22 The sharp social patterning of candidatures in the early twenties helps to explain the general form of English trends in polarisation. Polarisation began at a maximum and declined. There was no period of slow growth.

CHAPTER 6

Variations from Basic Alignments
1918–74

1 Varieties of Non-conformity within England 1918–74

There were important differences within the English state church and at least until the turn of the century these could have political implications. Since Parliament determined the rituals and beliefs of the Anglican church it was sometimes not enough for a parliamentary candidate to be Anglican; he was asked to define his position on the High versus Low or Anglo-Catholic versus Evangelical spectrum. However varieties of Anglicanism are hard to quantify and we shall have to neglect them. Varieties of non-conformity, on the other hand, can be measured by the numbers of members, adherents or clergy belonging to the different non-conformist sects.

Membership of the five largest non-conformist sects has been analysed and tabulated by Kinnear and we shall use, in modified form, his data on the spatial distribution of these sects.[1] From largest to smallest they were the Wesleyan Methodists, Baptists, Congregationalists, Primitive Methodists and Presbyterians. This is not the place for a history of the sects but several points are relevant to our analysis.[2] First, Kinnear's data covered 88 % of all non-conformists in England. Second, the divisions between Methodists were disappearing in our period and in 1932 Wesleyans, Primitives and also the United Methodists came together in a single Methodist Church. So we should not perhaps expect enormously different responses among branches of Methodism. Third, the English Presbyterian Church in our period was not entirely English. It was the product of a union in 1874 between the old English Presbyterians of 16th century origin and the 19th century church of the Scots living in England, the United Presbyterians. Its strength was concentrated in the counties close to the Scottish border and in towns throughout England. In Wales the Anglican church, disestablished in 1920, grew in numbers until 1936, but even then its strength was exceeded by a single non-conformist sect, the Calvinistic Methodists. Despite this name they were linked to the Presbyterian Church of Scotland and have become known as the Presbyterian Church of Wales. By the

sixties Anglican communicants in Wales exceeded Calvinistic Methodist adherents, though both were in decline. Welsh non-conformity was distinctive not
only because of the Calvinistic Methodists but because Welsh-speaking congregationalists had formed the Union of Welsh Independents within the
Congregational Union of England and Wales. Between them, these two
specifically Welsh non-conformist organisations maintained 2495 places of
worship in 1931 and depending upon one's choice of measure their strength per
capita in Wales was between two and four times the size of the Anglican Church's
strength in England.

Statements about the political responses associated with different churches are
often confused and confusing. It has been said, for example, that the Wesleyan
Methodists were the 'aristocrats' of non-conformity, drawn by their wealth and
social standing towards the Conservatives – which sounds like a statement about
religious effects on partisanship, but on examination turns out to be a statement
about class effects.[3] In the analyses that follow we always impose controls for
class and for rural effects so that the results relate to sect itself, not its correlates.
The question to be answered is not whether Wesleyans were more Conservative
than other non-conformists but whether they were even more Conservative than
their higher class status would indicate.

In Chapter Five we chose not to use Kinnear's membership figures for non-
conformists because he gave no corresponding figure for Anglicans and thus his
data was the joint product of non-conformity and religiosity. That objection still
applies. So instead of using the membership figures themselves we divided the
non-conformist clergy reported by the 1931 Census in the same proportions as
Kinnear's membership figures. Then for seventy seven constant units in England
we had notional numbers of Wesleyan, Primitive, Congregational, Baptist and
Presbyterian clergy. Since certain of these denominations relied heavily on lay
preachers and others did not, these notional numbers of clergy are intended to be
a cross-sectarian comparable clergy-equivalent rather than estimates of the
actual numbers of clergy. Nonetheless aggregate figures show that in 1931
Wesleyans, Primitives and Baptists all had between 184 and 202 members per
clergyman while the Congregationalists had only 140 and the Presbyterians
probably had a little over 200.[4] (Presbyterians recorded congregations but not
clergy in 1931. There were 239 members per congregation but Presbyterians in
Scotland, where figures are available had considerably more clergymen than
congregations.) This suggests that the combined Kinnear and census figures
probably were, by chance, not too far from the actual numbers of clergy, even
though that was not the intention.

The spatial distributions of all varieties of non-conformist clergy were less
biased than the Anglicans towards rural and middle class areas, but only
Presbyterians correlated positively with urban and working class areas. Wesleyans were the most correlated, of any non-conformists, with middle class areas,
although the Congregationalists were not much less so. Primitive Methodists,
and to a lesser extent Wesleyans, were most correlated with rural areas. However
since Anglican clergy were much more correlated with both middle class and

rural areas, each non-conformist sect, when expressed as a proportion of total clergy, had both a working class and an urban bias.

One method for relating party votes to the multiple subdivision of non-conformist sects is to predict party shares of the vote from multiple regression equations containing the following seven predictors

CL251, AGRI, RATWES, RATPRM, RATCONG, RATBAPT, RATPRES

where CL251 and AGRI are the class and rural indicators used before, and the other five predictors are the clergy of one denomination taken as a proportion of total Anglican plus non-conformist clergy.

The sum of these five ratios is

RATWES + RATPRM + RATCONG + RATBAPT + RATPRES
= 1 − RANG

where RANG is the Anglican proportion of clergy used in the last chapter. To interpret the coefficients in this multiple regression we note that each slope will show the political effect of an increase in one particular non-conformist sect when there is no change in class, rurality or any other non-conformist sect since these are all explicit predictors. Thus each slope shows the political effect of substituting one particular non-conformist sect for Anglicans. Anglicans provide the benchmark against which all the sectarian effects are measured.

Table 1 shows the results of such analyses. For brevity it does not display the party by party regressions but just the size and orientation of the generalised sectarian polarisations. Similarly it does not show the class and rural polarisations although both these variables were included as predictors.

The analyses do not single out the Wesleyan tradition as having a uniquely low anti-Conservative or even pro-Conservative effect. At every election the Wesleyan effect was anti-Conservative. Until the fifties it was usually pro-Liberal but pro-Labour thereafter. It was somewhat smaller than Congregational and Baptist effects in most of the interwar years but similar to them after the Second War.

The Baptist effect was also consistently anti-Conservative and again showed the tendency to be pro-Liberal in earlier years, veering more pro-Labour from 1945 onwards. It was particularly strong in the twenties.

Primitive Methodist and Presbyterian effects were also anti-Conservative and pro-Liberal in general between the wars. However afterwards, particularly from the mid fifties, they became consistently pro-Labour and generally anti-Liberal. In the twenties they were intermediate in size between the smaller Wesleyan and larger Congregational and Baptist effects, but later the Presbyterian effect was left as the largest for it maintained its size while all the other effects declined.

That leaves the Congregationalists. They had a direct connection with the Civil

Table 1
Size and Orientation of Non Conformist Effects 1918–74

	Size					Orientation				
	WES	PRM	CONG	BAPT	PRES	WES	PRM	CONG	BAPT	PRES
1918	8.2	5.7	3.8	4.5	5.8	117 C→I	123 C→I	172 C→L	87 *→I	121 C→I
1922	3.5	3.7	4.2	5.3	3.0	140 C→*	104 *→I	267 I→*	123 C→I	141 C→*
1923	2.4	1.5	6.0	5.0	3.1	115 C→I	104 *→I	252 I→L	108 C→I	158 C→*
1924	1.9	2.4	4.7	4.7	2.9	130 C→I	114 C→I	251 I→L	104 *→I	157 C→*
1929	1.7	2.3	2.3	2.6	2.2	136 C→*	152 C→*	241 I→L	112 C→I	131 C→I
1931	1.9	2.6	3.2	1.8	2.8	150 C→*	135 C→*	284 I→*	122 C→I	125 C→I
1935	0.8	1.2	1.8	1.8	2.0	153 C→I	127 C→I	280 I→*	117 C→I	122 C→I
1945	1.7	1.1	1.5	0.7	0.9	108 C→I	286 I→C	258 I→L	172 C→L	209 *→L
1950	1.1	1.2	0.7	1.2	1.0	106 C→I	185 C→L	304 I→C	155 C→*	123 C→I
1951	0.7	0.9	0.3	1.5	0.8	120 C→I	204 *→L	18 L→*	225 *→L	143 C→*
1955	0.8	1.0	0.5	0.9	0.6	127 C→I	235 I→L	264 I→*	170 C→L	180 C→I
1959	1.5	1.4	1.8	1.6	1.2	151 C→*	243 I→L	266 I→*	125 C→I	240 I→L
1964	0.9	1.6	2.2	1.1	2.5	174 C→L	251 I→L	267 I→*	156 C→*	239 I→L
1966	1.1	1.9	1.8	1.3	2.0	175 C→L	252 I→L	267 I→*	151 C→*	216 I→L
1970	1.1	1.2	0.3	1.1	2.4	162 C→*	223 *→L	292 I→C	198 *→L	209 *→L
1974 F	1.4	2.1	0.8	1.5	2.6	161 C→*	266 I→*	133 C→I	157 C→*	214 *→L
1974 O	1.3	0.2	1.3	1.5	2.8	173 C→L	123 C→I	237 I→L	176 C→L	198 *→L

Note: (1) WES = Wesleyan Methodist Clergy as a proportion of the total Anglican plus non-conformist clergy.

(2) PRM, CONG, BAPT, PRES are defined similarly for Primitive Methodists, Congregationalists, Baptists and Presbyterians.

(3) The tabulated figures for the sizes of the sectarian effects provide the best basis for comparison both with each other and with the overall non-conformist effects associated with RANG and tabulated in Chapter Five.

(4) These figures are unstandardised slopes multiplied by 5.35%. Unstandardised slopes are appropriate for measuring the relative sizes of political responses to equal numbers of clergy from different denominations. The standard deviations of the different non-conformist clergy ranged from 3.90% for Primitive Methodists to 6.51% for Baptists with an average of 5.35%. Multiplying by this scale factor makes the Table more comparable with Tables in Chapter Five. However note that the standard deviations of the different non-conformist denominations are generally lower than the effects in Chapter Five for non-conformity as a whole. This is because they correlate and cumulate. The standard deviation of non-conformity as a whole, was 12.14% because in non-conformist areas all the non-conformist sects tended to be strong and vice versa.

(5) With these provisos, calculations for this Table followed the method of Chapter Five.

(6) Each sectarian effect is for that sect compared to the Anglicans.

(7) Slopes are taken from equations that included CL251 and AGRI as additional predictors. So all results are controlled for class and rurality.

War days and quite recently had been strongly connected with politics. Blewett showed that in the 1910 elections they had provided well over twice as many non-conformist candidates as any other sect, 88 of the 215 Liberal non-conformists.[5] So we might have expected a particularly strong Congregational effect. The results show that the Congregational effect was strong but anti-Liberal, not pro-Liberal. Until 1931 Labour was the chief beneficiary. In 1918 the orientation was anti-Conservative pro-Labour. From 1923 to 1929 it was from Liberal to Labour and even in 1922 it was closer to a pro-Labour anti-Liberal than a pro-Conservative anti-Liberal effect. It would be possible to interpret the results up to 1931 as a switch to the most radical of the parties by a sect with strong radical traditions. However in 1931 and 1935 the Congregational pattern stayed anti-Liberal while becoming more pro-Conservative than pro-Labour. In 1945 it was again rather more pro-Labour and the entire effect was very small in 1950, 1951 and 1955. From 1959 to 1966 it increased again remaining slightly more pro-Labour than pro-Conservative (i.e. less than 270 degrees). It was again very small in 1970 and February 1974 and then clearly anti-Liberal pro-Labour in October 1974. Generally when it was very small it benefitted the Conservatives.

The Congregational pattern of a pro-Labour anti-Liberal effect in the twenties was the same as the pattern associated with the Primitive Methodists and Presbyterians after the Second War. As such it was just a foretaste of things to come. However the pro-Conservative bias which was strong in 1931, less so in 1935 and just detectable in 1950 and 1970, was unique. Perhaps the explanation is that the 1931 crisis, if it discredited any party, discredited Labour. In that situation the alignments most at risk would be pro-Labour alignments based on political choices not social interests.

2 Middle England, England, England and Wales: a Search for Homogeneity

For most purposes England and Wales was administered as a single entity, but whatever the unity in law the English and Welsh parts were clearly very different in partisanship. Table 2 shows the trends in voting and seats contested for Wales. It should be compared with the English trends shown in Table 1 of Chapter Five. Before 1918 Wales returned far more Liberal M.P.s for its size than England. Centre candidates did outstandingly well in Wales in 1918 and 1922; although the reunited Welsh Liberals did only a little better in 1923 than their English colleagues, from 1924 onwards Liberals were again far more successful in Wales than England; but their advantage slowly faded away over the next fifty years. Labour also enjoyed a large, if fluctuating advantage in Wales and from 1929 the Welsh Nationalists (Plaid Cymru) began to accumulate support. The sum of all these advantages equalled the Conservative disadvantage. They never obtained as much as a third of the Welsh votes.

Yet none of this implies any lack of political homogeneity throughout England and Wales, for Wales had more agriculture and far more non-conformity and religiosity than England; all of which might explain the political response.

Table 2
Trends in Votes and Candidatures in Wales 1918–74

| | Adjusted % of Vote | | | | | % of Seats Contested | | | | |
	CON	CEN	LIB	LAB	PC	CON	CEN	LIB	LAB	PC
1910 JAN	32		52	15	—	97		85	15	—
1910 DEC	24		62	15	—	59		88	21	—
1918	8	41	12	35	—	23	57	29	71	—
1922	22	24	10	39	—	54	51	31	80	—
1923	18	—	39	42	—	54	—	88	77	—
1924	22	—	27	51	—	49	—	60	94	—
1929	22	—	34	44	0	100	—	97	94	3
1931	20	11	17	48	0	40	17	40	86	3
1935	17	9	12	60	0	40	14	34	94	3
1945	16	7	15	60	1	51	26	49	97	17
1950	21	6	13	58	1	81	17	58	100	19
1951	28	3	8	61	1	83	8	25	100	11
1955	27	3	7	58	3	78	11	28	100	31
1959	30	3	5	57	5	86	8	22	100	56
1964	28	2	7	58	5	94	6	33	100	64
1966	28	—	6	61	4	100	—	31	100	56
1970	28	—	7	52	12	100	—	53	100	100
1974 FEB	26	—	16	47	11	100	—	86	100	100
1974 OCT	24	—	16	50	11	100	—	100	100	100

Note: (1) Votes adjusted for unopposed returns.

At the other extreme we can define Middle England as another sub-area of England and Wales to exclude the North, North West, Yorkshire/Humberside and South West of England. Some of these areas were noted for their non-conformity and their anti-Conservatism. While we may look at England and Wales to see if non-conformity might explain the apparent Welsh deviance, we may compare analyses in Middle England with those in all England to see whether regional peripherality may explain the apparent sectarian effects on voting in England. If the peripheral areas of England were against the Conservatives as a national centrist (geographically) party and were also more non-conformist, then our England-wide analyses would falsely attribute peripheral effects to sect.

Table 3 shows the results of some attempts to investigate homogeneity. Regressions predicting the Conservative share of the vote in 1923, 1929, 1950, 1964 and 1974 used class, sect and rurality as predictors. There were four regressions taken over three data sets. First, the slopes were calculated for Middle English data, then for all English, then for English and Welsh units. Finally a second regression was run on the English and Welsh data using the same three social predictors but including, as a fourth predictor, a dummy

Table 3
Regressions over Different Areas within England and Wales
Slopes predicting Conservative share of vote

Year	Span	CL251	RANG	AGRI	R^2
1923	E	9.3	4.7	−2.0	48
	ME	10.8	4.2	−2.4	57
	EW	5.4	8.6	−5.0	38
	EWD	6.4	6.1	−3.5	43
1929	E	7.4	4.1	−3.2	53
	ME	9.3	3.6	−3.2	65
	EW	5.9	5.9	−4.4	54
	EWD	6.4	4.5	−3.5	57
1950	E	8.3	2.1	−0.8	71
	ME	9.8	2.5	−0.5	80
	EW	5.4	5.3	−2.9	48
	EWD	5.9	3.0	−1.5	57
1964	E	5.4	1.8	1.3	62
	ME	6.4	2.2	1.4	68
	EW	2.9	4.7	−0.9	40
	EWD	3.4	2.5	0.4	50
1974 OCT	E	7.4	2.3	0.9	72
	ME	5.9	3.0	0.4	63
	EW	4.4	5.2	−1.0	48
	EWD	5.4	2.9	0.4	57

Note: (1) E = England, ME = Middle England (as defined in Chapter Three), EW = England and Wales.

(2) EWD indicates regression used all units from England and Wales, but the regression predictors included a dummy variable with values 1 in Wales and 0 otherwise, to take out a purely constant Welsh bias against the Conservatives. The slope on this predictor is not shown but its use alters all the other slopes.

(3) Tabulated values are scaled unstandardised slopes, that is unstandarised slopes multiplied by the standard deviation of each predictor within England. See note to Table 1.

variable for Wales. This extra predictor allowed a constant anti-Conservative disadvantage throughout Wales.

The Welsh shift was never a redundant predictor as may be seen from the increase in fit (R^2) when it was applied. So even allowing for the social variation, Wales was indeed politically deviant. Turning to the social predictors, sect was as effective in Middle England as in all England. On three occasions sect was slightly more powerful in Middle England, on two it was slightly less. The slopes on agriculture were also very similar in Middle and all England. The class effect was most variable but not consistently higher or lower in the different parts of England.

Adding Wales to the data set produced marked changes in slopes. The class effect went down, the sectarian effect shot up and the rural effect became considerably more anti-Conservative. However a part of these changes was spurious, caused by a confusion of national and social effects. When the Welsh national predictor was included as a control all the slopes moved back towards their English values, but not completely. Even allowing for a Welsh national effect, the sectarian effect was a little larger when Wales was included. This suggests that Calvinistic Methodism and Welsh Congregationalism produced a greater anti-Conservative effect than English brands of non-conformity, but only a little greater. Again, even with a Welsh national control, agriculture had a larger anti-Conservative or smaller pro-Conservative effect when Wales was in the data set, but again this deviance was small. What the Welsh national control did not do was to restore the class effect to the size it had for England alone. The reason for this is partly technical: social class Two, as measured by the census, was designed to group together those of similar 'general standing within the community'. As such it may have been entirely successful judged from a sociological viewpoint. However, in parts of Wales and even more in Scotland, it grouped together people with highly dissimilar political traditions. (see the section below on Scotland). Allowing for this, or ignoring the class variable, Table 3 shows that, while a national Welsh effect existed and the sectarian and rural effects had the anticipated biases in that direction, the biases were small and there was a remarkably homogeneous response to sect and rurality throughout England, Middle England and Wales.

The search for homogeneity can be taken a stage further by repeating the multi-denominational sectarian analyses within Middle England and comparing them with our previous results. This is done in Table 4. Over five elections the Wesleyan effect averaged 0.6 higher in Middle England, the Primitive effect 0.1 lower, the Congregational 0.5 lower, the Baptist 0.1 higher and the Presbyterian 0.5 higher. Orientations were also similar, except in 1950. In the other four years the average bias in orientations was greatest for the Wesleyans at 36°, but only 19° for Primitives, 14° for Baptists, 8° for Presbyterians and 5° for Congregationalists. In 1950, when the size of effects was particularly low, the orientations were especially inconsistent; indeed, the relatively high average discrepancy for the Primitives was almost completely due to an enormous discrepancy in 1974 when the Primitive effect was even lower than in 1950. Overall, the only evidence of an important difference in Middle England is of a less pro-Liberal and more pro-Labour effect associated with the Wesleyans.

3 Scotland 1918–74

Scotland has one city, Glasgow, which dominates all others in terms of population, communications links with the outside world and social problems. Too often it also dominates discussion about Scotland. The standard work on Scottish political behaviour, for example, is based on data from Glasgow.[6] Yet

Table 4
Size and Orientation of Non-Conformist Effects in Middle England

		Size					Orientation				
		WES	PRM	CONG	BAPT	PRES	WES	PRM	CONG	BAPT	PRES
1923	E	2.4	1.5	6.0	5.0	3.1	115 C→I	104 *→I	252 I→L	108 C→I	158 C→*
	ME	2.3	0.4	5.5	4.3	2.8	162 C→*	98 *→I	247 I→L	110 C→I	173 C→L
1929	E	1.7	2.3	2.3	2.6	2.2	136 C→*	152 C→*	241 I→L	112 C→I	131 C→I
	ME	2.9	2.1	2.5	2.6	1.9	125 C→I	161 C→*	244 I→L	111 C→I	155 C→*
1950	E	1.1	1.2	0.7	1.2	1.0	106 C→I	185 C→L	304 I→C	155 C→*	123 C→I
	ME	1.2	0.8	0.8	1.5	1.8	215 *→L	227 I→L	270 I→*	130 C→I	180 C→L
1964	E	0.9	1.6	2.2	1.1	2.5	174 C→L	251 I→L	267 I→*	156 C→*	239 I→L
	ME	2.9	2.3	0.9	1.2	3.9	251 I→L	260 I→*	280 I→*	185 C→L	235 I→L
1974 OCT	E	1.3	0.2	1.3	1.5	2.8	173 C→L	123 C→I	237 I→L	176 C→L	198 *→L
	ME	1.3	0.8	0.4	2.3	3.6	203 *→L	35 L→*	247 I→L	200 *→L	195 *→L

Note: (1) All the notes for Table 1 apply here.
(2) In addition the unstandardised slopes for Middle England have been scaled using the English standard deviations. This makes Table entries comparable.
(3) Taking 30° as the maximum discrepancy between 'similar' orientations (it equals one point on the compass e.g. the difference between CON v LAB and LAB v the rest) the numbers of similarly orientated effects were four in 1923, five in 1929, only one in 1950, four in 1964 and four in 1974.

between the wars the city only returned fifteen of Scotland's seventy one M.P.s and today it returns less.

Following our standard procedures for constructing constant units produced twenty three units for Scotland. Glasgow was compressed into just one of these units. So analyses of the data set for Scotland can say nothing about partisan variation within Glasgow and the whole analysis is biased against within-city explanations. Although this is an inescapable consequence of the way census data was tabulated, it provides a useful corrective bias against the usual tendency to concentrate too much attention on a tiny area and a small part of Scotland's population.

Trends in votes and candidatures within Scotland are shown in Table 5. These figures are for the whole of Scotland with no bias. Before 1918 Scotland had been much more pro-Liberal than England and in 1918 and 1922 Centre votes were higher than in England, though lower than in Wales. However, from 1923 onwards, the Liberals either had only a small advantage in Scotland or, as was more usual after the Second War, a substantial disadvantage. Labour had a Scottish advantage from 1918 to 1931; from 1935 to 1955 and in 1974 the party

Table 5
Trends in Votes and Candidatures in Scotland 1918–74

| | Adjusted % of Vote | | | | | % of Seats Contested | | | | |
	CON	CEN	LIB	LAB	SNP	CON	CEN	LIB	LAB	SNP
1910 JAN	40		54	5	–	100		97	14	–
1910 DEC	37		60	3	–	81		96	7	–
1918	30	29	13	22	–	52	44	46	59	–
1922	24	18	22	31	–	51	46	68	61	–
1923	30	–	32	34	–	73	–	83	68	–
1924	39	–	20	39	–	79	–	48	89	–
1929	36	–	18	42	0	92	–	63	93	3
1931	49	7	12	29	1	79	13	20	80	7
1935	44	7	7	36	1	82	15	23	89	10
1945	37	4	5	48	1	87	8	31	96	11
1950	37	8	7	46	0	80	15	58	100	4
1951	40	9	3	48	0	80	18	13	100	6
1955	42	9	2	47	1	83	17	7	100	3
1959	40	8	4	47	1	83	15	23	100	7
1964	37	3	8	49	2	92	8	37	100	21
1966	38	–	7	50	5	100	–	34	100	32
1970	38	–	6	45	11	99	–	38	100	92
1974 FEB	33	–	8	37	22	100	–	48	100	99
1974 OCT	25	–	8	36	30	100	–	96	100	100

Note: (1) Votes adjusted for two member seats and unopposed returns.
   (2) The breakaway Independent Labour Party (ILP) gained 5% in 1935 and almost 2% in 1945.
   (3) The ILP contested 15% of seats in 1935 but only 4% in 1945.

fared the same or worse than in England; but from 1959 until 1970, it again did better. Conservatives often did less well in Scotland than in England, nevertheless they could claim, correctly, to be the only party since 1918 to get over half the Scottish vote which, with their Centre allies, they achieved in 1955. During the thirties when the area close to Glasgow was known as 'Red Clydeside' it is worth recalling that the Conservatives alone took 49 % of the 1931 vote and 42 % in 1935, and the National Coalition which they led scored 64 % in 1931 and 50 % in 1935.

The Scottish Nationalist Party or its predecessors contested every election from 1929 onwards but failed to win sizeable numbers of votes until the mid sixties. In 1970 it contested most seats but still gained only 11 % of votes. Then in 1974, with only a slight increase in candidatures it pushed its vote up to 31 %.

One important feature of Scottish elections throughout the twenties was the low number of Conservative candidates. In the six constituencies of the crofting counties and islands, for example, Centre candidates took five seats in both 1918 and 1922. Although the Liberals reunited and ended any coalitions with the Conservatives, three of these seats were won in 1923 by a Liberal without a Conservative opponent and four in 1924.

3.1 Crofting, Scottish Politics and the Scottish Census

Following their rule that the social classes should be 'homogeneous' in 'general standing within the community' the Census put crofters into social class two. They also included self-employed farmers and market gardeners without employees in this class. As a result CL251 which we have used as a basic class control in England had an average value in the crofting counties that was well over twice as high as in central Scotland. Maybe it measured social standing, but it was an exceedingly poor indicator of the employers and managers versus operatives distinction. Moreover crofters had a very specific political tradition in Scotland. The franchise reform of 1885 coincided with a period of intense reaction by the crofters against established systems of land tenure. Along with riots and violent attacks on property 'Crofter' candidates appeared throughout the crofting lands. Out of seven seats in the crofting counties: Crofter candidates won four, an 'Independent Liberal' associated with the crofters beat an official Liberal to win a fifth and in the remaining two seats crofters took 38 % and 48 % of the votes although they were defeated. Most of the Crofter candidates obtained the support of local Liberal associations as well as specifically Highland organisations like the Highland Land League; as Liberal governments delivered pro-crofter legislation and agitation died away, the Crofters turned into ordinary Liberal candidates. The exception was in Inverness where Fraser-Mackintosh was a Liberal Unionist Crofter who became a straight Liberal Unionist in 1892. He was promptly defeated by a Liberal Crofter. The speed and totality of the Crofters' election successes outclassed the 1974 SNP breakthrough and, over its much smaller area, was far more dramatic even than Labour's jump from six to twenty nine M.P.s in 1922.

So for our comparative analysis of Scotland we have taken 1951 employers and managers as a percent of the economically active as our class indicator. This was not a single census category but its component parts were available for all Scottish constant units.

Table 6, however, shows the correlations between party shares of the vote in Scotland and CL251 which could be regarded as a measure of crofting and similar economic activities. (In the South CL251 was also much higher than in central Scotland although the term crofter was not used. It reflected own account farming.) In 1918 crofting correlated strongly with Centre votes and in 1922 with both Centre and Liberal. Thereafter, right through to 1974, there remained a close correlation between crofting and Liberal voting. Crofting was always strongly negatively correlated with Labour votes and weakly correlated, sometimes positively, sometimes negatively with Conservative votes. It did not correlate with SNP voting in 1974.

Table 6
The Crofting Fringe: Correlations between Voting and CL251

		Correlations with		
	CON	*CEN*	*LIB*	*LAB*
1918	− 51	73	− 14	− 65
1922	− 43	52	54	− 73
1923	4	−	61	− 75
1924	− 28	−	72	− 90
1929	2	−	80	− 82
1931	− 33	−	71	− 76
1935	21	−	59	− 85
1945	9	−	76	− 75
1950	14	−	67	− 85
1951	18	−	63	− 87
1955	1	−	77	− 88
1959	− 21	−	60	− 78
1964	− 4	−	74	− 81
1966	6	−	81	− 79
1970	15	−	58	− 73
1974 FEB	16	−	78	− 71
1974 OCT	31	−	73	− 75

Note: (1) Crofters were specifically named as a group, within Scotland only, to be included in social class two. However throughout Britain this class included self–employed farmers and gardners without employees. Social classes were defined according to the Census Office's view of public esteem. No doubt the crofters and farmers without employees merited that esteem, but their political traditions were very different from those of the industrial managers also included in class two.
(2) The percentages in CL251 were 19.7% in the North, 17.0% in the South, 11.0% in East Central and 10.9% in West Central Scotland. In that part of the North described as Crofting Counties the figure was 24.1%
(3) A control for AGRI makes the Conservative link to CL251 consistently and severely negative.
(4) Correlations with SNP voting were − 17 in February 1974 and − 9 in October.

When CL251 and AGRI were used in a multiple prediction scheme, to separate the effects of agriculture itself from crofting or own account farming, the strong positive link with Liberal votes and the negative link with Labour remained; but with agriculture controlled the link between Conservative votes and crofting became strongly and consistently negative.

It is perhaps a little surprising that Labour never inherited the strong link with crofting areas. As early as 1888 the Crofter M.P. for Caithness was Honorary Vice President of the Scottish Parliamentary Labour Party and in the same year Kier Hardie had the support of the Highland Land League when he fought the very non-Highland seat of Mid-Lanark. CL251 must be a middle class biased measure of crofting since it is a mixture of the two; with an agricultural control the negative link between crofting and Labour was usually much smaller than the negative link with the Conservatives. Between the wars Labour's weakness in crofting areas could also be attributed to candidature. Of the six Highlands and Islands constituencies, one got its first Labour candidate in 1923, two in 1924, one in 1929 and two in 1945. Three of the six constituencies elected Liberals unopposed in 1924. However purely technical effects of candidature do not explain the continuation of the crofter's voting patterns after the Second War and right up to the present, although failure to contest seats between the wars could not have helped local organisation or party identification in later years.

3.2 Class, Religious and Rural Alignments in Scotland 1918–74

Now, for comparison with the analyses of English voting, we must attempt to replicate the class, religion and agriculture scheme for predicting partisanship. Some alterations are necessary for Scotland: first, EMPL51, the percent employers and managers must be substituted for CL251 for the reasons given; second, the religious structure was different in Scotland. The established church was the presbyterian Church of Scotland which was used as the basis for sectarian analyses. The Anglicans were not an established church and were called Episcopalians. We distinguish two other sorts of Protestant non-conformity: the Free Churches and other non-conformists. In the Scottish context, Free Churches means the remnants of those Presbyterian churches which had broken away from the established church and refused to reunite with it: the United Free 'continuance' and the Free Church of Scotland (or 'wee Frees'). The final reunion of the Church of Scotland occurred in 1929, just prior to our 1931 Census measures and almost half the post-1929 Church came from the former breakaway churches.

So there are five sectarian groups: the established and reunited Church of Scotland (CS); the Free Presbyterian Churches (FC); Catholics (PRS); Episcopalians (EP); and other non-conformists (NC). For sectarian analyses we use the clergy of each church other than the Church of Scotland, each taken as a percentage of total clergy. For religiosity analyses we use clergy from each of the five groups, each taken per capita of population. In any analysis it is necessary to impose controls for class and rurality. Consequently the multiple regressions contain either six or seven predictors even though we have only twenty three data points: these are more predictors and fewer data points than any analyst would like. Results are not susceptible to chance or sampling distortions since all the data for Scotland is included. Standard tests of significance are thus not strictly appropriate even if their statistical presumptions were justified which, with voting data, they are not. However the results are susceptible to the decisions of parties about whether to field candidates in some set of half a dozen seats and to the charisma of a handful of candidates, to an extent that was not true for analyses of the larger English data set.

A related problem is that the square of the multiple correlation coefficient, R^2, is not a suitable measure of the proportion of partisan variation explained when the data set is small and the number of predictors relatively large. In particular, it is a misleading measure of the increase in variation explained as more predictors are added to the predictive scheme. With twenty three data points we could get an R^2 value of 100% with any twenty three linearly independent predictors; the annual rainfall in twenty three successive years would do. Table 7 shows the values for R^2 and for an 'adjusted R^2' which takes account of degrees of freedom – essentially the excess of the number of data points over the number of predictors used. It is these adjusted values which should be compared with the R^2 values for England.[7] Even allowing for the decreasing number of degrees of freedom the addition of sectarian and religious predictors improved the fit. Averaging over the nine elections from 1950 to 1974, the adjusted R^2 for the Conservatives increased by 13%, for the Liberals by 27% and for Labour by 8% when sect and religiosity were used in addition to class and agriculture. For Labour and the Liberals the fit was better than in England, but not for the Conservatives. By contrast all the social predictors, class and rurality as well as sect and religiosity were poor predictors of 1974 SNP votes. Allowing for the restricted degrees of freedom the predictive fit for the SNP was negligible. Despite the small number of data points and the number of predictors the adjusted R^2 values suggest that it is reasonable to proceed with the analysis, at least of Labour, Liberal and Conservative votes.

Slopes and generalised polarisations associated with class and rurality are set out in Tables 8 and 9. The comparable results for England are in Table 17 of Chapter Five. As in England, the Liberals were the main beneficiary of the rural effect and the Conservatives of the class effect, but the Scottish rural effect did not veer towards a pro-Conservative anti-Labour effect in the sixties; it remained both anti-Labour and anti-Conservative. The class effect was also orientated differently: in England it was Labour versus Conservative until 1955 veering Labour versus the rest from 1959 to 1970 as the Liberals made gains in middle class areas. In Scotland the class effect was Conservative versus the rest on most occasions. After controls for sect and agriculture Liberal votes in Scotland unlike England remained biased towards working class areas (with the outstanding but temporary exceptions of 1931 and 1935).

Size differences were greater than orientation differences. In England the class effect was large, usually more than twice the size of the rural effect. The class effect was also stable and the rural effect variable. In Scotland the class effect

Table 7
Raw and Adjusted R² values for Regressions in Scotland

	Raw			Adjusted		
Predictor Sets	EMPL51 AGRI	EMPL51 AGRI RPRS RFC REP RNC	EMPL51 AGRI CS PRS FC EP NC	EMPL51 AGRI	EMPL51 AGRI RPRS RFC REP RNC	EMPL51 AGRI CS PRS FC EP NC
Conservative						
1923	9	13	19	−1	−19	−18
1924	28	54	53	21	37	31
1929	25	46	51	18	26	28
1950–74	45	58	67	39	43	52
Liberal						
1923	40	55	55	34	39	34
1924	43	68	68	37	55	53
1929	59	72	72	54	62	59
1950–74	35	60	69	28	47	55
Labour						
1923	74	84	85	72	78	78
1924	80	88	88	79	83	82
1929	67	82	82	64	75	73
1950–74	80	87	90	78	83	86
SNP						
1974 FEB	10	29	38	1	3	10
1974 OCT	12	25	28	3	−3	−5

Note: (1) The adjusted R² value takes account of the declining number of degrees of freedom as the number of predictors is increased. It is calculated as one minus the ratio of the variance of residuals to the original variance in the dependent variable. Both these variances depend on the degrees of freedom as well as the sum of squared deviations.

(2) A negative value for the adjusted R² means that the predictors perform so badly that, after allowing for degrees of freedom, the estimated variance of residuals is larger than the original variance.

(3) EMPL51 = % employers and managers 1951; AGRI = % in agriculture; RPRS, RFC, REP, RNC are the Catholic, Free Churches, Episcopalian and other non-conformist clergy as percentages of total clergy; CS, PRS, FC, EP, NC are the Church of Scotland, Catholic, Free Churches, Episcopalian and other non-conformist clergy per capita. Agriculture and clergy are 1931 measurements.

(4) The 'Free Churches' used in this chapter are a composite. At the Disruption in 1843 the Free Church of Scotland was set up. In 1900 a dissenting minority of this Free Church refused to join the United Free Church. Then in 1929 a dissenting minority of the United Free declined to amalgamate with the Church of Scotland. Our Free Churches clergy comprise both sets of dissenting Presbyterians. It should remembered that our

1931 Church of Scotland was the newly reunified church, almost half of it old Free Churchmen. In 1921, for example, there were 1457 parish churches of the established church of Scotland versus 1482 congregations of the United Free, but the established church claimed rather more communicants. Although our files contain 1921 clergy data, we have used the 1931 figures, partly for comparability with England and because the date is more central, but mainly because the 'Wee Frees' and the United Free Continuance may be better measures of the strength of Presbyterian non-conformity. By 1921 both Church of Scotland and United Free had set up pervasive parish church systems; so their clergy were similarly distributed. They had also drawn close together, as witness their 1929 reunion.

(5) Figures for 1950 to 1974 were so similar that they can be represented adequately by an average value.

Table 8
Class and Rurality in Scotland 1918–74

Semi-standardised slopes
(after controls for five-way sectarian division)

	EMPL51				AGRI			
	CON	CEN	LIB	LAB	CON	CEN	LIB	LAB
1918	−0.3	10.8	−4.5	−6.2	−13.8	22.6	−0.7	−7.9
1922	2.6	−0.5	0.7	−2.6	−10.5	4.7	21.9	−16.0
1923	5.1	−	4.7	−9.9	−4.1	−	15.9	−11.8
1924	14.0	−	−10.9	−3.1	−17.9	−	30.7	−12.8
1929	5.7	−	−2.3	−3.4	−5.6	−	16.4	−10.8
1931	1.0	−14.9	20.0	−6.0	−19.2	12.2	14.5	−7.6
1935	12.6	−14.1	14.4	−12.7	−9.1	13.6	0.3	−4.9
1945	14.4	−7.1	0.0	−7.2	−9.7	7.6	8.7	−6.5
1950	14.2	−	−6.3	−7.8	−9.4	−	13.6	−4.3
1951	9.0	−	−2.5	−6.4	−2.3	−	9.5	−7.3
1955	9.6	−	−4.0	−5.7	−5.2	−	13.4	−8.1
1959	11.7	−	−7.6	−4.1	−5.3	−	15.9	−10.6
1964	10.1	−	−5.1	5.0	−9.3	−	20.3	−11.0
1966	9.2	−	−3.5	−5.8	−5.7	−	15.9	−10.3
1970	10.5	−	−4.8	−5.6	−4.8	−	14.2	−9.4
	CON	LIB	LAB	SNP	CON	LIB	LAB	SNP
1974 FEB	6.5	−3.3	−8.0	4.8	−3.0	12.6	−6.1	−3.3
1974 OCT	7.4	−5.3	−8.7	6.5	−2.6	12.6	−6.1	−3.9

only exceeded the rural effect at three elections and although both fluctuated, the class effect was the less stable. Rural polarisation in Scotland was clearly much more important than in England. Our estimates put the Scottish class polarisation since the Second War at roughly equal to English class polarisation.

Sectarian polarisation, after controlling for class and rurality, is set out in Tables 10 and 11 which compare the political effect of substituting each non-established sect for the Church of Scotland. The comparable table for England is Table 1 of this chapter, although here the benchmark was the Anglican Church. Sectarian effects in Scotland were larger than in England even during the twenties

Table 9
Size and Orientation of Class and Rural Polarisations in Scotland

| | Size | | Orientation | |
	EMPL51	AGRI	EMPL51	AGRI
1918	6.2	19.2	61 L →I	100 * →I
1922	2.6	23.2	3 L →C	83 * →I
1923	8.5	14.3	28 L →*	74 L →I
1924	12.8	26.7	312 * →C	95 * →I
1929	4.8	14.4	355 * →C	79 * →I
1931	17.7	12.6	103 * →I	89 * →I
1935	13.7	4.7	66 L →I	3 L →C
1945	7.3	7.9	0 L →C	73 L →I
1950	12.3	12.1	334 * →C	102 * →I
1951	8.0	8.6	344 * →C	73 L →I
1955	8.4	11.7	336 * →C	83 * →I
1959	10.3	14.0	320 * →C	79 * →I
1964	8.7	17.6	330 * →C	87 * →I
1966	8.1	13.9	338 * →C	81 * →I
1970	9.1	12.5	333 * →C	79 * →I

Note: These figures were calculated from regressions that included sectarian controls.

and though both declined to a minimum in the early fifties and only partially recovered thereafter, the sectarian effects in Scotland never declined so far and by the sixties were much larger than those in England. It is worth noting that religiosity in Scotland was much higher than in England. In 1966, for example, the Church of Scotland had two communicants in Scotland for every three attending Anglican Easter Communion in England despite Scotland having only a ninth of England's population.[8] The largest sectarian effect was that for 'other' non-conformists. It was orientated from both Labour and Conservative towards the Liberals. The Free Churches effect also helped the Liberals but mainly at Labour's expense. The Episcopalian effect helped the Conservatives at the expense of both other parties, although it was more of a disadvantage to Labour. Thus the Episcopalian versus Church of Scotland effect was similar in orientation to the Anglican versus non-conformist effect in England, while the Scottish non-conformist and Free Church effects showed the Liberals retaining a non-conformist advantage far longer than they did in England.

In England we made little attempt to estimate a Catholic sectarian effect. The political consequences of Catholicism at any level are complicated by different tendencies among different Catholic traditions and at the aggregate level they are complicated by reactive effects. At the individual level we should distinguish indigenous Catholics drawn to the Conservatives by Conservative links with religiosity and Liberal and Labour links with free thinking and socialism, from immigrant Catholics drawn to Labour and the Liberals by their support for Irish Home Rule and their general concern for working class immigrants. Irish

Table 10
Sectarian Polarisations in Scotland 1918–74

Semi-standardised slopes
(after control for Class and Rurality)

	PRS				FC				EP				NC			
	CON	CEN	LIB	LAB	CON	CEN	LIB	LAB	CON	CEN	LIB	LAB	CON	CEN	LIB	LAB
1918	-4.0	8.3	-4.6	0.3	-1.6	4.8	-0.2	-3.1	0	3.1	-2.3	-0.9	-2.9	5.7	2.8	-5.4
1922	-2.4	-6.6	11.3	-2.4	-1.7	8.5	2.1	-8.7	0.4	-2.5	8.7	-6.4	-1.8	-2.2	8.5	-4.7
1923	-3.3		5.6	-2.2	-3.1		9.0	-5.9	-0.7		3.6	-2.9	-2.2		7.8	-5.6
1924	-4.3		4.8	-0.5	-3.0		7.4	-4.4	2.2		-1.7	-0.5	-11.6		15.0	-3.4
1929	-4.9		2.0	3.0	-4.7		6.1	1.3	-2.6		1.0	1.6	-0.7		5.9	-5.3
1931	-15.4	4.6	9.5	1.4	-1.1	7.6	-0.8	-5.6	3.1	1.8	-2.7	-2.1	-15.1	0.9	17.2	-3.2
1935	-6.5	4.5	2.3	-0.4	-2.9	3.9	3.3	-4.3	2.2	2.3	-4.1	-0.3	-2.5	0.8	8.0	-6.3
1945	-2.5	2.6	3.2	-3.2	-3.2	3.1	2.7	-2.5	-3.3	3.6	1.3	-1.7	-0.5	-1.5	5.7	-3.6
1950	0		0	0	0.8		0.7	-1.6	2.7		-1.4	-1.2	-2.6		5.8	-3.1
1951	1.9		0.3	-2.2	3.0		-1.4	-1.7	2.6		-1.1	-1.5	-3.2		7.1	-3.8
1955	1.0		1.6	-2.4	1.3		1.1	-2.5	2.0		-1.4	-0.8	-3.0		7.0	-3.8
1959	5.0		-0.1	-4.9	-1.1		2.6	-1.4	6.0		-1.7	-4.3	-4.5		8.5	-4.1
1964	-2.7		5.9	-3.1	-0.4		2.5	-2.2	3.7		-1.1	-2.6	-4.8		8.6	-3.8
1966	-0.4		3.5	-3.2	-1.5		3.4	-2.0	2.8		0.2	-3.0	-3.2		7.1	-3.7
1970	0.3		3.6	-4.0	-0.2		1.6	-1.6	3.8		-0.8	-3.0	-3.5		6.8	-3.2

	PRS				FC				EP				NC			
	CON	LIB	LAB	SNP	CON	LIB	LAB	SNP	CON	LIB	LAB	SNP	CON	LIB	LAB	SNP
1974 FEB	-1.7	1.7	-2.1	2.1	-0.9	2.6	-3.7	2.0	-0.4	-0.4	-3.1	3.8	-2.6	7.7	-1.3	-3.9
1974 OCT	-0.9	1.1	-2.6	2.5	2.3	1.0	-3.7	0.5	2.5	-0.3	-2.2	0.2	-2.1	6.9	-1.9	-3.0

Note: Tabulated figures are semi-standardised slopes as in Chapter Five. We revert to this choice particularly because the Free Churches measures of clergy are not directly comparable with other clergy measures. This situation is similar to the Anglican versus non-conformist analyses rather than the non-conformist denominational breakdowns.

Table 11
Size and Orientation of Sectarian Polarisations in Scotland

	Size				Orientation			
	PRS	FC	EP	NC	PRS	FC	EP	NC
1918	3.9	4.1	0.8	7.5	124 C→I	79 *→I	57 L→I	80 *→I
1922	4.1	9.9	6.3	5.6	90 *→I	69 L→I	57 L→I	75 *→I
1923	4.9	8.4	3.3	7.0	96 *→I	80 *→I	70 L→I	76 *→I
1924	5.0	6.5	2.0	13.6	115 C→I	84 *→I	313 I→C	108 C→I
1929	4.4	6.1	1.0	5.6	156 C→*	120 C→I	120 C→I	66 L→I
1931	10.3	6.1	3.7	15.9	126 C→I	353 L→C	326 *→C	110 C→I
1935	2.2	3.9	4.3	7.3	112 C→I	47 L→I	304 I→C	72 L→I
1945	3.2	2.6	1.5	5.0	59 L→I	63 L→I	49 L→I	81 *→I
1950	0	1.4	2.3	5.0	–	27 L→*	328 *→C	87 *→I
1951	1.6	2.6	2.3	6.2	9 L→C	333 *→C	335 *→C	87 *→I
1955	2.2	2.1	1.8	6.1	39 L→*	27 L→*	320 *→C	86 *→I
1959	0.1	2.3	5.4	7.4	–	86 *→I	344 *→C	92 *→I
1964	5.1	2.3	3.3	7.5	88 *→I	67 L→I	343 *→C	94 *→I
1966	3.4	3.0	2.9	6.2	66 L→I	85 *→I	3 L→C	88 *→I
1970	3.8	1.6	3.5	5.9	55 L→I	63 L→I	349 L→C	92 *→I

Note: (1) These figures have been calculated from those in table 10, using the method of Chapter Five.

(2) Each sectarian effect is for that sect compared to the established Church of Scotland. This is an important difference between this Table and those for England which took the established Church of England as the base for comparison. The Scottish Episcopal Church was in communion with the Church of England.

Catholic immigrants also produced indigenous and even imported Protestant reactions. Therefore, at the aggregate level, the partisanship associated with concentrations of Catholicism was an amalgam of a pro-Conservative 'religious' Catholic effect, an anti-Conservative 'ethnic' Catholic effect and a pro-Conservative Protestant reaction. To disentangle and quantify these separate effects would need a better data than we have at hand. We can only note that the net Catholic effect estimated by our regressions was a substantial anti-Conservative pro-Liberal effect between the wars and an anti-Labour, usually pro-Liberal, effect after the Second War. This post-war effect partially reflects the bias in our data against the Catholic non-Liberal area of Lanarkshire (including Glasgow) and its bias towards Catholic areas, like the small towns of Greenock and Paisley and the remote Western Isles where the Liberals did relatively well.

When clergy per capita for each of the five sectarian groups were used to assess the effect of religiosity as well as sect, the results revealed further differences from English patterns. In the multiple regression Labour votes were not associated with a general absence of clergy. Labour was positively linked with Catholic clergy throughout the interwar years, but not afterwards, and with Church of Scotland clergy at most times between 1918 and 1974. Similarly the Con-

servatives were usually linked positively with Church of Scotland and Episcopalian clergy and the Liberals with Free Presbyterian Churches and always
with the non-conformist clergy. None of the three parties in Scotland was clearly
disadvantaged by religiosity.

In the four party contest of 1974 the SNP appeared to share the Catholic and
Free Church sectarian effects with the Liberals, while Episcopalianism discriminated against the Liberals in favour of the SNP and the 'other' non-conformist
effect strongly discriminated against the SNP and in favour of the Liberals.
When the Liberals had a full slate of candidates in October the SNP versus
Liberal effect in Episcopalian areas was eliminated, but the others remained.
Where the bias in favour of the Liberals was already strong, it survived in 1974
producing a compensating anti-SNP bias if only because it blocked the SNP
advance.

4 Trends in Secondary Social Patterns within England 1918–74

4.1 Basic Controls

To assess the influence of a wide variety of social variables on deviations from
general alignments we used five predictors as basic controls; the influence of all
other variables was gauged by calculating the proportion of residual partisan
variation explained after a control for the best of these five predictors and again
after a multiple control for all five basic predictors used simultaneously. This
technique is biased towards those additional predictors of partisanship which are
themselves uncorrelated with the basic predictors and is biased against indicators
that apply to only a very few areas.

The five basic control variables were:

- (1) CL251 : percent Social Class Two in 1951.
- (2) AGRI : percent agriculture in 1931.
- (3) NON = 1 – RANG31: non-conformist clergy in 1931 as a percent of total Anglican plus non-conformist clergy.
- (4) CA = CL251 * AGRI: the product (interaction) of class and agriculture.
- (5) CN = CL251 * NON: the product (interaction) of non-conformity and class.

Of these variables one, two and three are the same as, or equivalent to, those we
have used in the earlier analyses; five is equivalent to the interaction between class
and Anglicanism (which we have used before), but only when used in conjunction
with three, by itself it is somewhat different; and four is new. It allows differential
class effects in urban and rural areas.

Table 12 shows the best of these five predictors for each party and election and
also the proportion of variation explained by it. Later Tables show what fraction
of the remaining variation can be explained by other social variables. For Labour
and Conservative class was always the best of the basic predictors. For the
Liberals the basic control moved from the interaction between class and non-

Table 12
Best Predictor from the Basic Set 1918–74

(England)	CON		LIB		LAB		TURN	
	Pred	R^2	Pred	R^2	Pred	R^2	Pred	R^2
1918	CL251	22	CL251	−6	CL251	−12	CL251	5
1922	CL251	30	CL* NON	8	CL251	−49	NON	4
1923	CL251	37	CL* NON	8	CL251	−44	NON	2
1924	CL251	44	CL* NON	5	CL251	−51	NON	6
1929	CL251	39	CL* AGR	42	CL251	−66	NON	4
1931	CL251	24	CL* AGR	10	CL251	−63	NON	2
1935	CL251	43	CL* AGR	21	CL251	−56	NON	4
1945	CL251	56	CL* AGR	20	CL251	−62	NON	10
1950	CL251	67	CL* AGR	18	CL251	−75	CL* NON	7
1951	CL251	66	CL251	9	CL251	−78	NON	7
1955	CL251	64	CL* AGR	19	CL251	−78	AGRI	5
1959	CL251	51	CL251	31	CL251	−77	AGRI	7
1964	CL251	54	CL251	32	CL251	−71	AGRI	15
1966	CL251	59	CL251	42	CL251	−73	CL251	20
1970	CL251	56	CL251	38	CL251	−71	AGRI	25
1974 FEB	CL251	56	CL251	32	CL251	−67	AGRI	24
1974 OCT	CL251	65	CL* AGR	37	CL251	−67	AGRI	24

Note: Here we follow our usual convention of attaching signs to indicate the directions of effects.
These are *not* adjusted R^2 and the R^2 themselves are all positive.

conformity, through the interaction with agriculture to just class itself. Until the sixties basic predictors explained negligible proportions of turnout variation. Then the best of the basic predictors was usually agriculture.

4.2 The Classes

Table 13 shows how well class variables, including CL251, explained political deviance. On those occasions where CL251 was the basic control it is indicated by an asterisk. Where a variable explained less than 10 % of deviance the exact figure is replaced by a plus or minus sign, or a dot if the exact figure was less than 1 %.

This Table can be used first, to check whether the timing of our basic class variable was critical and second, to check for complex class responses. On the first point it is best to use Labour votes since that party was most closely associated with the employers and managers versus workers division. If CL251, the 1951 measure of the English managerial classes, was significantly out of date by 1966, we should expect a growing negative correlation between residuals and EMPL66 as the years passed from 1951 to 1966. In the event, EMPL66 was always negatively correlated with the residuals, as we should expect of any second measure of the managerial classes, but the correlations were never large and they showed only the slightest tendency to grow. The size of the squared correlation was 6 % in 1951 itself, reached a peak of 11 % as early as 1959 and was

Table 13
Other Classes and Residual Variation 1918–74

YEAR	18	22	23	24	29	31	35	45	50	51	55	59	64	66	70	74F	74 Oct
							% of residual variation explained										
Conservative																	
CL151	19	11	12	21	30	17	25	12	14	+	12	+	+	+	+	+	+
CL251	*	*	*	*	*	*	*	*	*	*	*	*	*	*	*	*	*
CL351	·	+	−	−	·	+	+	+	+	+	+	+	+	+	+	·	+
CL451	−15	−	·	−	−	−	−	+	−	·	·	·	+	+	+	+	+
CL551	+	·	·	·	·	−	−	−	−	−	−12	−13	−18	−27	−28	−20	−24
PROF66	11	+	+	14	21	14	17	+	10	+	11	+	+	+	+	+13	+10
EMPL66	+	+	+	10	14	12	12	+	+	+	12	+	+	11	+	13	·
CLERK66	20	+	+	+	12	12	+	−	−	·	+	+	−	+	−	−	·
SKIL66	−18	−	−10	−18	−22	−11	−13	−	−	−	−	−	+	−	·	−	−
SEMI66	−12	·	−	−	−10	−10	−	−	−	−15	−	−	+	+	+	·	−
UNSK66	·		−	−	−	−	−10	−	−14	−	−19	−20	−23	−37	−36	−29	−35
Labour																	
CL151	−	−	·	·	·	−	−	−	−	−	−	−	−	·	·	·	·
CL251	*	*	*	*	*	*	*	*	*	*	*	*	*	*	*	*	*
CL351	·	·	·	·	+	+	+	·	·	·	·	·	−	−	−	−	−
CL451	+	+	·	−	−	·	−	+	+	+	+	+	+	−	−	−	−14
CL551	·	·	+	+	+	+	+	+	+	+	+	+11	12	11	14	14	18
PROF66	−	−	·	·	·	−	−	·	−	−	−	−	−	·	·	·	+
EMPL66	−	−	·	−	−	−	−	+	−	−	−	−11	−	−11	−10	−	−
CLERK66	−	−10	+	+	+	·	+	·	+	+	+	+	+	+	+	+	16
SKIL66	+	+	·	−	−	+	−	−	·	·	·	·	·	−	·	·	−
SEMI66	+	·	·	−	+	·	+	−	−	−	−	+	+	−	·	+	−
UNSK66	·	·	+	+	+	+	+	+	11	12	11	11	20	17	21	17	20

Table 13 [continued]

YEAR	18	22	23	24	29	31	35	45	50	51	55	59	64	66	70	74F	74 Oct
Liberal																	
CL151	-12	–	–	–	·	–	·	·	+	–	+	·	·	·	–	–	+
CL251	*	–	·	·	+	·	·	+	+	*	+	*	*	*	*	*	*
CL351	·	+	·	·	+	·	·	+	+	·	·	·	+	·	+	·	+
CL451	12	+	+	+	–	+	·	–	–	+	–	+	+	+	·	+	–
CL551	–	·	·	·	–	·	·	–	–	·	·	+	·	+	·	·	–
PROF66	–	–	–	·	·	–	·	·	+	–	·	–	·	–	–	–	+
EMPL66	–	–	–	+	+	–	·	+	+	–	+	–	·	·	+	·	10
CLERK66	-13	–	–	-12	+	–	+	+	·	–	+	·	–	·	–	–	·
SKIL66	+	+	+	+	–	+	+	+	–	+	–	·	+	+	+	+	·
SEMI66	+	+	+	+	–	+	+	–	–	+	·	+	–	+	·	+	·
UNSK66	·	+	–	·	–	+	+	–	–	+	·	+	–	+	·	·	–
Turnout																	
CL151	–	–	–	–	–	–	–	·	–	–	+	–	·	–	–	·	·
CL251	*	·	·	·	·	+	·	+	*	·	+	+	+	*	+	+	+
CL351	+	+	+	+	13	+	+	+	17	23	32	29	26	15	28	37	34
CL451	+	+	+	+	–	+	+	+	+	+	·	·	·	+	·	–	·
CL551	–	–	–	–	–	–	–	-10	–	-13	-19	-15	-22	-30	-29	-32	-27
PROF66	–	–	–	–	–	–	–	·	–	–	·	·	+	–	+	+	+
EMPL66	–	-19	-20	-12	-26	-12	-20	+	–	–	·	·	+	–	+	+	+
CLERK66	-12	18	18	20	35	16	25	15	28	22	14	18	10	25	·	·	12
SKIL66	23	18	+	–	+	·	+	–	·	–	–	–	–	·	·	·	12
SEMI66	·	+	–	–	–	–	·	–	–	–	–	–	–	·	·	-11	–
UNSK66	–	–	–	–	–	–	·	-10	–	-12	-16	-13	-22	-26	-27	-28	-25

Note: (1) '+' represents any positive value less than 10%, '–' any negative value under 10%, '·' represents zero.

(2) '*' indicates that this predictor, or any interactive term involving this predictor, was the single best predictor giving the basic explanation of partisan variation.

(3) 1951 classes: CL151 = professional, CL251 = intermediate, CL351 = skilled, CL451 = partly skilled, CL551 = unskilled. Only CL151 is entirely non-manual and CL551 entirely manual.

(4) 1966 classes: as in Chapter Two. The first three are non-manual.

down to 3% in 1974. Temporal inaccuracies in the basic class measure seem unimportant.

Much greater class effects show up in both 1951 and 1966 class measures. There was a long term trend towards pro-Labour anti-Conservative deviance in areas of unskilled workers. This effect stayed less than 10% between the wars, went above 10% in the forties and fifties and then took a quantum jump in the sixties. Two interwar class effects died away: the Conservatives' advantage in professional areas and their disadvantage in skilled working class areas.

Other classes had little effect on Liberal deviance but a lot on turnout. There was a long term trend, again in three stages, towards low turnout in unskilled working class areas. Between the wars turnout was high in skilled manual working class areas but deviantly low in routine non-manual areas. Over time the negative deviance of the non-manuals disappeared but the positive skilled working class effect persisted longer.

4.3 Sect and Religiosity

We have examined the effects of sect and religiosity in great detail, but Table 14 presents these effects in a form that enables comparison with other effects.

The basic predictor of Liberal voting in the early twenties was the interaction between class and non-conformity; at all other times until 1950 non-conformity correlated positively with Liberal deviations but the effect died out in the fifties. Meanwhile the correlation between religiosity and Liberal deviations which was only intermittent until 1959 was evident at every election thereafter and passed 10% in 1974. Both non-conformity and religiosity were consistently, if only slightly, correlated with high turnout.

There were larger correlations between non-conformity and Labour and Conservative voting deviations. Non-conformity always helped Labour and damaged the Conservatives. There was no trend in the size of the partial correlations with Conservative votes, though there was a temporary lull throughout the fifties, but the correlation with Labour deviations increased over time.

The largest correlations were between religiosity and anti-Labour deviations. Always negative, these explained around a quarter of Labour residual variation from 1923 onwards and they reached a maximum in 1974. Religiosity always correlated positively with Conservatiive deviations though not as strongly as with anti-Labour deviations.

4.4 Sect, Religiosity, Language and National Effects in England and Wales

Extending the data set to include Wales, we can repeat the analysis of main and secondary influences using the same methods but adding other non-religious cultural variables, particularly language and Welsh nationalism. Table 15 shows some of the results.

In all years class was the best predictor of Labour voting; the pattern of basic Liberal predictions, moving from the interaction between class and non-conformity, to the interaction with agriculture, to class itself, reflected English

Table 14
Sect, Religiosity and Residual Variation 1918–74

% of residual variation explained

YEAR	18	22	23	24	29	31	35	45	50	51	55	59	64	66	70	74F	74Oct
Conservative																	
NON	−	−13	−16	−15	−17	−	−16	−18	−12	−	−	−	−14	−12	−17	−13	−18
RELIG	+	+	16	+	11	+	10	21	10	12	+	+	13	14	15	11	15
Labour																	
NON	+	+	+	+	14	13	10	+	14	+	+	10	10	17	15	20	17
RELIG	−	−	−17	−22	−31	−25	−19	−29	−25	−20	−18	−19	−22	−28	−26	−31	−38
Liberal																	
NON	+	*	*	*	+	+	+	+	+	.	+	.	.	−	.	−	.
RELIG	.	.	+	+	.	.	.	+	+	.	.	+	+	+	+	10	11
Turnout																	
NON	+	*	*	*	*	*	*	*	*	*	+	+	+	.	+	+	+
RELIG	+	+	+	+	+	+	+	+	.	+	+	+	+	+	+	+	+

Note: (1) NON = non-conformist clergy as a proportion of total Anglican plus non-conformist clergy.
(2) RELIG = total Anglican plus Catholic plus non-conformist clergy per capita of population.

Table 15
Culture in England and Wales 1918–74

	18	22	23	24	29	31	35	45	50	'51	55	59	64	66	70	74F	74 Oct
Conservative																	
Best Predictor	NON in all years																
R²	−23	−29	−29	−28	−27	−20	−26	−30	−23	−22	−22	−23	−26	−24	−32	−26	−26
% of residual variation explained																	
NON	*	*	*	*	*	*	*	*	*	*	*	*	*	*	*	*	*
RELIG	−	−	.	−	+	.	.	.	+	.	−	−	.	+	.	+	+
WALES	−14	−	−	−	−	−	−	−12	−	−10	−18	−21	−	−	−12	−	−
ENG MON	10	12	+	16	+	+	17	18	12	15	22	22	11	+	17	+	+
WELSH MON	−	−	−	−	−	−	−	−	−	−	−12	−15	−	−	−10	−	−
WESLH BIL	−10	−10	−	−16	−	−	−17	−18	−10	−14	−20	−10	−	−	−14	−	−
Labour																	
Best Predictor	CL251 in all years																
R²	−13	−34	−41	−41	−59	−47	−39	−53	−61	−62	−59	−54	−53	−57	−56	−52	−54
% of residual variation explained																	
NON	+	14	+	14	24	22	18	12	26	24	22	26	25	28	14	30	28
RELIG	−	+	−	−	−	−	−	−	−	.	.	.	.	−	−	−	−
WALES	+	19	+	14	13	19	14	11	25	29	28	36	30	23	+	18	17
ENG MON	−	−23	−	−16	−17	−21	−20	−16	−25	−32	−28	−33	−29	−28	−10	−21	−18
WELSH MON	.	16	+	+	+	+	+	+	+	+	+	10	+	10	+	+	+
WELSH BILL	+	18	+	15	16	22	23	19	31	36	31	36	32	29	+	23	21

Table 15 [continued]

Liberal

Best Predictor R²	CN 18	CN 35	CN 32	CN 33	CN 49	CN 24	CA 27	CA 49	CA 43	CN 50	CA 32	C 44	C 39	C 44	C 48	C 30	CA 37
	% of residual variation explained																
NON	*	*	*	*	+	*	+	12	11	*	+	·	·	–	·	–	–
RELIG	+	+	+	+	+	10	+	10	+	15	+	+	·	+	+	·	·
WALES	14	+	+	+	+	+	11	17	12	+	10	·	–	·	·	–	–10
ENG MON	–	–	–	–	–	–10	–22	–19	–28	–14	–32	–	·	·	·	11	12
WELSH MON	+	·	+	+	+	+	16	11	22	12	21	+	+	+	·	–	–
WELSH BIL	+	+	+	+	+	+	18	17	21	+	27	+	–	+	·	–	–10

Note: (1) MON = monoglot, BIL = bilingual, CN = CL251*NON, CA = CL251*AGRI, C = CL251.
(2) CN was the best predictor of Plaid Cymru voting in both 1974 elections, explaining 26% each time. The percentages of residual variation explained by the other variables were:—

	NON	RELIG	WALES	ENG MON	WELSH MON	WELSH BIL
FEB	*	5	33	–56	48	34
OCT	*	6	30	–57	57	31

trends. However in England and Wales non-conformity, or the lack of it, was always the single best basic predictor of Conservative votes.

The Table uses three indicators of language: the percent English monoglots which is equivalent to the percent speaking Welsh (= 100% – ENGMON); the percent Welsh monoglots which is equivalent to the percent able to use English (= 100% – WELSHMON); and the percent bilingual. It also uses a dummy variable indicating whether units were in England or Wales.

At different times non-conformity, English monoglots and Welsh bilinguals were the best explanations of Labour deviations; the degree of explanation ranged between a fifth and a third. In the sixties Welsh bilinguals were the best explanation of pro-Labour deviation, but non-conformity was best in 1970 and 1974.

Since non-conformity was the basic predictor of Conservative voting it could not explain any deviance. Correlations with residuals were smaller than for Labour; linguistic indicators were more powerful than national and effects were small in all but one of the five elections since 1964.

Non-conformity also appeared in basic predictions of Liberal voting and when it did other cultural variables explained only small proportions of the residual. However, linguistic variables, particularly English monoglots or general Welsh speaking, were strongly correlated with Liberal deviations from 1935 to 1955. Welsh speaking helped the Liberals; but with the renewed support for English Liberals from 1959 onwards, this effect died out and in 1974 pro-Liberal deviations correlated with England and English monoglots.

It is not altogether surprising that even when the basic predictor was the interaction between class and non-conformity, the Welsh nation explained about a third of pro-Welsh Nationalist deviations in 1974. After all, they got no votes in England. However the Welsh national indicator was a relatively poor explanation of Welsh Nationalist (Plaid Cymru) votes which correlated most strongly with Welsh speaking (negatively with English monoglots). Even allowing for class and non-conformity Welsh speaking explained over half the residual. Significantly, Welsh monoglots was almost as powerful a predictor of Plaid Cymru success, whereas the correlation with bilinguals was far lower. This contrasts with the opposite pattern for Labour.

4.5 English Regions

Restricting the data set once again to England, we can examine the trends in regional explanations of partisan deviations. These were always weak except for three effects. First, a growing long term trend towards pro-Labour deviation in Inner London which, by 1974, explained a fifth of the residual. In 1918, 1922 and as late as 1931 Inner London had deviated against Labour. Meanwhile pro-Conservative deviation in London between the wars became anti-Conservative after the Second War. Apart from these trends, the only other large regional effects were two sizeable correlations with turnout. Turnout was so deviantly high in the North West throughout the interwar period that it explained about an eighth of turnout variation. In Inner London turnout was so low that this one region always explained over a quarter of turnout deviations. This effect intensified so that from 1959 onwards the difference between low turnouts in London and higher turnouts elsewhere explained almost half the residual. Against this background all the other regions, except for the South East between the wars, had relatively high turnouts.

All other regional effects were slight because the regions were small or their deviance small, or both. Some regions showed consistent, stable deviations even if they were small. The West Midlands were always pro-Conservative and anti-Labour. The South West was always pro-Liberal and anti-Labour. Yorkshire/Humberside nearly always deviated against the Conservatives and the South East towards them. The Liberals were always weak in Inner London. Others showed long term trends: the East Midlands from anti-Conservative to pro-Conservative, the North West from nothing or pro-Conservative to anti-Conservative.

4.6 The Urban-Rural Dimension

We have used two indicators of the urban-rural dimension. First, the percent in agriculture was a basic predictor and was indeed the best of the basic predictors for Liberal votes at seven elections (including the interaction between class and agriculture) and turnout at six elections. It explained relatively little of Conservative deviations, although there was a trend from Conservative disadvantages in agricultural areas between the wars to advantages after the Second War. Labour did badly in agricultural areas especially in 1929 and increasingly from 1966 onwards.

The second indicator was simply the number of persons per acre. This did not correlate so very highly with agriculture ($R = -0.51$, $R^2 = -26\%$). It correlated more with indicators of housing amenity and house tenure. We could also discuss it under the heading of affluence. It was an indicator that combined the rural versus urban distinction at one end with a suburban versus urban versus compact city distinction at the other. Correlations with persons per acre showed a sharp rise in anti-Conservative pro-Labour deviation in densely populated areas during the sixties. Density was also an increasingly good predictor of turnout: from 1918 to 1951 it explained about two-fifths of turnout deviations, but from 1959 onwards about two-thirds. Agriculture was the basic turnout predictor from 1955 onwards, except for 1966 when it was class; but irrespective of this control, the density still explained close to two-thirds of the residual. Since it was so much more powerful than any of the basic predictors, we should note that by itself population density explained almost three-quarters of all turnout variation at each election from 1964 onwards. It was a more powerful predictor of turnout than class was of the Labour share of the vote.

There was a technical reason for density accompanying low turnout. Electors could change their address but still vote at a nearby polling station only if they moved within a single parliamentary constituency. In densely populated places constituencies were small in area and a move of a few miles could be sufficient to make it inconvenient to return to the elector's old address for voting. However,

TABLE 16
Regions and Residual Variation 1918–74

YEAR	18	22	23	24	29	31	35	45	50	51	55	59	64	66	70	74F	74Oct
							% of residual variation explained										
Conservative																	
N	−	−	·	·	−	−	−	·	−	·	·	·	·	·	·	+	·
YH	−	−	−	−	−	·	−	−	−	·	·	·	·	·	−	·	−
EM	−	−	·	−	−	−	·	·	·	·	·	·	+	+	+	+	+
EA	+	·	·	·	−	+	+	+	+	+	·	·	+	+	+	·	+
SE	·	+	·	·	·	−	−	·	·	+	·	+	−	·	·	·	·
SW	·	−	+	−	·	·	+	+	+	·	−	−	+	·	·	·	·
WM	+	+	·	+	·	·	+	+	+	+	+	+	−	+	+	+	+
NW	·	+	+	+	·	+	·	−	+	+	+	−	−	−	−	−	−
Inner L	10	−	+	+	+	+	·	−	−	−	−	−	·	−10	−	−	−
Labour																	
N	·	·	·	+	·	·	·	−	−	−	−	·	·	·	·	+	·
YH	·	·	·	−	+	·	·	+	·	·	·	·	·	·	+	·	·
EM	+	+	+	+	+	+	+	+	·	+	·	·	·	+	·	−	·
EA	−	+	·	·	−	·	−	−	·	·	+	·	·	−	−	−	−
SE	·	−	·	·	·	+	+	−	·	·	·	·	·	−	−	·	−
SW	·	−	−	−	·	·	−	−	·	·	−	−	−	−	−	−	·
WM	·	·	−	−	·	·	−	−	·	·	−	−	−	−	−	−	−
NW	+	+	−	−	−	·	−	−	·	−	−	·	·	·	·	−	−
Inner L	−	−	·	+	·	−	·	+	+	+	+	+	13	10	14	11	19

Table 16 [continued]

Liberal

N	+	+	·	·	+	+	+	+	+	+	+	·	·	–	+	–10	·
YH	+	+	+	+	·	·	+	+	·	·	·	–	·	·	·	·	·
EM	+	+	·	·	·	–	–	–	–	–	·	·	–	–	+	–	–
EA	+	·	·	+	·	–	–	–	·	–	–12	·	·	·	–	–	–
SE	–	–	·	·	+	–	–	·	·	·	+13	·	+	+	+	+	+
SW	·	+	+	+	+	10	+	+	+	+	·	+	+	+	+	+	12
WM	–	–	–	·	·	·	·	·	·	·	–	·	·	+	·	–	·
NW	–	–	·	–	–	·	·	+	·	·	–	·	+	·	+	+	+
Inner L	–	·	·	–	–	·	·	–	–	·	·	·	–	–	–	–	–

Turnover

N	+	+	+	+	+	+	12	+	+	+	+	+	+	+	+	+	+
YH	·	·	·	·	+	+	·	+	+	·	·	·	·	+	·	·	·
EM	+	+	+	+	+	+	+	+	+	+	+	+	+	+	+	+	+
EA	·	·	+	+	+	·	+	·	·	·	·	+	+	+	·	+	+
SE	–	·	+	+	+	·	–12	–	·	+	+	+	+	+	+	+	+
SW	+	+	·	·	+	+	+	+	·	+	+	+	+	+	+	+	+
WM	+	+	+	+	+	+	13	+	+	·	·	·	·	·	·	·	+
NW	14	13	12	14	10	12	13	10	+	+	+	·	+	+	+	+	+
Inner L	–28	–42	–37	–27	–47	–39	–31	–32	–40	–31	–38	–48	–50	–48	–46	–40	–47

Table 17
Rurality and Residual Variation 1918–74

		18	22	23	24	29	31	35	45	50	51	55	59	64	66	70	74F	74 Oct
% of residual variation explained																		
Conservative																		
	AGRI	−10	−	.	.	−	−	.	+	.	+	.	+	10	+	14	+	+
	PPA	+	+	.	.	+	−	−	−	−	−	−	−	−	−20	−16	−15	−15
Labour																		
	AGRI	.	+	−	−	−20	−	−10	−10	−	−	−	−	−	−13	−13	−21	−25
	PPA	−	−	+	+	+	.	+	+	+	13	11	+	16	12	18	17	26
Liberal																		
	AGRI	10	.	+	+	*	*	*	*	*	.	*	.	.	+	+	11	*
	PPA	−	.	.	.	.	.	.	−10	−	.	.	.	−	−	−	−	−
Turnout																		
	AGRI	.	+	+	+	+	+	+	+	.	+	*	*	*	+	*	*	*
	PPA	−36	−42	−37	−26	−41	−40	−34	−40	−44	−39	−56	−65	−72	−67	−69	−65	−68

Note: AGRI = percent in agriculture 1931, PPA = persons per acre 1931.

this seems likely to explain only a part of the link between density and low turnout and it does nothing at all to explain the sharp increase in the correlation during the late fifties and early sixties.

4.7 Education

Education levels in 1951 were measured by the proportions with minimal schooling and with formal education beyond the age of seventeen. In 1951 itself education had very little effect on voting; but if the 1951 indicators can be taken as a guide to areas which had relatively high and low education levels for generations, then there was evidence that the Conservatives had done particularly well between the wars in areas of high educational attainment. Despite low sizes, the signs of correlations with party deviations were the ones we should expect: low education areas were biased against the Conservatives and towards Labour and the opposite was true for high education.

Not so obvious were the correlations with turnout deviations. They were always small and died away in the seventies, but they indicated higher turnouts in areas of low education. This could not be deduced from patterns among individuals in sample surveys, but was in agreement with the urban rural patterns. Comparing individuals in the same environment, the more educated might be more likely to vote but the patterns of work and living that went with high community levels of education went with low turnout.

4.8 The Property Owning Democracy

As measures of affluence and property ownership we have the house tenure variables and car ownership measured in 1966 and used in the constituency analyses. Earlier censuses were not so rich in such indicators, but we have taken the percent of households with 'full amenities' in 1951 and the number of persons per room in 1931.

Between the wars, none of these provided much of an explanation of partisan deviance. Those that did very occasionally explain over 10% of residual variation were 1966 measures. There is little doubt for example that Labour voting between the wars correlated strongly with 1931 persons per room, but only in as much as that stood as a surrogate for class. Persons per room was only weakly correlated with pro-Labour deviations from the class alignment.

After the Second War however, indicators from all the censuses began to correlate more strongly with Labour and Conservative deviations. Had we found, for example, that council housing in 1966 correlated with pro-Labour deviations in 1966, but equally well with pro-Labour deviations in earlier years before the houses had even been built, we might have concluded that Labour councils were more prone to build council houses i.e. that the direction of causation ran from politics to house tenure. This was not the pattern.

Not only did the socially patterned deviances spring up after the Second War and increase in size, but the best predictors of these deviances were 1931 persons per room and 1966 car ownership, widely separated in time but both measures of which places were more or less affluent. The affluent deviated to the Con-

Table 18
Education and Residual Variation 1918–74

% of residual variation explained

YEAR	18	22	23	24	29	31	35	45	50	51	55	59	64	66	70	74F	74 Oct
Conservative																	
LSU 15	−21	−	−	−14	−18	−	−14	−	−	−	−	−	−	−	−	−	−
LSO 17	20	11	12	20	29	14	19	+	+	+	+	+	+	+	+	+	+
Labour																	
LSU 15	+	+	+	+	+	+	+	·	+	+	+	+	+	+	·	·	·
LSO 17	−	−	−	·	·	−	−	·	−	−	−	−	·	·	·	+	+
Liberal																	
LSU 15	11	+	·	+	−	·	·	·	−	+	−	·	·	·	+	+	−
LSO 17	−12	−	−	−	·	−	·	·	+	−	+	·	−	−	−	−	+
Turnout																	
LSU 15	+	+	+	+	13	+	+	+	+	+	+	+	·	+	·	·	·
LSO 17	−	−	−	−	−14	−	−	−	−12	−	−	−	−	−13	·	·	−

Note: (1)LSU 15 = percent of adult population who had left school at fifteen or less in 1951 i.e. with minimum education.
(2)LSO 17 = percent who finished education at seventeen or over, including university and further education graduates.

Table 19
The Property Owning Democracy and Residual Variation 1918-74

% of residual variations explained

YEAR	18	22	23	24	29	31	35	45	50	51	55	59	64	66	70	74F	74 Oct
Conservative																	
PPR31	+	·	-	-	-	-	-10	-12	-20	-25	-22	-12	-14	-27	-28	-19	-33
AMEN51	·	·	+	+	+	+	+	+	+	+	14	+	+	15	+	14	11
COUN66	-	-	-	-	-	-	-	-	-11	-12	-12	-	-	+	+	+	+
OWN66	-	-	+	+	-	·	+	·	+	·	+	+	+	-	+	+	+
RENT66	14	10	+	+	+	+	+	-	+	·	+	·	·	-	-	-	-
CAR66	+	+	+	+	+	+	+	-	+	+	+	+	12	18	23	15	25
Labour																	
PPR31	·	·	+	+	+	+	+	12	14	21	22	18	27	24	30	32	34
AMEN51	+	+	+	·	+	·	+	+	+	-12	-	-	-10	-	-	-	-
COUN66	·	+	+	+	+	·	·	+	+	10	12	+	+	+	+	+	+
OWN66	+	+	·	·	·	+	+	+	-	+	-	+	-15	-10	-16	-14	-18
RENT66	+	+	·	+	+	+	+	-	-	+	-	·	+	+	+	+	12
CAR66	+	-	+	-	-21	-	-10	-	-	-	-	-12	-21	-24	-24	-23	-26
Liberal																	
PPR31	-	+	·	·	+	+	·	-	+	+	·	-	+	-	-	-	-11
AMEN51	·	-	-	-	-	·	·	11	+	·	·	·	+	·	·	-	+
COUN66	·	+	·	·	+	+	·	·	+	+	-	·	12	+	+	-	10
OWN66	+	·	·	+	+	·	·	15	+	·	+	·	-	-	-	+	14
RENT66	-	-	-	·	+	·	·	-	-	-	+	·	-	+	+	-	-
CAR66	-	-	-	·	+	-	-	+	+	-	+	+	+	+	+	+	+
Turnout																	
PPR31	-26	-15	-14	-10	-16	-15	-	-18	-14	-18	-28	-25	-33	-45	-42	-44	-41
AMEN51	18	23	15	15	17	25	17	28	27	23	31	40	52	31	53	53	54
COUN66	·	·	·	·	·	·	·	·	·	·	·	·	-11	·	-13	-14	-11
OWN66	31	30	25	21	36	29	23	34	48	41	50	55	59	56	58	65	65
RENT66	-25	-33	-30	-28	-46	-27	-31	-26	-50	-43	-40	-50	-45	-50	-39	-45	-51
CAR66	·	·	·	·	+	·	·	+	+	+	+	+	+	16	10	16	12

servatives, the others to Labour.

House tenure in 1966 and housing amenity in 1951 were quite good explanations of turnout variations. However, the areas which had high rates of owner occupation in 1966 had experienced high turnouts since 1918; similarly, house renting areas of 1966 had experienced low turnouts. Both correlations increased in the fifties. Turnout was always low where 1931 persons per room was high and usually high where 1966 car ownership was high; once again both correlations increased at the end of the fifties. Car ownership was always the least effective of these turnout predictors. Despite increases in all these correlations during the late fifties and sixties, their long history, and even the sharpness of the increases when they occurred, suggests that what produced these patterns was at once more fundamental and more potentially volatile than changes in the hardware of domestic living. Quite obviously the tenure patterns of 1966 were not the tenure patterns of 1918. Moreover, there was no tendency for affluence indicators to be specially effective predictors close to the date of their definition, which would have suggested a mechanistic link with politics. Rather, the evidence suggests: first, that after the Second War there was an increasing partisan polarisation between the perennially 'have not' areas and the 'haves'; and second, that the long term turnout polarisation which had been moderately strong between the wars intensified during the fifties.

4.9 Unemployment

Unemployment was measured in 1931, 1951, and 1966. The general level of unemployment was very low in 1951 and 1966 (1.0% and 1.2% respectively for England) while 1931 was close to the height of the depression. There is an extensive literature which claims that parties are automatically penalised for being in power during high unemployment.[9] Even on a national aggregate time series basis, the evidence for this is open to question. In terms of spatial distributions it was remarkable how little impact local unemployment made on local partisanship. Unemployment never correlated to any extent with deviations from basic, usually class, alignments. What has sometimes confused this question is that unemployment, especially in 1931, was correlated with working class areas which voted Labour for class reasons. Our class measure CL251 correlated at -0.54 with 1931 unemployment, -0.13 with 1951 and -0.18 with 1966.

Though effects were small there was a general tendency for areas of unemployment to deviate towards Labour. Between the wars this was true for 1931 unemployment areas and later for all unemployment areas. The correlations were largest in the seventies. Although Labour was in office between 1929 and 1931 when unemployment increased most rapidly, there was no evidence that areas of high unemployment gravitated towards Labour's opponents in an act of retribution, nor did they move towards Labour in an act of fear. Interwar unemployment explained just 4% of pro-Labour deviance in 1929 and 3% in 1931. This does not mean that the country at large did not hold Labour responsible for the depression or, more especially, for its inability to face a crisis. The (unadjusted) Labour vote in England went down by 7%, from 37%

Table 20
Unemployment and Residual Variation 1918-74

% of residual variation

YEAR	18	22	23	24	29	31	35	45	50	51	55	59	64	66	70	74F	74 Oct
Conservative																	
UN31	−	−	−	−	−	−10	−	·	·	·	·	−	−	·	−	·	−
UN51	+	·	·	·	·	−	−	+	·	−	−	·	−	−	−	−	−
UN66	·	·	·	·	·	−	−	·	·	−	−	−	−	−	−11	−	−10
Labour																	
UN31	+	+	+	+	+	+	+	−	·	·	·	+	+	+	+	+	+
UN51	−	−	·	·	·	·	·	·	·	·	+	+	+	+	+	13	11
UN66	−	·	·	+	+	·	·	·	+	·	+	+	+	+	+	+	10
Liberal																	
UN31	+	+	·	·	·	+	+	·	·	+	−	·	·	−	·	−10	−
UN51	−	·	·	·	·	+	+	−	·	·	·	−	−	−	·	−	·
UN66	·	·	·	·	·	+	+	−	·	·	·	·	−	·	·	−	·
Turnout																	
UN31	+	+	+	+	+	+	11	+	·	·	·	·	·	·	·	−	·
UN51	−13	−12	−12	−13	−21	−	−10	−13	−31	−31	−29	−26	−19	−29	−14	−21	−19
UN66	−	−	−	−	−	−	−	−	−21	−21	−18	−18	−16	−21	−10	−18	−14

in 1929 to 30% in 1931. But it does mean that this loss was not concentrated in areas of high or low unemployment. Either unemployment itself was less important than the Labour government's general incompetence revealed by the economic crisis, or those still with a job were as incensed as those who actually suffered the unemployment or greater bitterness in unemployed areas was offset by the details of the crisis in 1931 which included a strong Labour commitment to maintain or increase state unemployment benefits. All three explanations would be consistent with the data.

The largest correlations with unemployment were between deviantly low turnout and post Second World War unemployment. Turnout had always been low in 1951 unemployment areas, but the correlation increased very sharply in 1950; at the same time low turnout began to correlate noticeable with 1966 unemployment. The values fluctuated, but roughly a quarter of turnout deviations could be explained by post-war unemployment.

4.10 Immigration

New Commonwealth, specifically coloured, immigration began in large numbers at the start of the sixties; but the problem of immigration does not depend upon any particular set of immigrants. Any movement that imports obviously different, unassimilatable characteristics is likely to provoke an indigenous reaction. Moreover there may be a tendency for certain areas to be transit areas for successive waves of immigration. In England we have coded 1931 immigrants from Northern and Southern Ireland, and 1966 immigrants from the New Commonwealth. The correlation between 1966 Commonwealth immigrants and 1931 Southern Irish was 0.40, although the Northern Irish were located in very different areas.

In party terms, the outstanding feature was pro-Conservative deviance between the wars which correlated with Irish, particularly Southern Irish immigrants. Although both other parties suffered in Irish areas, the correlations with anti-Liberal deviance were greater throughout the twenties. This Irish immigrant effect died out gradually after the Second War eventually left a slight pro-Labour deviance. There was also an increasing pro-Labour deviance associated with high levels of Commonwealth immigration. This was particularly evident in the seventies by which time Labour had succeeded in keeping immigrants out, even more effectively than the Conservatives, while avoiding too much offence to the immigrants who had already arrived.

As we noted in the constituency analyses, areas of Commonwealth immigration were quite strongly associated with low turnout and this effect grew from the mid-fifties to the mid-sixties. However Table 21 shows that these same areas had been even more deviant towards low turnouts between the wars. Immigrant areas simply maintained a long standing tradition of low turnout.

4.11 Sector and Industry

Table 22 shows correlations between political deviance and industry. Ten industries, all measured in 1931, are used; they may be divided into the basic or

Table 21
Immigration and Residual Variation 1918–74

% of residual variation explained

Year →	18	22	23	24	29	31	35	45	50	51	55	59	64	61	70	74F	74 Oct
Conservative																	
NI31	10	+	+	12	16	+	+	+	11	15	10	+	+	+	·	+	+
EIRE31	19	18	14	18	29	11	14	+	13	+	+	+	+	+	·	·	·
CIMM66	15	+	·	+	+	+	·	−	−	−	−	−	−	−	−	−	−
Labour																	
NI31	·	−	−	·	−	−	−	−	−	−	−	−	·	·	·	+	+
EIRE31	·	−	·	·	−	−	−	·	−	−10	−	−	+	·	+	+	+
CIMM66	−	−	·	·	·	·	·	+	+	+	+	+	+	+	12	11	18
Liberal																	
NI31	−	−	−	−	−	·	·	·	+	·	·	−	−	−	−	−	·
EIRE31	−18	−11	−	−11	−	−	·	−	·	−	·	−	−	−	−	−	·
CIMM66	−11	−	−	−	·	·	·	−	−	−	+	·	−	−	−	−	−
Turnout																	
NI31	−	−	−	·	−	·	·	·	·	·	·	·	·	·	·	−	·
EIRE31	−	−10	−	−	−22	−	−10	−	−21	−22	−14	−17	−10	−26	−	−	−
CIMM66	−21	−41	−35	−26	−39	−39	−41	−26	−25	−19	−18	−32	−39	−36	−30	−20	−29

Table 22
Special Industries and Residual Variation 1918—74

% of residual variation explained

Year →	18	22	23	24	29	31	35	45	50	51	55	59	64	66	70	74F	74 Oct
Conservative																	
AGRI	-10	-	·	·	-	-	·	·	·	+	·	+	10	+	14	+	+
MIN	-	-	·	-	-	-	-	+	-	-	-	-	-	·	·	+	·
MET	·	·	+	+	·	·	+	·	+	+	+	+	+	+	+	+	+
ELEC	18	12	+	+	+	+	+	·	+	·	+	·	·	·	-	-	-
TEXT	-	-	-	-	-	-	-	-	·	·	·	-	-	-14	-16	-11	-15
TRAN	+	+	-	-	·	-	-	-	-	-	-	-	-	-	-	·	+
FIN	10	+	·	·	+	+	+	+	·	-	·	·	-	-	-10	-	-
ADMIN	+	+	+	+	+	+	+	+	+	+	+	+	+	+	+	+	+
PROF	19	+	+	14	22	12	12	+	+	+	+	+	·	·	·	·	·
RET	+	+	+	+	+	+	+	10	+	+	+	+	+	+	+	+	+
Labour																	
AGRI	·	+	-	-	-20	-	-10	-10	-	-	-	-	-	-13	-13	-21	-25
MIN	+	+	+	+	+	+	+	·	+	+	+	+	+	+	+	+	·
MET	+	·	·	·	+	·	·	12	·	-	·	-	-	-	-	-	-
ELEC	+	-	+	+	+	+	+	·	+	+	+	·	+	+	+	+	11
TEXT	+	+	·	·	+	+	+	-	·	-	+	·	·	·	·	·	·
TRAN	-	-	-	·	·	·	+	-	+	+	-	+	+	+	14	14	17
FIN	·	-	+	+	+	+	+	+	+	+	+	+	+	12	14	19	26
ADMIN	·	-	-	·	-	-	-	+	-	-	-	-	·	-	-	-	-
PROF	·	-	·	+	+	-	-	+	·	+	+	·	·	+	+	+	·
RET	·	-	-	-	-	-	-	-	-	+	+	-	-	-	-	-	10

Table 22 [continued]

	C1	C2	C3	C4	C5	C6	C7	C8	C9	C10	C11	C12	C13	C14	C15	C16
Liberal																
AGRI	*	11	+	+	·	·	*	·	*	*	*	*	+	+	·	10
MIN	·			·	·	·	·	·	+	·						·	·	·	·	·
MET	·			·			+	·			·	·							·	·	·	−22
ELEC	·											·			·	+					−12			−13	+
TEXT	+	+	+	+	+	·	·	+	+			+	+	+	+	+		
TRAN						·			·	+	·	·			·	·	·	·	·	·	
FIN								·	+			+	+	+	+								
ADMIN	+					·					·			·	·	·	·	·	·				
PROF	+	·	·	·					·			+	·	·	·							−13
RET	13	−12							+	+	+	+	+	+	+	·	+	·		
Turnout																
AGRI	*	*	*	+	*	*	*	+	·	+	+	+	+	+	+	18
MIN	+	+	+	+	+	+	+	+	+	+	+	+	+	+	+	−
MET	+	+	+	+	+	+	+	+	12	15	18	14	16	13	14	15
ELEC	·	+	·			·	·	·	·					−10	−18	−10	−21	−21	−
TEXT	·	+	10	+	11	12	11	+	12	15	14	13	13	13	14	15
TRAN	−33	−33	−34	−34	−32	−31	−32	−26	−28	−28	−27	−31	−22	−27	−27	−25
FIN	·	+	·	−10	·			·			−10					−14			−14	−11		
ADMIN																																	
PROF	·	+	+			·			·					·											
RET	+	+	+	+	+	·	+	+	·	+	+	·	·	+	+	+

primary industries of mining and agriculture; the secondary or manufacturing industries of metals, textiles, electrical, and transport; and finally, the tertiary or pen-pushing industries of finance, public administration and the professions. The ultimate industry, being retired, is also included. All measures were for males as a proportion of the male workforce. Females in textiles were also used but produced results so similar to the pattern for male textile workers that they have not been separately recorded.

Of these industry measures several are closely related to class. The professions are really an ambiguous indicator, being both a class and an industry. Finance and administration include the lowest status employees in these industries. So although finance has a strong class bias it is to clerks rather than financiers. Similarly agriculture and mining include farm and mine managers. Concentrations of the retired reflect the ability of some retired people to come together, thus producing a class bias.

Industries were also biased regionally. The four most notable biases, in order from largest to smallest, were: textiles and the North West; transport and London; agriculture and East Anglia; and finally, metals and the West Midlands.

The electrical industry was an indicator of prosperous new industry. In the depression unemployment never went beyond 16% in electrical engineering even when shipbuilding had rates of over 60%. It was located near London and the South East and correlated spatially with clerks and finance.

Because industries were different in location, type of work and prosperity, we might expect that political deviance might vary by individual industry rather than by sector. Agriculture and mining might both be primary sector industries but their associations with Labour were notoriously different. The closest approximation to sector effects was on turnout where both primary sector industries correlated with high turnout and all tertiary sector industries with low turnout. However these were small correlations; the largest were positive links between turnout and metals and textiles and negative links with transport and electrical, all secondary sector industries.

Most correlations with party deviance were small but they were frequently consistent over time. Mining always correlated with pro-Labour deviance and almost always with anti-Conservative. Agriculture has been discussed already, but was almost always anti-Labour and pro-Liberal, latterly pro-Conservative as well. It was the best of the industrial predictors of party deviance.

Metals showed few non-zero correlations between the wars but consistent pro-Conservative anti-Labour correlations after the Second War. The electrical industry went with anti-Liberal deviance, textiles with pro-Liberal anti-Conservative and transport with increasing pro-Labour anti-Conservative deviations.

The Conservatives always did a little better and Labour worse in public administration and retired areas. Liberals, too, did better in retirement areas. In 1918 there was a relatively strong pro-Conservative anti-Liberal correlation in professional areas which died away by the end of the twenties and was replaced a generation later by pro-Labour anti-Liberal correlations. Finally, there was an increasing pro-Labour and eventually anti-Conservative bias in financial areas which would have been surprising if the finance industry had consisted mainly of high level capitalist financiers instead of routine non-manual clerks.

4.12 Summary of Best Explanations of Residual Variation from Simple Regression Predictions

These broad ranging checks for socially patterned political deviance confirm that our basic model of class, religion and agriculture was a good choice. All three concepts were the best predictor of some type of partisanship over some data set at some election; all three were also relatively good explanations of residual variation when they were not the basic predictor. So a simpler model would be too simple. Only a few of the other variables added much to single basic variable predictions of partisanship. The best explanation of residual variation in each year is listed in Table 23. For Liberal voting there really were none. For Labour, religiosity and persons per room were the only two to appear; religiosity

Table 23
Best Explanations of Residual Variation 1918–74

Best explanation of residual variation after single control (provided the best explains more than 10%)

	CON	LAB	LIB	TURN
1918	− 21 LSU 15	−	− 18 EIRE	− 36 PPA
1922	18 EIRE	−	none	− 42 PPA
1923	− 16 NON	− 17 RELIG	thereafter	− 37 PPA
1924	21 CL151	− 22 RELIG		− 28 RENT
1929	30 CL151	− 31 RELIG		− 47 LOND
1931	17 CL151	− 25 RELIG		− 40 PPA
1935	25 CL151	− 19 RELIG		− 41 CIMM
1945	− 18 NON	− 29 RELIG		− 40 PPA
1950	− 20 PPR	− 25 RELIG		− 50 RENT
1951	− 25 PPR	21 PPR		− 43 RENT
1955	− 22 PPR	22 PPR		− 56 PPA
1959	− 20 UNSK	− 19 RELIG		− 65 PPA
1964	− 23 UNSK	27 PPR		− 72 PPA
1966	− 37 UNSK	− 28 RELIG		− 67 PPA
1970	− 36 UNSK	30 PPR		− 69 PPA
1974 FEB	− 29 UNSK	32 PPR		− 65 PPA
1974 OCT	− 35 UNSK	− 38 RELIG		− 68 PPA

Note: (1) For the Liberals there were occasions after 1918 when some variable explained over a tenth of the residual, but so little over a tenth, 10% or 11%, that it is less misleading to say that the residuals were relatively unpatterned. See the individual Tables for details.

(2) UNSK = unskilled, PPR = persons per room, RELIG = religiosity, CL151 = class one (professionals), PPA = persons per acre. Occasional influences included education (LSU15), immigration (EIRE, CIMM), London (LOND), tenure (RENT) and nonconformity (NON).

alone between the wars, both intermittently afterwards. Both were measured in 1931. For Conservative votes there was more variety in the best residual predictors, although all but four elections were covered by a sequence that began with pro-Conservative deviations in Social Class One (professional) areas, then anti-Conservative deviations in areas with high numbers of persons per room and finally, anti-Conservative deviations in unskilled areas.

The basic model for partisanship was a poor explanation of turnout; various other variables, notably persons per acre, were good and became increasingly so, for explanations of turnout deviation and indeed of turnout itself.

4.13 Residual Variation after Multiple Controls for Class, Sect, Rurality and Interactions

A rather more stringent way of assessing explanations of residual variation is to record the proportion of residual variation explained after a multiple control for all the five basic predictors. For the years 1923, 1929, 1951, 1964 and 1974, Table 24 shows all variables which explained over 10% of residual variation in partisanship or over 20% in turnout. Entries are ranked from the most to least powerful explanations. Obviously a less powerful variable may be doing nothing more than reflecting a stronger political pattern associated with a correlated predictor.

For Liberal votes the only predictors to explain over a tenth of the residual were house owning in 1964 and the South West region in 1974 and both only marginally exceeded the 10% threshold.

Between the wars the only variables to explain more than 10% of Conservative or Labour deviations were religiosity (Labour 1923 and 1929) and Southern Irish immigration (Conservative 1929). This contrasts with a lengthening list after the Second War in which the property owning democracy variables were prominent.

The list was always long for turnout with persons per acre always in top or second place and tenure variables also near the top.

4.14 Another look at the Property Owning Democracy

These findings suggest that if anything was to be added to the basic model for partisanship it should be some measure of the property owning democracy that would capture the growing postwar party polarisation, and turnout polarisation too, between the property owning, affluent and skilled areas versus the rest. One survey study has even concluded that tenure not occupational class was the basis of 1970 voting alignments.[10]

In Table 25 we report a number of multiple regression results using one measure of class, and zero, one or two measures of tenure. They show standardised slopes. Since the standard deviation of the tenure measures was greater than the standard deviation of the class indicators, this choice maximises the sizes of the path coefficients (slopes) from tenure as compared with the path coefficients from class. However, the aggregate data analyses at either constituency or constant unit level, with either CL251 or EMPL66, put most of the predictive weight on occupational class. Even when both council housing and

Table 24
Residual Variation after Multiple Controls for Class, Sect, Rurality and Interactions

	1923	1929	1951	1964	OCT 1974
Conservative R^2	55	62	73	65	79
% residual variation explained if over 10%	none	19 EIRE	−17 PPR	−17 UNSK	−22 UNSK
			−12 COUN	−15 CL5	−20 PPR
			10 AMEN	12 AMEN	−17 CL5
			10 OWN	10 MET	17 AMEN
			−10 LOND		17 MET
					12 OWN
					11 CL3
Labour R^2	50	77	82	79	79
% residual variation explained if over 10%	−14 RELIG	−12 RELIG	−17 NW	−22 OWN	−26 OWN
			15 AMEN	−19 CL3	25 PPR
			14 PPR	16 PPR	−23 CL3
			−14 NI	−16 AMEN	19 LOND
			−13 OWN	15 LOND	−17 MET
			12 COUN	12 UNSK	16 PPA
			12 LOND	12 PPA	−16 AMEN
			11 PPA	10 COUN	14 UNSK
			−10 CL3	10 RENT	13 CL5
				−10 MET	13 RENT
					10 COUN
					−10 SKIL
Liberal R^2	20	52	10	34	44
% residual variation explained if over 10%	none	none	none	13 OWN	10 SW
Turnout R^2	9	15	15	31	38
% residual variation explained if over 20%	−42 PPA	48 SEMI	46 OWN	−68 PPA	−62 PPA
	−34 LOND	−47 PPA	−44 PPA	55 OWN	−61 RENT
	29 OWN	44 OWN	−43 RENT	−53 RENT	59 OWN
	27 SKIL	−43 LOND	36 SKIL	−52 CIMM	52 AMEN
	−27 CLERK	−40 RENT	31 CL3	50 AMEN	51 SKIL
	−27 RENT	−33 CIMM	−30 LOND	−49 LOND	−46 LOND
	−27 PPR	−32 PPR	−26 EIRE	45 SKIL	−40 CIMM
	−25 TRAN	32 AMEN	−26 UN51	−30 LS017	−37 PPR
	23 AMEN	−29 TRAN	25 AMEN	−28 PPR	31 CL3
		−28 CLERK	−23 TRAN	−24 TRAN	−31 LS017
		24 LSU15	−20 PPR	23 LSU15	−26 TRAN
		22 MET		−22 EIRE	24 LSU15
				22 CL3	−21 EIRE

Note: For interpretation of mnemonics see text.

Table 25
Class, House Tenure and Voting in 1970

(A) Path coefficients from class alone or class plus one tenure variable

Data Set	Party Vote	Class	Tenure	Path coefficients for	
				Class	Tenure
English constant units	VCON	CL251	–	75	–
	VLAB	CL251	–	– 84	–
	VCON	CL251	OWN	65	21
	VLAB	CL251	OWN	– 73	– 25
British constituencies	TWOCON	EMPL66	–	82	–
	VCON	EMPL66	–	72	–
	VLAB	EMPL66	–	– 83	–
	TWOCON	EMPL66	OWN	75	12
	TWOCON	EMPL66	COUN	74	– 14
	VCON	EMPL66	OWN	60	18
	VCON	EMPL66	COUN	61	– 17
	VLAB	EMPL66	OWN	– 75	– 12
	VLAB	EMPL66	COUN	– 76	13

(B) Path coefficients using class plus two tenure variables

Data Set	Party Vote	Path coefficients for		
		EMPL66	COUN	OWN
British constituencies	TWOCON	73	– 11	5
	VCON	58	– 11	11
	VLAB	– 74	10	– 6

Note: (1) VCON, VLAB are percents of vote, TWOCON is percent of Conservative plus Labour vote.

(2) Path coefficients are standardised slopes. Since CL251 and EMPL66 are small categories of people compared to the tenure categories, and their variences are correspondingly small, use of unstandardised slopes would make the point of this table *even more strongly*.

house owning were used as predictors, which effectively allowed for three different partisan biases among council tenants, house owners and private renters, the coefficients from class were not a great deal less than when no tenure predictor was used and were still five or six times as large as the tenure coefficients.

Where aggregate and survey analyses agree is on the increasing importance of tenure in the sixties and seventies. Where they appear to disagree is on the relative power of class and tenure. The explanation may be that in a sample survey tenure is an indicator both of tenure itself and also of the class environment. Since survey results are seldom controlled for environment, which we know to be more important than individual characteristics, the apparent tenure effects in surveys are likely to be greatly inflated.

The multiple regressions using class and tenure only compare the direct effects of these variables on partisanship. Tenure was itself quite strongly dependent on class. The path coefficients between CL251 and tenure for English constant units were 0.47 for ownership and -0.66 for council tenancy; between EMPL66 and tenure for British constituencies they were 0.53 for ownership and -0.49 for council tenancy. Private renting was only slightly correlated with the managerial classes, but negatively so.

The causal direction between occupation and tenure seems likely to run from occupation to tenure. So between a third and a half of even the small direct effects from tenure were class determined, in the sense that tenure itself was dependent to that extent on class.

5 Summary

1 We can use data on the membership of five non-conformist sects by dividing the census measure of non-conformist clergy in the same proportions as the membership figures. Multiple regression analysis of constant units using class, rurality and five sectarian measures simultaneously produced the following results, where each sectarian effect is relative to Anglicans.

2 Wesleyan effect: usually smaller than Primitive, Baptist and Presbyterian; anti-Conservative pro-Liberal until 1955, then anti-Conservative pro-Labour.

3 Baptist effect: larger but similar orientation to Wesleyan.

4 Primitive Methodist effect: also anti-Conservative pro-Liberal between the wars, but later pro-Labour and even anti-Liberal.

5 Presbyterian effect: similar orientation to Primitive, but recovered its old strength after 1951 better than any other.

6 Congregational effect: anti-Liberal pro-Labour in twenties, 1945, 1959 to 1966 and 1974; occasionally anti-Liberal pro-Conservative especially in 1931–35.

7 Sect, class and rurality were each as effective in central England as in the whole of England.

8 Extending the analysis to England and Wales reduced the effect of class and increased the other effects.

9 Including a dummy variable for Wales to remove a national Welsh effect brought sectarian and rural effects back close to the English level but left the class effect low. This may be due to problems of class definition in rural Wales.

10 Reanalysis of sectarian subdivisions in central England compared to all England produced slightly lower Congregational and Primitive effects but higher Baptist, Presbyterian and Wesleyan effects. Orientations were similar except for a less pro-Liberal more pro-Labour Wesleyan orientation in central England.

11 Our Scottish data set was biased against Lanarkshire, including Glasgow.

This is opposite to the usual biases in Scottish voting studies.

12 There were only twenty three Scottish constant units and we used multiple regressions with six or seven predictors. An R^2, adjusted for the reduced degrees of freedom, showed that sectarian effects did improve partisan predictions, but estimated effects are obviously susceptible to biases caused by only a few deviant units.

13 The census included crofters in our standard class measure – 1951 social class two. It was a good measure of crofting but a poor measure of class.

14 Crofters had a special political tradition going back to the crofting M.P.s of 1885–92. There remained, even until 1974, an extremely strong link with Liberal voting.

15 A control for agriculture confirmed and even sharpened this link.

16 Scottish analyses comparable with those for England were run using 1951 Employers and Managers (specially constructed), agriculture and five measures of sect. In these analyses sectarian effects were relative to the Church of Scotland (Presbyterian).

17 As in England, agriculture helped the Liberals; employers and managers helped the Conservatives.

18 Unlike England, the rural effect did not veer anti-Labour, nor the class effect pro-Liberal.

19 Unlike England, the rural effect was much larger than the class effect. At least after the Second War class effects in the two nations were similar.

20 As in England, sectarian effects declined to a minimum in the early fifties and then partially recovered.

21 Unlike England, sectarian effects were always larger in Scotland than England.

22 Unlike England, but like the class effect on Scottish Liberal votes, the Liberals retained their advantage associated with 'other' non-conformists and the 'free' Presbyterian churches.

23 As in England, Episcopalians went with Conservative advantages.

24 Catholic effects must be net of action and reaction. Our Scottish estimates indicated Conservative disadvantage and Liberal advantage which was particularly evident in small towns and the Highlands.

25 Unlike England, no party clearly suffered or gained from religiosity in general.

26 SNP votes in 1974 were analysed but were not strongly related to social divisions.

27 Political deviance from basic social alignments in England was examined using class (CL251), non-conformity and rurality as basic controls.

28 Possible explanations of deviance were other classes, religiosity, regions, population density, education, the property owning democracy, unemployment, immigration, industrial sector and nine individual industries and retired persons.

29 Using only the best of the basic controls as a control, the best explanations of deviance were: for Liberal votes, none; for Turnout, population density;

for Conservative, professions early on, then overcrowded housing, then unskilled workers; for Labour, religiosity, later religiosity and overcrowded houses.

30 The basic variables were poor predictors of turnout, but the main candidates for inclusion in predictions of party votes were variables associated with the property owning democracy. A careful check showed that for constant units and constituencies, occupational class remained far more powerful than the property owning variables even in 1970.

31 This contrasts with some survey data findings about individuals, although survey and aggregate studies agree that property owning was an increasing explanation of deviance.

32 Expanding the analysis to include Wales resulted in Anglicanism always being the best predictor of Conservative votes, while class remained best for Labour.

33 The Welsh language was better than Wales itself as an explanation of deviations from these alignments.

34 The best basic predictor of Plaid Cymru votes in 1974, zero outside Wales, was the interaction between class and non-conformity. The Welsh language explained over half the deviation from this alignment, far more than was explained by Wales itself.

35 Among the language indicators, Labour was more associated with bilinguals than Welsh monoglots, the Liberals were equally correlated with both and Plaid Cymru more with Welsh monoglots.

CHAPTER 7
Review

At the start we described the issues in British politics since 1910 and the appeals made by the parties to the electorate. From these alone there was reason to expect certain patterns and trends in social alignments. Our empirical findings have confirmed such expectations. On some points the implications of party appeals were ambiguous and on all points they were inevitably imprecise; but party appeals matched electoral responses in several important ways.

1 Party Control of Social Alignments

An obvious fact, which could easily have been overlooked if it had not shown up so strongly in the data analysis, is that parties in a constituency system could coerce the electorate into social alignments by rejecting potential support as well as issuing appeals. With no candidate in a locality a party was sure to get no votes there.

A lack of candidates affected the level of votes and variations in the numbers of candidates had an immediate effect on trends. Between 1918 and 1929, for example, the Labour vote went up from 23 % to 37 % (English unadjusted votes). So in 1929 it got 1.6 times its 1918 share of the vote; but in 1929 it had exactly 1.6 times as many candidates as in 1918.

Similarly a lack of candidates was likely to have an immediate effect upon voting patterns and variations in candidature upon trends in constituency level social polarisations. Labour candidates, particularly in 1922 and 1923, were aimed at working class and non-conformist electorates, while Conservatives avoided them. In 1918 and 1931–45 Conservatives also avoided rural areas. Liberal candidates were initially aimed at rural, non-conformist and working class electorates, but they migrated to middle class areas later. Socially biased candidature patterns did not explain voting polarisations completely but they were a contributory element.

A lack of candidates at one time could have more than an immediate effect. Survey analysts have drawn attention to the very close connection between voting and party identification in Britain.[1] British voters changing their votes were likely to alter their party identification as well. Since there were three way contests in less than half the constituencies at all elections except 1929, 1950 and 1964–74, the electorate may have been coerced into party identification as well as voting choice, particularly in the earlier years.

The 1918 electorate was three times as large as in 1910; much less than a third had ever voted before and the party choice available after 1918 was a new one. In these circumstances some development of new social alignments could be expected but the pattern was established in 1918 and 1922 and polarisations tended to decline, not grow, thereafter. The coercive effect of candidature patterns helps to explain why alignments began at the extreme.

2 Class Appeals and Responses

Class related issues were a major ingredient of party appeals. An empirical check using the 1966 Election Survey confirmed that there were large class differences in attitudes on class related issues, particularly trade union power. However there were other points of agreement between class appeals and responses. It was Labour which emphasised class issues in its appeals and class polarisation was always orientated between Labour versus Conservative and Labour versus the rest, often close to the unipolar Labour versus the rest orientation. Labour began, and continued, in close association with the trade unions. Many of its candidates were trade union sponsored and it frequently advocated more power for the unions. The aspect of class that proved the most powerful predictor of voting generally, and especially of Labour voting, was the distinction between the managerial classes and the rest. Trade unions and the employers and managers defined the opposite ends of a particular class spectrum.

The course of party appeals had several contradictory implications for class polarisation. Before 1918 Labour's fundamental policy was simply to put working class individuals into Parliament. When Labour attempted to replace the Liberals as the main opponent of the Conservatives, the background of its candidates and its pre-war policy would imply a much greater class polarisation between Labour and Conservative after 1918 than between Liberal and Unionist before 1918. However, in the process of attempting to replace the Liberals, Labour began to resemble the pre-war Liberals. Under the guise of adopting a socialist constitution it reduced its commitment to class representation: in the first few elections after 1918 its manifestos gave first place to internationalist, non-class issues. Its candidates gradually became almost as middle class as the full pre-1918 Liberal-Labour alliances'. All of which would imply a steadily declining class polarisation after 1918. In an effort to contradict this trend there was what Fabians called the 'inevitability of gradualism'. By putting a quota of socialisation and redistribution in each manifesto, never accepting the status quo, always demanding some more nationalisation of industry and some more redistribution of consumption (a much wider demand than redistribution of income) Labour's policy inevitably became more extreme. This implied steadily increasing class polarisation. Our basic measures of class polarisation showed that after 1923 the size of class polarisation remained remarkably constant. In earlier chapters we have discussed minor variations in the basic class alignment and complex class related deviations from it, but the broad pattern was one of stability.

Survey data, cross-tabulated to show the partisanship of middle and working class individuals without controls for the class environments in which they lived, indicated a drop in class polarisation in 1970. Such a drop might have been expected since the Labour government and the trade unions had come to the brink of open warfare in 1969 over legislative proposals to curb strikes. One study suggested class polarisation had dropped by a third between 1966 and 1970. Nothing like this change was apparent in constituency analyses. Environmental influences made communities vote as communities not just as cumulations of individuals. So constituency class polarisation was at least two and a half times as large as individual class polarisation, and by some measures much more than that. Yet the same mechanisms which made for local consensus appear to have made for continuity and stability. The spatial amplifier was a temporal dampener.

3   Religious Appeals and Responses

Open religious confrontation in Britain was over by 1918 or 1922 at the latest. So we expected the sectarian polarisations that remained to follow the trends in intensity of patriotic versus internationalist issues which were traditionally linked with sectarian divisions. The 1966 Election Study data showed that sect was associated with attitudes on such internationalist issues as unilateralism, immigration and the Queen (there is an important difference between international*ist* issues as defined here and international issues). There was also evidence of a 'social gospel' dimension to sectarian divisions which was particularly strong among the oldest cohorts in 1966; but even in the complete sample, sectarian differences on tax cuts versus social services were greater than class differences on that issue.

In a three party contest the political orientations of social alignments are as significant as their sizes. The question of trends in the orientation of social alignments is particularly familiar when applied to sectarian polarisation—when, if ever, did Labour inherit the Liberal position as the party of non-conformity? If we focused on policy appeals we should have to say 1918 or 1923 (the tariff election) at the latest. Labour politicians claimed they had inherited the non-conformist tradition as soon as Labour received more votes than the Liberals, certainly from 1924. However the area analyses show that sectarian polarisation was between the Conservatives and both other parties until 1950. Until 1931 its orientation was tilted more towards Liberal versus Conservative than Labour versus Conservative. From 1951 onwards the sectarian alignment was at last between Labour and the Conservatives, but the trends continued and from 1966 to February 1974 it orientated between Labour and the rest. All trace of the Liberal non-conformist link had gone and there was even a slight tendency for Liberals to do better in Anglican areas. (These results are for England excluding Wales).

Trends in the size of sectarian polarisation were influenced by candidature patterns particularly in 1918 and 1922. For the rest of the twenties sectarian polarisation was roughly 40% of the size of class polarisation. Thereafter, it declined to a minimum in the early fifties before partially recovering. Although analyses restricted to the changing collections of seats with three way contests suggest that trends were small, it is also true that throughout the twenties internationalist issues such as the Peace Treaties and economic nationalism were major topics of debate while the decline in sectarian polarisation coincided with Hitler's rise to power and the Cold War tensions following the 1945 victory. Sectarian polarisation increased as fear for survival diminished and divisive internationalist issues such as nuclear weapons, decolonisation, immigration and Home Rule reappeared.

Some estimates of religiosity put the total 'membership' of Anglican and non-conformist churches at only 12% in 1966 which appears too low to maintain any sectarian polarisation.[2] However the same estimation methods put the total at only 20% in 1901, the year before Balfour's Education Act. By comparison only about half the Election Study respondents thought of themselves as belonging to a class and the best class predictor of voting, employers and managers, only averaged 11% of economically active males and a tiny percent of the population at large. While 96% of survey respondents were willing to place themselves in a class if pressed, 95% were willing to state a sectarian preference.

Just as our analyses showed that individuals of all classes shared the class character of their environment, so they also showed that Anglicans and others were infected by the non-conformist tradition in areas of relatively high non-conformity.

The largest religious effect evident in our analyses was not sectarian: it was the anti-Labour religiosity effect. It occurred despite efforts to keep religiosity issues, 'moral' issues, out of party politics. Some of these, like abortion, had considerable political potential and their relevance has increased rather than decreased with time, but the parties have tried to avoid holding well defined, well publicised positions on them.

4   Rural Appeals and Responses

Rural polarisation favoured the Liberals at all elections until 1955, although the effect was reduced by a control for religiosity. Conversely the greater religiosity of rural areas helps to explain the Liberals greater success there.

It was the Conservatives who made the most explicit appeals to rural and agricultural interest. Labour tried to appeal to the rural working class on class grounds, but the priority it gave to cheap food for the urban working class must have reduced its attractions for agricultural labourers. Liberal manifestos were not noteworthy for their appeal to rural interests but they did appeal to attitudes which were more common in rural areas.

Table 1 shows, in summary form, a comparison of attitudes in rural and urban

Table 1:
Summary of Differences in Political Attitudes between Rural Areas and Big Cities

Attitude	Class	Rural Bias = % among rural respondents minus % among big city respondents		
		A	N	Av
% more nationalisation	M	3	−9	
	W	1	−14	−5
% too much TU power	M	−14	−8	
	W	−6	−2	−8
% unilateralist	M	−6	−23	
	W	−10	0	−10
% very strongly against immigration	M	−15	−34	
	W	−16	5	−15
% gave up Empire too fast	M	−8	−4	
	W	2	5	−1
% accept UDI or negotiate	M	−3	2	
	W	14	2	4
% feel Queen and Royal Family very important	M	2	20	
	W	19	−12	7
% no increase in social services	M	−6	35	
	W	1	2	8
% prefer tax cut to more social services	M	4	18	
	W	10	−3	7
% class conflict inevitable	M	−7	14	
	W	−13	18	3
% close to own class	M	−15	6	
	W	−6	−28	−11

Note: (1) Table restricted to English respondents only (even Wales excluded).
     (2) Av = average of four entries.

areas. Respondents in rural areas were less worried by trade union power and immigration which would imply an anti-Conservative bias. They were also less keen on nationalisation and less in favour of high taxes and big government which would imply an anti-Labour bias. Rural respondents of both classes felt less close to their own class which would make Labour versus Conservative battles less relevant to them. While the Liberals often voiced their social concern they never tired of denouncing waste and bureaucracy in government or the class struggle in politics.

Liberals in rural areas were also helped by accidents of timing which enfranchised greater percentages of rural than urban electors before 1918 and by Conservative and Labour tendencies to avoid contesting rural seats.

One purpose of the 1885 franchise extension had been to break the grip of the Conservatives on rural seats. The Liberals did well in rural areas in 1885, but almost at once the architect of the franchise reform, with his slogan of 'three acres and a cow', formed an alliance with the Conservatives on the Irish question. This had two effects. In 1886 there was an above average swing to Unionists in rural areas but there were ex-Liberal MPs standing as Liberal Unionists in 18% of rural seats compared with only 10% of urban seats. While they contributed to Unionist strength in Parliament, they denied electors the chance to vote Conservative. Even with their contribution to the Unionist Alliance, Blewett's categorisation of pre-1918 constituencies suggests that the combined Unionist vote in rural England was no better than in 'mixed class' urban areas in 1886 and by 1900 more like their vote in urban 'working class' areas.[3]

The allocation of the 1918 coupon again prevented rural electorates from voting Conservative. So at the critical opening elections of the post-1918 period the Liberals had a history of reasonable success in rural areas and a useful lack of opposition for the moment. In addition, much of the restriction on the pre-1918 franchise came from the operation of the residence requirement which was specially significant in urban areas with high rates of mobility. While rural areas did experience a major increase in their electorates by the enfranchisement of women, the increase in male enfranchisement was small. Conversely, the rural working class was already used to voting before Labour became a contender for power. Thus, in rural areas the Liberals had already formed a connection with most of the anti-Conservatives. The lack of Conservative candidates in 1918 gave them a voting connection with Conservatives too.

Altogether a combination of circumstances made the Liberals better prepared to face post-1918 elections in rural areas and there was also less opposition to be faced. These circumstances and also the pattern of rural attitudes combine to explain the longstanding Liberal advantage in rural areas over the Liberal performance in urban areas. It is important to remember that we are not trying to explain a Liberal advantage over the other parties in rural areas. At most elections in our period the Conservatives were the leading party in agricultural areas, but they also did well in the towns.

Over time the Liberals relative advantage in rural areas declined and when, after the fifties, rural polarisation increased again it was more anti-Labour than pro-Liberal. This new orientation was more consistent with the directions of interest-related appeals.

5 Convergence

One finding links the class, sectarian and rural polarisations: their convergence in political orientation. Between the wars class polarisation was between Labour and Conservative, sect between Conservatives and the rest, and rurality between Liberals and the rest. In 1923, for example, these three polarisations were spread over an arc of 137° while in 1966 they ranged over a mere 9° and even in October 1974 they spanned only 55°. Thus, even though the sectarian and rural polarisations recovered some of their former strength after the fifties and the Liberals again achieved sizeable shares of the vote, the distribution of partisanship remained much more unidimensional than between the wars, partly because the orientations of different social alignments had come closer together.

The focus of this study has been narrow even if the range of data, time and method has not. We sought to examine the social patterns in constituency voting and relate them to the appeals parties made to electorates of different kinds. Attitude surveys have been used only in so far as they could help explain why electorates voted as they did; in particular, to show why appeals that were not about social groups were nonetheless relevant to social groups and how concentrations of one social group affected the attitudes and partisanship both of those within and those outside it. Similarly, the only aspect of constituency voting which we have discussed in detail is its relationship to social groups. Many related topics on British voting have been omitted, but what is included is an important, central and well-defined aspect of British politics since 1918.

The methods and approaches we have used are particularly appropriate to Britain since 1918, but are in no way limited to this time and place. Wherever there is a need to analyse multiple political options without arbitrarily dichotomising them or forcing them onto a unidimensional spectrum, the methods used here should prove of value.

REFERENCES

Chapter 1

1. N. Blewett, *The Peers, the Parties and the People: The General Elections of 1910*, Macmillan: London, 1972, p. 359.
2. D. Butler and A. Sloman, *British Political Facts 1900–1975*, Macmillan: London, 1975, p. 200.
3. Blewett, p. 317–318, gives a complete analysis of topics mentioned by all candidates in 1910.
4. H.C.G. Matthew, R. I. McKibbon and J. A. Kay, The Franchise Factor in the Rise of the Labour Party, *Eng. Hist. Rev.*, v. 91, 1976, p. 723–752 but especially p. 729.
5. An explicit statement of this process is contained in one of Gladstone's letters quoted by R. C. K. Ensor, *England 1870–1914*, O.U.P.: Oxford, 1936. Unfortunately for Gladstone others could recall the precedents and took care that history did not repeat itself in 1885. But it was easier to renounce Irish Home Rule than avoid a European war.
6. T. Wilson, *The Downfall of the Liberal Party 1914–1935*, Collins: Glasgow, 1966, p. 193.
7. LG papers BL C/16/9/1 or for a more accessible summary and lengthy extracts see, for example, Peter Rowland, *Lloyd George*, Barrie and Jenkins: London, 1975 pp. 236–238.
8. F. W. S. Craig, *British Parliamentary Election Results 1885–1910*, Macmillan: London, 1974, gives cross-voting results for each constituency at each election, pp. 595–645.
9. R. E. Dowse, The Entry of Liberals into the Labour Party 1914–20, *Yorkshire Bulletin*, v. 13, no. 2, 1961, p. 78–87, especially pages 84–85. Compare Keir Hardie's comments on infiltration by the Miners Federation a decade earlier, quoted by Blewett p. 58.
10. F. W. S. Craig, *British General Election Manifestos 1900–1974*, Macmillan: London, 1975, reprints all the relevant manifestos in full.
11. Wilson, p. 196 quoting *Liberal Magazine*, February 1919.
12. A. J. P. Taylor, *English History 1914–1945*, O.U.P.: London, 1965 p. 40.
13. Blewett, p. 232 analyses all 1910 candidates by sect and, on page 230, by occupation.

14. Compare Blewett, p. 230, with D. Butler and D. Kavanagh, *The British General Election of October 1974*, Macmillan: London, 1975, p. 215.
15. On the significance of party manifestos in British politics see, for example, D. Butler and D. Kavanagh, *The British General Election of February 1974*, Macmillan: London, 1974, chapter 4.
16. Wilson, p. 138.
17. Cmnd 6171, *Report No. 1 of the Royal Commission on the Distribution of Income and Wealth*, 1975, table 25, p. 64.
18. Cmnd 6171, table 22, p. 57.
19. Cmnd 6171, table 18, p. 52, for details of working wives, table 10, p. 36, for distribution of income by tax units.
20. Department of Employment and Productivity, *British Labour Statistics 1886–1968* (and annual updates), HMSO, 1971, table 197.
21. See D. Winch, *Economics and Policy: a Historical Survey*, Hodder and Stoughton: London, 1969. The "most rapid decline in American economic history" (p. 242) occurred in 1937–38, not in the twenties or early thirties, but it did not cause a comparable slump in Britain. The credit for this is. usually assigned to war preparations rather than voluntary economic policy (Winch p. 212).
22. Butler and Sloman, p. 271. The ratio of public to private housebuilding has followed trends in accord with the governing party's ideology for most of the period since 1918.
23. Butler and Sloman, p. 316. In 1960, for example, the total expenditure on furniture, electrical and other durables, plus cars and motorcycles came to only $7\frac{1}{2}\%$ of consumer spending. By comparison, tobacco took 7%, alcohol 6%.
24. British Labour Statistics, table 164.
25. British Labour Statistics, tables 168 and 169.

Chapter 2

1. *Census 1966: United Kingdom General and Parliamentary Constituency Tables*, HMSO, 1969.
2. D. Butler and D. Stokes, *Political Change in Britain: the Evolution of Electoral Choice*, Macmillan: London, 1974 (2nd Edit). All further references are to the 2nd edition unless specifically to the contrary.
3. Butler and Stokes, p. 90.
4. Butler and Stokes, p. 460.
5. Butler and Stokes, p. 461.
6. Butler and Stokes, p. 459.
7. Butler and Stokes, p. 465.
8. Butler and Stokes, p. 461–462.
9. Butler and Stokes, p. 315.
10. There is a large and growing literature advocating the analysis of survey

cross tabulations in terms of relative odds ratios instead of percentage differences. Chiefly for simplicity that approach is not used here despite its technical advantages. See, for example, L. A. Goodman, Causal Analysis of Data from Panel Studies and Other Kinds of Surveys, *Amer. J. Sociol.*, 1973, v. 78, p. 1135–1191.

11. Butler and Stokes, p. 72, table 4.2.

12. Butler and Stokes, p. 72, table 4.3. See also the footnote on p. 75.

13. Compare Butler and Stokes p. 72 of 2nd Edition with p. 70 of 1st Edition.

14. R. Rose, Britain: Simple Abstractions and Complex Realities, in R. Rose, (ed), *Comparative Electoral Behaviour,* Free Press: New York, 1974, p. 501.

15. Butler and Stokes, p. 70.

16. Rose, p. 510.

17. Taylor, p. 129.

18. Rose, p. 505.

19. Butler and Stokes, p. 101.

20. Butler and Stokes, p. 203.

21. See L. A. Goodman, Some Alternatives to Ecological Correlation, *Amer. J. Sociol.*, 1959, v. 64, pp. 610–625 for this basic but often misleading result. For a fuller discussion in the context of British voting see W. L. Miller, G. Raab and K. Britto, Voting Research and the Population Census 1918–71: Surrogate Data for Constituency Analyses, *J. Roy. Stat. Soc.*, Series A, 1974, v. 137, pp. 384–411.

22. Miller, Raab and Britto, p. 392.

23. Butler and Stokes, pp. 134–135.

24. R. Putnam, Political Attitudes and the Local Community, *Amer. Pol. Sci. Rev.*, 1966, v. 50, pp. 640–654.

25. B. Berelson, P. F. Lazarsfeld and W. N. McPhee, *Voting*, Chicago Univ. Press: Chicago, 1954.

26. A. Przeworski and G. A. D. Soares. Theories in Search of a Curve: A Contextual Interpretation of Left Vote, *Amer. Pol. Sci. Rev.,* v. 65, 1971, pp. 51–68.

27. D. R. Segal and M. W. Meyer, The Social Context of Political Partisanship, pp. 217–232 but especially p. 223 in M. Dogan and S. Rokkan, eds., *Quantitative Ecological Analysis in the Social Sciences,* Cambridge: MIT Press, 1969.

28. See, for example, J. K. Linsey, A Comparison of Additive and Multiplicative Models for Qualitative Data, *Quality and Quantity*, v. 9, 1975, pp. 43–50, or L. A. Goodman, The Relationship between Modified and Usual Multiple Regression Approaches to the Analysis of Dichotomous Variables, in D. R. Heise, ed, *Sociological Methodology* 1976, Jossey-Bass: San Francisco, 1975.

29. A. E. Hoerl and R. W. Kennard, Ridge Regression: Biased Estimation for Nonorthogonal Problems, *Technometrics*, v. 12, 1970, pp. 55–68.

30. For a more political definition of marginality and its relationship to turnout see D. T. Denver and H. T. G. Hands, Marginality and Turnout in British General Elections, *Brit. J. Pol. Sci.*, v. 4, 1974, pp. 17–35.

Chapter 3

1. W. L. Miller and M. Mackie, The Electoral Cycle and the Asymmetry of Government and Opposition Popularity: An Alternative Model of the Relationship between Economic Conditions and Political Popularity, *Pol. Stud.*, v. 21, 1973, pp. 263–279.
2. Butler and Stokes, p. 269.
3. Butler and Stokes, p. 203.
4. The defeat of the 1964 Labour Government's Foreign Secretary, Patrick Gordon-Walker, at Smethwick in 1964 was widely attributed to a campaign on immigration in this midlands constituency. In 1966 New Commonwealth immigrants made up less than 7% of the Smethwick population. The constituency was distinguished as much by the local political campaign as by the level of immigration. See A. W. Singham, Immigration and the election, pp. 360–368 in D. E. Butler and A. King, *The British General Election of 1964*, Macmillan: London, 1965 and J. Byrne, Smethwick, pp. 249–253 in D. E. Butler and A. King, *The British General Election of 1966*, Macmillan: London, 1966.
5. Butler and Stokes, pp. 414–415.

Chapter 4

1. G. H. Gallup, *The Gallup Poll 1935–1971*, Ramdom House: New York, 1972, lists results from British as well as American Gallup Polls. The first entry for Britain (1938) records 60% support for membership of the League of Nations, the second (also 1938) records 56% opposition to Chamberlain's foreign policy and 73% support for Eden's resignation. The first time respondents were asked the 'most important problem' facing government they opted for 'shipping losses.'
2. Miller and Mackie.
3. H. M. Blalock, *Causal Inferences in Nonexperimental Research*, Univ. of North Carolina Press: Chapel Hill, 1961, p. 103.
4. Miller, Raab and Britto.
5. F. W. S. Craig, *British Parliamentary Election Statistics 1918–1970*, Chichester: Political Reference Publications, 1971, p. 74.
6. See W. L. Miller, Cross-voting and the Dimensionality of Party Conflict in Britain during the Period of Realignment; 1918–31, *Pol. Stud.*, v. 19, 1971, for more details of cross-voting in this period.
7. M. Kinnear, *The British Voter: An Atlas and Survey since 1885*, Batsford: London, 1968, p. 122.
8. Blewett, pp. 488–489.
9. Kinnear, p. 133.
10. Kinnear, p. 129.

11. For further details see W. L. Miller, Symmetric Representation of Political Trends in Three-Party Systems with Some Properties, Extensions and Examples, *Quality and Quantity*, v. 11, 1977, pp. 27–41.

12. These measures of political change are more familiar within Britain than outside. They have been used by David Butler and his co-authors in the Nuffield Studies of British Elections published after each election since 1945, and notably by Michael Steed in the Appendices he has contributed to each volume since 1964. See also H. B. Berrington, The General Election of 1964, *J. Roy. Stat. Soc.*, Series A, v. 128, 1965, pp. 17–66 for alternative swing concepts.

13. The principal components output by a standard programme applied to only two input variables x_1 and x_2 are always $x_1^* + x_2^*$ and $x_1^* - x_2^*$ where x_1^* and x_2^* are the standardized (zero mean, unit standard deviation) versions of x_1 and x_2. Thus, using 1924 English data and various input combinations produced the following outputs, from the SPSS factor programme.

Input Set	Principal Component Output expressed in terms of *un*standardized Conservative and Labour percents
1) CON, LAB	LAB − 0.98 CON
2) CON, LIB	LAB + 1.99 CON
3) LEAD (= CON − LAB), LIB	LAB + 3.73 CON
4) CON, LIB, LAB	LAB + 4.14 CON

The power of the principal factor is also indeterminate, ranging from a proportion of variance explained of 50.7% for input set 4 up to 75.8% for input set 2.

14. For a simple description of the canonical regression method see the SPSS manual, N. H. Nie, C. H. Hull, J. G. Jenkins, K. Steinbrenner, D. H. Bent, *Statistical Package for the Social Sciences*, McGraw-Hill: New York, 1975, pp. 515–518. More technical descriptions are given in W. W. Cooley and P. R. Lohnes, *Multivariate Data Analysis*, Wiley: New York, 1971, and in J. P. Van de Geer, *Introduction to Multivariate Analysis for the Social Sciences*, Freeman: San Francisco, 1971. The method is arithmetically equivalent to some of the basic calculations in multiple discrimant analysis. Despite its obvious relevance to multi-party voting analysis, excellent technical descriptions and widespread availability in standard computer packages for the social sciences it has not been widely used. (But see, for example, the application to German and Italian voting in V. E. McHale and R. T. Partch, Canonical Ecology and the Analysis of Aggregate Voting Models, *Quality and Quantity*, v. 9, 1975, pp. 245–264.) One cause of this failure to exploit a powerful and relevant procedure has been the problem of finding some simple way of presenting the results of canonical analysis. We hope that problem has now been solved.

Chapter 5

1. Craig, *British Parliamentary Election Results 1918–1970*, gives party shares of the vote broken down by the four nations of the United Kingdom.
2. Butler and Stokes, pp. 155–233. The cohorts are defined on p. 59.
3. Butler and Stokes, p. 205.
4. Rose, p. 521.
5. For more details of similarities and differences see W. L. Miller and G. Raab, The Religious Alignment at English Elections between 1918 and 1970, *Pol. Stud.*, v. 25, 1977.
6. Miller, *Pol. Stud.*, 1971.

Chapter 6

1. Kinnear, p. 195.
2. For a brief summary of sectarian divisions see R. Currie and A. Gilbert, Religion, pp. 407–450, in A. H. Halsey, ed., *Trends in British Society Since 1900*, Macmillan: London, 1972.
3. Blewett, p. 348, describes the Primitive Methodists as 'most proletarian of Nonconformist denominations' and the Wesleyans as 'the aristocrat of Nonconformist denominations'. While such language has its charm it almost wilfully confuses wealth, social prestige, occupation and sect.
4. Currie and Gilbert, pp. 418–450, for tables of members and clergy.
5. Blewett, p. 232.
6. I. Budge and D. W. Urwin, *Scottish Political Behaviour*, Longmans: London, 1966.
7. The adjusted R^2 is 1 minus the ratio of the estimated variance of deviations from the regression to the estimated variance of the dependent variable. Both these estimates require division of a sum of squares by a number of degrees of freedom and when there are many predictors the numerator is divided by a relatively small number which depresses the R^2 value. For the arithmetical formula etc. see the SPSS manual, p. 358.
8. Compare p. 425 and p. 424 of Currie and Gilbert.
9. Perhaps the best known paper on this topic is C. A. E. Goodhart and R. J. Bhansali, Political Economy, *Pol. Stud.*, v. 18, 1970, pp. 43–106. The logic of that paper has been attacked by various authors since then but others have defended the conclusions if not the logic and similar work has been done on Australian and American elections (see recent numbers of *Amer. Pol. Sci. Rev.*, for example). It is difficult to resist the feeling that political scientists the world over believe that governments *should* be massively punished for economic misfortunes, but it is less obvious that electorates concur.
10. Rose, p. 525.

Chapter 7

1. So close that the concepts have often been used interchangeably in Britain. Private polls for the Conservative Party in 1967–1969 showed a large discrepancy between stated vote intention in mid-term sample surveys and current party identification but even then the natural interpretation was that actual votes in a real election would have followed party identification more closely than stated vote intention. See p. 346 of D. Butler and M. Pinto-Duschinsky, *The British General Election of 1970*, Macmillan: London, 1971. Other evidence for a strong link between identification and voting is provided by recent Scottish surveys. Although the Scottish National Party vote rose from only 5 % in 1966 and 11 % in 1970 to over 30 % in 1974 fully 68 % of SNP voters claimed an SNP identification in 1974. While 68 % is a long way short of 100 % it is a high figure given the rapidity of the SNP's voting gains. (The strength of SNP identification was less than for other parties, however.) Since the SNP's voting gains in 1974 occurred even more quickly than the comparable Labour gains in 1918–24 current surveys of the Scottish electorate may give the best guide to the likely attitudes of British electors in that earlier period of rapid electoral change for which no direct evidence is available.
2. Currie and Gilbert, p. 449.
3. Blewett, p. 20.

Index